THE CANADIAN GRAIN TRADE

THIS book traces in an accurate and objective manner the sequence of events during the last twenty years which have influenced the organization of the Canadian grain trade. During these years problems arising out of the production and marketing of western grain have been under continuous review in Canada, leading at different times to royal commissions of inquiry. The production and sale of cereals have become such a vital part of the economic life of the three prairie provinces and, indeed, of Canada, that anything affecting this great industry becomes at once a subject of general interest.

These twenty years have witnessed momentous changes. The period marks a shift from free trading on the open market to the compulsory marketing of Canadian wheat and other grains through the medium of a Federal board endowed with wide powers. Basically, this change stems from conditions arising out of the Great Depression and World War II. And in one form or another the Canadian Wheat Board will continue to be a significant factor in the marketing of Canadian wheat.

Noteworthy also have been the dramatic recovery of the Pools and the negotiation of international agreements; and, on the farm front, the establishment of a permit system to control deliveries of grain to country elevators, and the enactment of legislation to protect producers against losses arising from the hazards of nature.

THE AUTHOR

DUNCAN ALEXANDER MACGIBBON was born at Lochaber Bay, Quebec, in 1882. He received his B.A. and M.A. from McMaster University, and his Ph.D. from the University of Chicago. He has lectured at various universities in Canada, and for six months at the Khaki University in England after the first World War. He was Professor of Political Economy and Head of the Department at the University of Alberta from 1919 to 1929. In 1929 he was appointed a Commissioner of the Board of Grain Commissioners for Canada. He served in this post for twenty years, at the end of which time he retired from the Board to return to academic life. He is at present Visiting Professor of Political Economy at McMaster University and the University of Toronto.

Professor MacGibbon was a Commissioner for the Alberta Government on Banking and Credit with respect to the Industry of Agriculture, 1922, and a member of the Royal Grain Inquiry Commission, Canada, 1923-24. He was attached to the Canadian delegation to the Imperial Conference at London in 1930, and to the Imperial Economic Conference, Ottawa, 1932. He was a member of the Royal Commission on Taxation of Annuities and Family Corporations, 1944-45.

Professor MacGibbon is the author of several volumes in economics; his *The Canadian Grain Trade*, published in 1932, is the standard work in its field.

THE CANADIAN GRAIN TRADE 1931-1951

BY

D. A. MacGIBBON

Member of the Royal Grain Inquiry Commission, 1923-4; Member of
the Board of Grain Commissioners for Canada, 1929-49

UNIVERSITY OF TORONTO PRESS: 1952

ISBN 978-1-4875-8699-7 (paper)

TO DOROTHY

Preface

DURING the last twenty years problems arising out of the production and marketing of western grain have been under almost continuous review and discussion in Canada. They have been a source of constant preoccupation to the Dominion Government, leading at different times to royal commissions of inquiry. They have also required, on certain occasions, consideration by the governments of the three Prairie Provinces. The production and sale of cereals is such a vital part of the economic life of these provinces and, indeed, of Canada, that anything affecting this great industry becomes at once a subject of general interest. In the present volume, which follows my study *The Canadian Grain Trade* (1932), I have endeavoured to trace as accurately and as objectively as possible the sequence of events which have occurred in the interval and which have exerted an influence upon the organization of the trade. I hope that this study may be of assistance to future scholars who wish to judge and assess the significance of these events.

Momentous changes have occurred since 1931. The period marks a shift from free trading on the open market to the compulsory marketing of Canadian wheat and other grains through the medium of a federal board endowed with wide powers. Basically this change stems from conditions arising out of the Great Depression and World War II. Whether it reflects permanent institutional changes in the methods of conducting international trade in cereals depends upon the future course of world affairs. In this sphere it would be rash to prophesy; the only certainty is uncertainty. What can be said with reasonable confidence is that in one form or another the Canadian Wheat Board will continue to be a significant factor in the marketing of Canadian wheat.

Noteworthy also have been the dramatic recovery of the Pools and the negotiations of international agreements; also on the farm front

the establishment of a permit system to control deliveries of grain to
country elevators and the enactment of legislation to protect producers
against losses arising from the hazards of nature.

With respect to the present volume I wish to express my thanks
to Mr. H. L. Griffin, Mr. Stanley N. Jones, Mr. W. A. MacLeod, and
Dr. T. W. Grindley, whose reading of the manuscript enabled me to
clarify various points of interpretation. Any opinions expressed in the
study, however, are entirely my own responsibility. I should add that
owing to a delay in publication the text has since been drastically
revised and enlarged to bring the record down to the present time.
I also wish to thank the general managers of the three provincial Pools
for making available to me information respecting the growth and
position of these organizations. I am very grateful to Miss Francess
Halpenny and to Miss M. Jean Houston, of the editorial staff of the
University of Toronto Press, for their painstaking care in assisting me
in the final revision of the manuscript. I have a further acknowledg-
ment to make: to the Canadian Social Science Research Council and
to the Publications Fund of the University of Toronto Press for gen-
erously providing financial underwriting for the publication of the
book.

D. A. MacGibbon

McMaster University, Hamilton, Ontario
August, 1951

Contents

PREFACE   vii

I   The Prairie Provinces Suffer a Setback   3

II   Government Intervention: The International Wheat Agreement of 1933   17

III   The Establishment of the Canadian Wheat Board: The Turgeon Commission   33

IV   Wheat Growing Becomes a Protected Industry   49

V   Wheat Politics and the Taxation of Co-operative Profits   67

VI   The Canadian Wheat Board and the War   89

VII   The British Wheat Agreement   119

VIII   The International Wheat Agreement of 1949   145

IX   Post-War Developments in the Grain Trade   162

X   The Growth of the Pool Organizations   173

XI   The United Grain Growers Limited   188

XII   The Independent Companies: The Winnipeg Grain Exchange   199

XIII   Summary and Conclusion   221

INDEX   225

THE CANADIAN GRAIN TRADE

1

The Prairie Provinces suffer a setback

THE years that intervened between the collapse of prices in 1929 and the outbreak of war in 1939 were years of extreme difficulty for the grain growers of Western Canada. The great depression that followed 1929 affected with especial severity the producers of farm products everywhere. From agricultural regions in all quarters of the globe came evidences of distress. Nor was this surprising since it is well known that in periods of violent price change agricultural products usually exhibit wider variation in price than do manufactured goods. Between 1929 and 1933 the world index number for industrial prices registered a decline in price levels of 48 per cent for manufactured goods, but agricultural prices receded much farther. The index number for agricultural prices went down from 100 in 1929 to 44 in 1933, or a reduction of 56 per cent.[1] This fact in itself, without further elaboration, is an indication of the magnitude of the disaster that struck agriculture throughout the world after the great boom of the nineteen-twenties.

In no country was this collapse in agricultural prices accompanied by greater distress than in Western Canada, where the one-crop system of commercial agriculture generally prevails and wheat is the chief cereal cultivated. While the percentage of decline in wheat prices in Western Canada was not markedly greater than that of the decline in the prices of other agricultural products, the general economic position of the wheat growers was not such as to enable them to

[1]*World Economic Survey, 1933-34* (Geneva: League of Nations, 1934), p. 134.

3

sustain a drastic reduction in income. The average price for No. 1
Manitoba Northern wheat, basis in store at Fort William, fell from
124.3 cents per bushel for the crop year of 1929-30 to 54.2 cents per
bushel for the crop year of 1932-33. Wheat prices had in fact begun
to decline, though slowly at first, as early as 1925. The highest average
price between 1920 and 1930 was realized during the crop year of
1924-25 when No. 2 Manitoba Northern wheat was reported at 168.5
cents per bushel.[2] In December of 1932, under the impact of record
deliveries by farmers, the price of wheat on the Winnipeg Grain
Exchange dropped to 38 cents per bushel delivered at Fort William.
This price was equivalent to about 22 cents per bushel for No. 1
Northern wheat at country elevators located on the railway in the
central regions of the western wheat belt.

The downward drift at the outset was due chiefly to two circumstances, a long-term trend in the world generally towards an excessive
production of wheat relative to demand aggravated by declining per
capita consumption, and the recurrence in Western Canada of especially bountiful harvests. Between 1928 and 1933 the Canadian carryover increased from 91,000,000 to 217,000,000 bushels. Then came the
effects of widespread and severe depression. The result was that the
average price of wheat which, throughout the period of 1925-29 had
been 141.7 cents per bushel, was approximately 66 cents per bushel
under conditions of depression during 1930-34. The depressed level
of wheat prices in the later period meant a sudden drastic change in
the western grain growers' financial situation. Within a few months
they passed from relatively high prosperity and seeming security to
the menace of bankruptcy and disaster and extreme hardship.

Nor did this situation improve quickly. When wheat prices began
to exhibit some substantial degree of recovery after the low point of
the depression had been reached, other circumstances unfortunately
intervened that largely nullified in Canada the benefits of advancing
prices. Unfavourable weather conditions affected the crops and reduced the yield for the five years between 1933 and 1937 far below
the long-term average. The average annual yield of wheat in Manitoba,
Saskatchewan, and Alberta for these five years inclusive ranged from
the abnormally low average of 6.4 bushels per acre in 1937 to 11.3
bushels per acre in 1935, compared with the long-term average of
approximately 17 bushels per acre. In 1937 the western wheat crop in
large parts of the grain-growing area, especially in Saskatchewan, was

[2]*Canada Year Book,* 1929, p. 262.

a complete failure. In that year the western wheat crop amounted in all to only 156,800,000 bushels, the average yield per acre being the lowest since Canada had become an important producer of wheat.[3] The distress of the depression years is often attributed almost solely to low prices with insufficient attention being given to the lengthening-out of distress because of crop failures.

With the return of better crops and some improvement in prices, the prospect for Canadian exports, already unstable because of excessive production, became more decidedly unfavourable. The deepening shadows of the approaching world war darkened the outlook. Those wheat-producing countries in Europe which normally looked to external sources such as Canada for part of their annual supply actively endeavoured, for purposes of security, to increase their domestic production so that they would not be dependent upon external purchases in the event of war. As the Nazi threat grew increasingly ominous, the trend towards increased production of cereals in Western Europe became more pronounced. All these developments tended to reduce purchases from overseas. When in 1939 war finally became a fact, the subsequent overrunning of Norway, Denmark, the Netherlands, and Belgium by Germany effectively eliminated from the Canadian export field some of the best continental European markets. Canadian export outlets for wheat were reduced by at least 30,000,000 bushels annually. For all practical purposes Great Britain alone remained. The grain growers of Western Canada, who had believed that ·the war would create during its progress such an overpowering demand for wheat that all their difficulties would, for the time being at least, disappear, found their expectations unfulfilled.

One result of the loss of continental European markets, coinciding with a return to large yields per acre in Western Canada, was that immense carryovers of wheat began to accumulate. These carryovers overhung the market and tended to depress prices while creating at the same time difficult warehousing and financing problems. By the end of the crop year of 1940-41 the Canadian carryover was estimated at 480,129,000 bushels, an amount not only far in excess of any previous carryover accumulated in Canadian history, but sufficiently great in itself to supply normal export possibilities for at least two years. To prevent greater declines in wheat prices in 1940-41 the Government set a minimum price of 70 cents per bushel for No. 1 Northern in store at Fort William. Subsequently, as a result of strong protests from the

[3]*Ibid.*, 1939, p. 212.

producers that this price was too low, the Government increased the minimum price for 1942-43 to 90 cents per bushel.

TABLE I[4]

(a)	(1) Acreage	(2) Yield per acre	(3) Produc- tion	(4) Domestic wholesale price	(5) Exports wheat & flour	(6) Value of exports	(7) Carryover July 31
	acres 000	bu.	bu. 000	cents	bu. 000	$ 000	bu. 000
1928	23,159	23.5	544,598	124	407,564	451,820	91,156
1929	24,297	11.5	279,336	124/3	186,267	227,317	127,239
1930	23,960	16.6	397,300	64/2	258,694	188,421	126,582
1931	25,586	11.8	301,181	59/7	207,030	128,117	138,598
1932	26,395	16.0	422,947	54/2	264,304	151,321	135,941
1933	25,177	10.4	263,004	68	194,780	140,488	217,657
1934	23,296	11.3	263,800	81/6	165,751	136,665	202,902
1935	23,293	11.3	264,096	84/5	254,425	210,196	213,852
1936	24,838	8.1	202.000	122.5	209,773	221,825	127,362
1937	24,599	6.4	156,800	131/4	95,586	114,581	37,049
1938	24,946	13.5	336,000	62	160,034	106,037	24,536
1939	25,813	19.1	494,000	76/4	192,674	165,004	102,911
1940	27,750	18.5	513,800	74	231,206	185,902	300,473
1941	21,140	14.0	296,000	76/5	225,828	187,301	480,129
1942	20,653	25.6	529,000	94.4	214,701	198,029	423,752
1943	16,091	16.6	267,800	123/2	343,755	445,814	594,626
1944	22,443	17.5	391,700	125	342,946	456,238	356,531
1945	22,566	13.1	294,600	125	343,186§	523,588	258,073
1946	23,731	16.6	393,000	138/4*	239,421	444,852	73,600
1947	23,357	13.7	319,000	155†	194,690	367,253	87,367
1948	23,045	15.5	358,000	200‡			75,993

*Fixed price of $1.25 from August 1–February 17, inclusive. Price increased to $1.55 effective midnight February 17. Carrying charges of 3½ cents per bushel to be added.
†Plus 3½ cents carrying charges.
‡Plus 5 cents carrying charges.
§Flour exports have been adjusted to remove effects of time-lag in customs returns.

NOTES RE PRICES

(a)   Prices quoted are annual averages of daily spot prices No. 1 Northern basis Fort William–Port Arthur.

(b)   From August 1, 1942 to September 15, 1947, net price to millers on wheat for domestic consumption was 77 3/8 cents, the difference between this and the quoted price being made up by government subsidy.

(c)   From September 15, 1947 to July 31, 1948, the subsidy was discontinued.

(d)   During August 1948, the rebate on wheat milled for domestic consumption was reinstituted at 45 cents per bushel.

(e)   Effective September 1 the subsidy was increased to 46½ cents per bushel.

[4]Agricultural Division, Dominion Bureau of Statistics, Ottawa, Oct. 27, 1948.

The main facts are conveniently summarized statistically in Table 1. Up to 1940 the figures reveal a trend towards increased acreage devoted to wheat, with violent fluctuations in yield per acre, in total production, and in prices. Except for the short crops of 1936 and 1937 the total annual amounts exported and the value of total exports did not fluctuate violently, but except for four years, from 1944 to 1947 inclusive, the annual total value of the wheat and flour exported did not exceed the sum reported for 1928. Excessive carryovers which had made the situation more difficult up to 1937 again began to appear in 1939 and continued to pile up until the stupendous amount of nearly 600,000,000 bushels was reached in 1943-44.

To appreciate fully the depressing effect of conditions in the nineteen-thirties, not only upon the individual grain grower's standard of living and financial solvency, but also upon western business generally and upon the maintenance of the institutional conveniences and amenities of community life on the prairies,[5] one must take into account the importance of wheat to the prairie farmer as indicated by the proportion of cash income received by him from that source. This is shown in Table II. The figures are given by provinces since the break-down

TABLE II[6]

CASH INCOME FROM WHEAT

Calendar year	Million dollars				Percentage of total cash income			
	Man.	Sask.	Alta.	Total	Man.	Sask.	Alta.	Total
1926	41.6	240.3	107.4	389.3	46.6	83.1	66.7	72.1
1927	31.8	216.3	116.7	364.8	40.5	80.2	69.1	· 70.6
1928	34.4	256.4	149.9	440.7	41.9	80.2	71.1	72.0
1929	29.3	184.3	110.0	323.6	40.4	75.9	64.9	66.7
1930	19.3	86.8	52.6	158.7	40.5	70.2	56.2	59.9
1931	9.3	44.2	38.6	92.1	30.2	63.1	55.4	54.1
1932	13.3	55.1	42.8	111.2	46.7	75.1	63.7	65.8
1933	15.6	52.9	40.5	109.0	48.5	72.0	61.0	63.4
1934	20.9	61.3	54.1	136.3	47.4	66.8	58.3	59.6
1935	11.9	74.6	55.2	141.7	33.0	69.0	57.1	58.8
1936	16.8	75.6	41.9	134.3	36.6	63.6	45.8	52.4
1937	34.5	34.8	61.6	130.6	46.7	42.0	50.7	47.1
1938	28.6	64.3	81.1	174.0	45.5	71.2	61.3	61.0
1939	27.9	120.0	65.0	212.9	43.8	77.0	54.8	62.9
1940	23.3	101.5	57.8	182.6	36.9	68.3	46.2	54.2
1941	25.2	88.0	54.8	168.0	31.9	56.1	36.7	43.6

[5]See G. E. Britnell, *The Wheat Economy* (Toronto, 1939). Also Bulletin 105, Agricultural Extension Department, University of Saskatchewan, 1942.

[6]Agricultural Division, Dominion Bureau of Statistics.

makes especially clear the plight of Saskatchewan where, except in the event of extensive crop failures, in excess of two-thirds of the farmers' total cash income normally is derived from wheat. In Alberta over one-half of the farmers' cash income comes from wheat, and it is only in Manitoba that other forms of cash income become of large significance to them. Even in Manitoba until 1939 cash income from wheat was roughly double the amounts received by the farmers from livestock and animal products.

Another unfavourable aspect of the situation during these years was the steady decline in the purchasing power of a bushel of wheat. In other words the terms of trade were moving against the western grain grower from year to year. The index number published by the Searle Grain Company computes the costs of goods prairie farmers have to buy for living and production using the years 1913 and 1914 as a base. "The index is computed on the basis of an average farming family of five, mother, father and three children, on what might be termed an average half-section farm in the prairie provinces." It takes account of the cost of a total of 147 items including household goods, farm equipment, and local taxes, but no luxuries or expenses for higher education. This index by April of 1942 stood at 151.6, indicating that farmers' costs on that date were 51.6 per cent greater than in 1913-14. Under these conditions the purchasing power of a bushel of wheat was estimated at 58 per cent of what it was in 1913-14. A comparison between less remote periods showed that the purchasing power of a bushel of wheat during the lean years between 1931 and 1935 was only 46.4 per cent of what it had been between 1926 and 1930.[7] The Searle index number is sufficiently representative to establish clearly the downward trend of wheat values during the depression years relative to the goods farmers had to purchase.

The net effect of all these adverse circumstances was a very severe reduction in the western farmers' cash income. Nor must it be overlooked in this connection that while wheat was the farmers' main source of cash income, drastic declines were also taking place in that portion of it obtained from livestock and animal products. In 1929 the cash income from livestock and animal products obtained by the farmers of Alberta, Saskatchewan, and Manitoba amounted to $105,600,000. In 1932 this total had shrunk to $40,800,000. The full magnitude of the disaster is revealed in the figures for gross cash

[7]The Searle index published by the Searle Grain Company, Limited, Winnipeg.

income for all farm products. The average annual gross cash income received for the four years from 1926 to 1929 inclusive is estimated at $538,500,000, contrasted with an average annual gross cash income of $194,000,000 for the four succeeding years of 1930, 1931, 1932 and 1933. The range of fluctuation was from $612,400,000 in 1928 to $169,000,000 in 1932. Not until 1939 did the farmers of the Prairie Provinces have a gross cash income from the sale of their wheat and other products in excess of $300,000,000.

It is painfully obvious that in the face of such disastrous circumstances no possible adjustments in the farmers' standard of living or in the scale of their operations could be sufficient to cope with the situation and that it must have its repercussions in various financial expedients designed to ameliorate their condition. These measures involved direct payments for relief made necessary by complete or partial crop failures aggravated by the low prices for farm products. Between 1931 and 1937 total relief expenditures for the three Prairie Provinces amounted to approximately $282,782,000, of which around $100,000,000 was contributed by the federal Government.[8] The necessity of providing for direct relief, however, was but a small part of the financial difficulties created by agrarian distress. Naturally under the conditions prevailing arrears in taxes and contractual payments developed while debts accumulated wherever credit could be obtained. Professor Waines of the University of Manitoba estimated that as late as the end of 1937 school and municipal arrears amounted to over $56,000,000; of this amount $27,000,000 was attributable to the province of Saskatchewan.[9] In order to maintain a minimum of municipal and school services it became necessary for the municipalities and school boards to borrow money. Rural municipal debt increased in both Saskatchewan and Alberta between 1930 and 1937, the significant item in this increase being bank loans. In 1930 in Saskatchewan these amounted to $6,800,000, in 1937 to $12,866,000. In Alberta municipal bank loans increased from $1,800,000 to $3,469,000.[10]

The strain placed upon provincial finances in each of the three provinces by falling revenues and increased demands upon the

[8]*Report of the Royal Commission on Dominion-Provincial Relations* (Ottawa, 1939), Book III, p. 109 and Appendix 4, "National Income."

[9]W. J. Waines, *Prairie Population Possibilities* (Ottawa, 1939), p. 55; mimeographed study prepared for the Royal Commission on Dominion-Provincial Relations.

[10]*Report of the Royal Commission on Dominion-Provincial Relations,* Book III, p. 159.

exchequer is revealed by the rapid growth of provincial debt. In this respect, however, the situation did not differ materially from that in the other provinces of Canada which were also facing problems arising out of depression and unemployment, though it should be pointed out that part of the difficulty of Eastern Canada was caused by the shrinkage in western markets for goods manufactured in the East.

TABLE III[11]

PRAIRIE PROVINCES—OUTSTANDING DEBT

	1930	1937	Increase
	(millions of dollars)		
Manitoba	107.6	122.4	14.8
Saskatchewan	98.4	215.2	116.8
Alberta	137.0	169.9	32.9
	343.0	507.5	164.5

With respect to the vast accumulation of private debts of a current nature that occurred, Professor Waines has estimated that at the end of 1937 the farmers of the West owed the implement companies $30,000,000, the oil companies somewhat under $4,000,000, retail merchants and various liens $75,000,000, and the banks and financial corporations and miscellaneous creditors $63,000,000. In all, this is a total of approximately $171,000,000.

There must also be considered the fact that during the course of the depression large amounts of debt were written off by one process or another. It is estimated that in the drought area of Saskatchewan private lenders on mortgages and agreements of sale up to March 1938 wrote off debts to the extent of $27,129,510.[12] The provincial Government in its dealings with rural municipalities cancelled claims amounting to $27,310,000, and in its dealings with individuals, claims amounting to $14,640,437. Municipalities in turn wrote off relief claims of $23,171,300 and unpaid taxes of $23,222,640. Finally, the federal Government absorbed treasury bills of the Saskatchewan Government for $17,959,606 and advances for direct relief and winter maintenance for 1934-35 of $9,000,000. In Manitoba and Alberta, conditions of extreme distress did not extend over such a large area as in Saskatchewan. In Manitoba, in the drought area, the total of the write-offs by the various bodies amounted to $4,390,399.16.

[11]Bank of Canada, *Statistical Summary*, April-May, 1942, p. 41.
[12]See Farmers' Creditors Arrangement Act, Statutes of Canada, 1934, c. 53; also various provincial statutes.

In addition, the mortgage-lending institutions wrote off over $2,000,000 in other parts of the province and also reduced interest rates. Detailed data are not available for the province of Alberta. Debt adjustment acts have been in force there since 1923, and it is estimated that the total reduction in claims handled exceeded $15,000,000, but what proportion of this amount relates to the period under review has not been disclosed.[13]

A natural result of this prolonged period of depression and difficulty was a great decline in the value of farm lands. The optimism that surrounded the settlement of the West in the earlier part of the present century, and which reached a peak during the boom period of the twenties, ebbed away under the succession of reverses in the thirties. The old axiom that in the long run the value of an income bearer is determined by the net income secured from it capitalized at the appropriate rate of interest received one more exemplification. Farm land values fell sharply in the Prairie Provinces. Thus, added to all their current difficulties, western farmers saw the value of their capital investment disappearing.

At the close of the First World War farm land values had been comparatively high, reflecting the high prices that were the rule at that time. Falling prices and drought led to some recession in 1923 and 1924, but with the return of good times and large harvests the prices of farm lands began to climb again, though not attaining the level reached in 1920. By 1928 this rising impulse had spent itself, and by 1930 a trend downward was clearly discernible. In Manitoba the estimated value per acre of occupied farm lands in 1920 was $39; by 1923 it had fallen to $28, rising to $29 in 1926 and thereafter declining to $16 per acre in 1940. The comparative figures for Alberta are: 1920, $32 per acre; 1923, $24 per acre; 1928, $28 per acre; and 1940, $16 per acre. In Saskatchewan values fell from $32 per acre in 1920 to $24 in 1923, rising again to $27 in 1928 and falling to $15 per acre in 1940.[14]

Nevertheless, in spite of the discouraging agricultural outlook, the area in farms continued to expand in the Prairie Provinces. This was rather surprising. The increase was apparently to be explained partly by a backward trek to the land from urban communities caused by the prevalence of unemployment in the cities, and partly by the con-

[13]Waines, *Prairie Population Possibilities*, p. 69. See also W. T. Easterbrook, *Farm Credit in Canada* (Toronto, 1938).
[14]*Canada Year Book*, 1941, p. 154.

tinuance of a small flow of emigrants from other countries seeking homes. Expansion of farm area was more marked in Saskatchewan and Alberta where there was a larger area of reasonably good virgin soil available for settlement. Between 1926 and 1936 the area in farms in Manitoba increased from 14,411,597 acres to 15,668,927 acres. In Saskatchewan the increase for the same period was from 45,945,410 acres to 56,903,799 acres, and in Alberta from 28,572,987 acres to 40, 539,934 acres.

When this increase in acreage is considered along with the decline in total farm values, the result is startling. In the decade between 1926 and 1936 total farm values in Manitoba fell from approximately $476,000,000 to $302,000,000. This sum includes the estimated value of land, buildings, implements, and livestock. In Saskatchewan total farm values in 1926 were estimated at $1,343,000,000; in 1936 at $1,004,000,000. In Alberta the reduction was somewhat less, and this was to be expected since the largest increase in acreage had occurred in Alberta. Farm values in Alberta in 1926 were placed at $790,000,000 and in 1936 at $675,000,000. Thus in ten years in these three predominantly agricultural provinces, notwithstanding a substantial increase in acreage devoted to agriculture, the total decline in farm values amounted to approximately $625,000,000. In 1936 total farm values were 76 per cent of what they had been in 1926.[15]

It is not possible to measure in any precise fashion the effect of economic vicissitudes of this magnitude upon the standard of living of the farm households of Western Canada.[16] In itself, the expression "standard of living" represents a complex notion which includes the actual amounts of consumption goods and services enjoyed by a family, the abstinences voluntarily accepted with a view to a future betterment in conditions, the general quality and nature of the goods consumed, and a general sense of security and stability. Standards of expenditure have usually been relied upon as the most satisfactory available measure of actual standards of living. In urban communities where the real income of the household is derived from goods and services practically all of which are purchased, price data are largely available, if recorded and gathered, upon which to form conclusions. But when dealing with farm standards of living it is found that between 20 and 35 per cent of the income contributing to the maintenance of the household is derived from the farm itself. Under conditions of depres-

[15]*Ibid.*, 1937, p. 270.
[16]Britnell, *The Wheat Economy*, p. 150.

sion this percentage may increase. It is apparent also that, apart from the actual consumption of goods, other elements in real income cannot be measured. For this reason, in discussing farmers' standards of living, it must always be remembered that there exists, to a greater extent than elsewhere, a lack of exactness in the primary data available upon which to base precise conclusions.

With respect to the farmers of Western Canada, a further difficulty appears. The value of examining standards of living lies in the comparisons that can be instituted either between the standard of living of different groups in the same community or between different periods of time for the same group. In Western Canada there is lacking any thorough basic examination of farmers' standards of living either before or during the depression. There is, however, plenty of evidence of one sort or another indicating a catastrophic drop in the level of welfare among western farmers after 1930.

While low prices for wheat and other cereals affected directly the welfare of the prairie farmer, their effects were not confined to this class alone. Agriculture is the mainspring of western economic life, and conditions of depression and hardship on the land quickly spread throughout all other classes in the West. The villages and small towns serving as local distributive points for the surrounding areas and, in effect, maintained by them, were as hard hit in the nineteen-thirties as the farmers themselves. Many found difficulty in maintaining their schools and other public services. In the larger centres and cities of the West unemployment and distress were rampant. Without proper administrative machinery or adequate financial resources these centres found they had to cope with the task of providing for large groups of people who were absolutely destitute. For the first time in half a century the West seemed seriously to doubt its future.

Awareness of the difficulties of the wheat producer bit deeply into the minds of everybody and drove home the vital relationship between the prosperity of the western grain grower and that of his urban centres. For example, during the prosperous twenties the number of automobiles, including motor trucks, on prairie farms doubled, but during the depression car registrations fell rapidly, and by 1933 nearly half the farm automobiles of the prairie region had been taken off the roads.[17] Between 1930 and 1937 the number of farm telephones in the wheat belt declined by 50 per cent. In rural areas in the West there was an obvious neglect of painting and repairs to farm buildings.

[17]*Ibid.*, p. 181.

Everything appeared to be "running down." In various regions, particularly where drought had occurred, whole communities were able to subsist only upon the basis of public relief. In some districts in Saskatchewan medical men reported evidence of malnutrition, and signs of scurvy were observed for the first time. Numerous examples came to light of lack of proper clothing and household equipment. The most telling confirmation of western difficulties was revealed in the decennial census of 1941. Census figures show that not one of the three provinces retained its natural increase of population for the decade. Saskatchewan, the province most severely affected, suffered an actual decrease in numbers of 34,308. In spite of new settlements in various parts of the western farm region, it is estimated that there was an exodus of a quarter of a million people from the West. Thus, while it is not possible to compute an index number registering in exact terms the deterioration in community life under depression conditions, the evidence is overwhelming that during the nineteen-thirties the standards of living declined below the level of social stability.

The conditions outlined in the preceding paragraphs were the background against which Canadian wheat production and the marketing policies of the period developed. The measures adopted must be viewed in the perspective of the fears and social disillusionment engendered by these acute difficulties.

Until 1928 the increase in the Western Canadian wheat area had gone forward under the optimistic assumption that no matter how much wheat the Canadian West produced, there would always be a ready market for it in the more densely populated countries of the Old World. The current viewpoint found expression in the saying that "wheat sold itself." On account of its high protein content Western Canadian wheat is particularly valuable for mixing with wheat of lower strength. Western wheat growers believed that Canadian hard red spring wheat for this reason would always find a market in competition with the wheat produced by other exporting countries so that even in the event of world over-production Canada would not suffer severely. It was argued that while other countries might have to reduce their exports on account of over-production, Canada would largely escape this necessity because of the high quality of her product. The progress of the West was conceived of in terms of increasing wheat exports. Scientists engaged in plant breeding were continually developing new strains of wheat which would extend the area of production of the yield per acre. Public men confidently predicted that Canadian wheat production would ultimately reach a yield of 1,000,000,000 bushels annually.[18]

Throughout the years of expansion, while wheat was becoming Canada's major export product, every care was being taken to ensure that Canadian wheat would be marketed under conditions that would increase demand for it abroad. Its quality and reputation were carefully safeguarded by official regulations; official weights and grades constituted a guarantee of fair dealing.[19] Nevertheless, despite these precautions, excessive carryovers of Canadian wheat began to appear. The first of these to attract attention, small in the light of later events, was reported for the crop year ending with July of 1928. There was an increasing accumulation in the following year with an accelerated downward trend in wheat prices in the autumn of 1929. These developments effectively disposed of the idea that, because of the high quality of her wheat, Canada could dictate the prices at which she would sell her surpluses to importing countries. The Wheat Pools, which had over-estimated the effective demand for Canadian wheat, found themselves in difficulties. Presently, the provincial governments, and later the federal Government, had to come to their assistance; with the onset of the depression the main burden of maintaining the wheat growers of Western Canada on a livable income fell to the latter. It was obvious that the situation was one of grave difficulty.

The record reveals that the problem of meeting this crisis was considered from many points of view. All kinds of solutions were put forward, not all of which were worthy of trial. Consideration of the Canadian wheat problem bulked large in every forum of discussion in Western Canada as well as in Parliament. There it was a question of the first magnitude. It will be seen, however, that the steps taken from time to time by the federal authorities were often merely stopgap remedies. These remedies were adopted in the hope that the international wheat situation would improve to such an extent that it would restore the wheat grower in Western Canada to prosperity while permitting him to continue to grow as much wheat as he wished. Only towards the close of the nineteen-thirties, when even the advent of war failed to support the growers' expectation of a satis-

[18]For various estimates see D. A. MacGibbon, "The Future of the Canadian Export Trade in Wheat," Supplement to vol. XIX, *Transactions of the Royal Canadian Institute* (Toronto, 1932).

[19]D. A. MacGibbon, *The Canadian Grain Trade* (Toronto, 1932), p. 375.

factory market for Canadian wheat, were comprehensive measures of a corrective nature taken.

Although in the next decade Western Canada was blessed with a series of good harvests and the grain producers worked themselves out of their difficulties during a period of high prosperity, the dark days of the early thirties were not forgotten, and memories of them remain as a disquieting portent of what might occur again. The continuing impact of these memories is an effective force in determining the grain producers' attitude to the marketing methods employed in the disposal of their products up to the present time.

2

Government Intervention: The International Wheat Agreement of 1933

THE preceding chapter gives a general idea of how deeply the great depression and later the drought affected the economic and social life of the people of Western Canada. From being one of the most prosperous farming sections of the Dominion, the prairies suddenly declined in large areas to submarginal levels of living conditions. But one is impressed by the fact that, when it became necessary for the Dominion Government to intervene, the various steps taken to relieve the situation were not made as the result of a thorough investigation into the causes but were largely a response to popular attitudes. At a time when depression was general throughout Canada the deeper significance of the severity of the crisis on the prairies did not really come home to the authorities at Ottawa.

In tracing the course of events it is convenient to begin with the appointment in the late autumn of 1930 of John I. McFarland to the position of General Manager of the Canadian Co-operative Wheat Producers Limited, the name given to the Wheat Pools' central selling agency. This appointment occurred in the second year of the Pools' difficulties in financing the crop in the face of declining prices.[1] In 1929 the governments of Alberta, Saskatchewan, and Manitoba had come to the Pools' assistance by guaranteeing their credits at the banks. When in 1930 the Pools again found their credit position imperilled by further declines in wheat prices, the Pools and the banks

[1]See D. A. MacGibbon, *The Canadian Grain Trade* (Toronto, 1932), p. 79.

united to appeal to the federal Government for aid. The banks were heavily committed, and to protect both groups the federal Government agreed to come to their assistance. As the price of this assistance the Government imposed the condition that a manager in whom it had confidence should be placed in charge of the central selling agency. With Mr. McFarland's appointment to this position the federal Government became directly involved in the marketing of the Canadian wheat crop.

This intervention of the Government was thought to be purely of a temporary nature. The Pools were in difficulties because initial payments to members when they delivered their wheat turned out to be too generous in view of the fact that the Pools did not protect themselves against fluctuations in market prices by hedging their receipts in the futures market. The larger general problem raised by the drastic decline in world values of wheat was thought of as being the result chiefly of a run of bumper crops which time itself would soon reverse. With respect to the international competitive situation, the Canadian Government under Mr. Bennett had decided views about how the Canadian wheat grower could be placed permanently in a more advantageous position in his principal market, the United Kingdom. At the Imperial Conference in London in 1930 the Canadian Government sought a preference for Canadian wheat in Britain. It had encountered the free trade policy of the British Labour Government, then in office, and failed to achieve its purpose. It did not, however, relinquish its design, and at the Imperial Economic Conference held at Ottawa in 1932 made the obtaining of such a preference once more a matter of firm policy.

Mr. McFarland went about his task of disposing of the Pools' surplus. At the outset he endeavoured to allay any ill feeling that had been created in trade circles abroad by discontinuing the Pools' marketing policy of dealing directly with the mills. His efforts did not noticeably alleviate the general situation, since they did not go to the roots of the trouble. Wheat prices continued to decline. Between November of 1930, when McFarland took over, and June of 1931, the average cash price of No.1 Northern wheat at Fort William fell from 64.4 cents to 60.8 cents per bushel with no prospects of a significant increase. As a result of reductions in the initial delivery price that was being paid to Pool farmers and the general fall in prices on the Winnipeg market for those who sold to the trade, the western grain growers soon began to feel the pinch of reduced income and were forced to draw upon whatever reserves they had accumulated during the preceding years of comparative plenty.

Among the members of the Saskatchewan Pool a strong agitation developed for placing the marketing of all wheat under Pool control. This was the demand for a "100 per cent pool." Behind this demand there lay the fallacious idea, widely propagandized, that if the producer organizations could obtain complete control of the marketing of Western Canadian wheat this monopoly would enable them to exact satisfactory prices for their export surplus on the world's markets. Combined with this notion was the general desire of the Saskatchewan Pool to eliminate private competition with its own system of country elevators. So strong did the agitation become that, under the pressure of this demand, the legislature of Saskatchewan passed a grain-marketing act[2] which would give effect to this proposal, subject to the provision that a referendum should be held on the principle of a grain-marketing monopoly. Enemies to this proposal were not lacking, not only among the private grain-trading interests but among the farmers themselves. The Grain Marketing Act was referred to the courts and was held to be *ultra vires* the powers of the province by the Saskatchewan Court of Appeal. When the Saskatchewan Pool sought to secure a decision on this point from the Privy Council the appeal was held up by an injunction.[3]

In the province of Manitoba, where the demand for a compulsory pool was not as strong as in Saskatchewan, the Premier announced that the Government would not introduce legislation similar to that passed in Saskatchewan, chiefly on the ground that the legal status of such legislation required clarification. In the province of Alberta agitation took another turn. A majority of the members of the Alberta Pool voted against the "100 per cent pool" in favour of other remedies. The Alberta grain growers demanded that there should be a reduction in freight rates for the carriage of grain and that the federal Government should establish a fixed minimum price for wheat. The latter demand implied some form of federal organization, and a movement for a centralized grain marketing system subsequently crystallized among the organized grain growers of the prairies in favour of a federal grain marketing board.[4]

The tendency of western grain producers to find an explanation for low wheat prices in defective marketing organization had a further

[2]The Grain Marketing Act, Statutes of Saskatchewan, 1931, c. 87.
[3]*Regina Leader-Post*, June 26, 1931.   [4]*Winnipeg Free Press*, Dec. 5, 1933.

result. As might be expected by anyone familiar with the development of grain growers' organizations in the West, the Winnipeg Grain Exchange came in for another attack. It was held by many producers that the true cause of low prices was speculation in the futures market of the Exchange. This view received powerful support from the Pool organizations; partly, undoubtedly, from a genuine belief that futures trading in the long run was injurious to the grain grower, and partly as a method of undermining the strength of their competitors, the privately owned grain companies, who used the futures market to hedge their purchases from the farmers until the grain was in a position to be sold to the exporter.

The upshot of the agitation against the Exchange was the appointment by the federal Government in the spring of 1931 of the Royal Commission to Enquire into Trading in Grain Futures.[5] This commission was headed by Sir Josiah Stamp, and its sittings in the West were attended by immense crowds of farmers, indicative of the interest taken in the subject. The report of the commissioners supported the conclusion that futures trading was of distinct benefit to the producer by enhancing the price that he received for his grain. A mild suggestion was made that the Exchange should be placed under the surveillance of a "person of independent judgment and position" whose function essentially would be to allay suspicion that the market was rigged. The recommendation to appoint such an officer was understood to be acceptable to the Dominion Government but at the time no action was taken.[6]

To return to conditions in the wheat market, as we have seen, despite Mr. McFarland's efforts to stabilize the market, the decline in wheat prices continued. Premier Bennett's failure to secure any concessions in favour of the Canadian wheat grower from the British Government at the Imperial Conference in 1930, and unfavourable prospects for a good crop in 1931, combined to produce an embarrassing situation for the federal Government. The West was pressing it to take steps to ameliorate the lot of the grain growers and to act without delay. The need was manifest. Up to this time the remedies applied had not had any noticeable success. In response to western demands for a measure of relief Premier Bennett announced, when introducing the budget on June 1, 1931, that it was proposed to adjust

[5]See MacGibbon, *The Canadian Grain Trade*, pp. 302-3.
[6]The recommendation was repeated by Mr. Justice Turgeon in *Report of the Royal Grain Inquiry Commission, 1938* (Ottawa, 1938), p. 190; see p. 44, *infra*.

the freight rates by the Government's absorbing 5 cents per bushel of the rate on all wheat exported during the year. Subsequently, probably partly in deference to criticisms that the only one to benefit from such a measure would be the exporter, and partly because of technical difficulties in disbursing the subsidy, when the resolution came before the House on July 24 Mr. Bennett announced that the payment of 5 cents per bushel was to be made to the person who was the producer of the grain. The payment was limited to wheat growers in the western provinces. This bonus was to be distributed through the Board of Grain Commissioners.[7] The distribution involved the sum of $12,720,121 and occasioned the use of 2,891,313 certificates.[8]

This modest, not to say parsimonious, contribution to the western farmer's income was clearly not a solution to his problem. Nor was it considered to be such by the Government, though there was always the feeling that, if the situation could be left alone to work itself out, time would bring the supply of and demand for wheat into a healthier relationship. Moreover, the federal Government was looking forward to the Imperial Economic Conference to be held in Ottawa in 1932, when it was hoped that concessions in the British market might be obtained from the British Government which would be of substantial value to the Canadian wheat growers. It is important to note, however, that this bonus was a direct subsidy to the western grain grower. Up to the onset of the great depression the belief had been prevalent in the West that no matter what quantity of wheat he produced, the western farmer could stand on his own feet and sell his wheat in the markets of the world at prices that would yield him a reasonable living. He now became, for the first time, a direct beneficiary under the federal Government. Wheat growing in Western Canada entered into the category of a government-aided industry, though under exceptional circumstances.

When the free trade convictions of Philip Snowden, Chancellor of the Exchequer in the British Labour Government, blocked the Canadian attempt to secure a preference in the British market for agricultural products at the Imperial Conference of 1930, it was agreed on Premier Bennett's motion that the conference would be adjourned to meet within twelve months at Ottawa. Various circumstances conspired to prevent this meeting, but after the election in Great Britain

[7]An Act Respecting Wheat, Statutes of Canada, 1931, c. 60.
[8]*Annual Report of the Board of Grain Commissioners for Canada for the Year 1932* (Ottawa, 1933), p. 9.

in 1931 returned the National Government to power, Premier Bennett invited the members of the British Commonwealth of Nations and of the Empire to an economic conference in Ottawa in 1932. This invitation was accepted by all, and the conference was held in the late summer of that year.

It is unnecessary to enter here into all the aspects of the agreement that was eventually signed by Great Britain and Canada as a result of this conference, but out of the arrangements concluded Canada secured a preference on wheat entering the British market of 2 shillings a quarter or approximately 6 cents a bushel. This preference remained effective for six years until it was abrogated with the consent of Great Britain as part of the terms of the trade agreement negotiated between Canada and the United States in 1938. It will be recalled that this Canadian-American agreement was linked up with a trade agreement made at the same time between Great Britain and the United States.

When the wheat preference was secured in 1932 its value to Canada was sharply questioned. In fact, opinion was divided in Canada over whether, on balance, the preference gave the western wheat producer any real advantage over his competitors in Argentina and the United States. In European countries the widespread imposition of high import duties on wheat and the encouragement they gave to home production had so narrowed the international market for exporters that for all practical purposes Great Britain remained not only the only market of magnitude, but the only one where wheat could be sold on a free trade basis. Britain, however, did not provide a large enough market to absorb all the wheat grown in Canada for export. For this reason it was argued that what Canada might gain in the British market she would lose on the Continent where she would have to meet in competition the wheat displaced from the British market by reason of the preference.

The situation was not quite so simple. European wheat is harvested roughly within the same periods as wheat in Canada and the United States. As a result European countries, except Great Britain, are characteristically not large purchasers of wheat from abroad during the autumn months when their own domestic stocks are available, except in so far as they require strong protein wheat to mix with their own weak wheats to improve the quality of their flour for bread-making purposes. For this purpose Canadian wheat with its high protein content commands a quality preference in European markets during these months. This advantage was greatly reinforced by the high rate of duty per bushel of wheat levied under European tariffs. With a high rate of duty per bushel it was cheaper for the European importer to import wheat of the best quality. As the quality of the wheat declined the effect of heavy import duties became more pronounced. Canada had thus a decided advantage in the protected European market during that part of the crop year when Europe came into the world markets chiefly to buy high protein wheat.

In Britain the situation was different. Britain did not produce at this time, in relation to her needs, a large home crop. Britain imported throughout the year not only high protein wheat to give her flour "lift," but also wheat of lower quality for "filler" purposes. With the preference in effect under open marketing conditions it would be cheaper for the British miller to buy lower grade Canadian wheat suitable for "filler" purposes than to import the softer wheats from the United States or Argentina. In brief, it would be advantageous to the British miller to use a larger proportion of Canadian wheat in the mixture he ground into the flour. This would mean that Britain would tend to import more Canadian wheat than she had previously done.

On the Continent as the season advanced, if domestic supplies proved insufficient to carry through until the new crop, Europe would be in the market both for high protein wheat and for wheat for "filler" purposes. The competition for this class of wheat would then be keen. Canadian exporters, however, would continue to have the advantage in Europe created by the levy of high import duties per bushel on all wheat imported. They would also be in a strong position to make price concessions on the lower grades of wheat in the face of competition since earlier in the season they would have disposed of a larger portion of their current stocks by reason of the preference to Great Britain.

Under these conditions the general effect of the preference, it was considered, would be to increase the proportion of Canadian wheat entering into the total volume of wheat imported annually from abroad by deficit countries. Since nationalistic policies were markedly reducing the magnitude of the international wheat market, this was an important consideration, especially to a country such as Canada where opportunities to shift to other crops were not great. It meant that the volume of Canadian exports would tend to be maintained at least to some degree at the expense of such exporting countries as the United States and Argentina. If carryovers were to accumulate and exert a pressure to reduce acreage there would be a greater likelihood that they would build up in these countries than in Canada.

Alternatively, it was conceivable that rather than lose their markets in Great Britain, Argentina and the United States might choose to absorb the duty and continue to compete in the British market. In this event the effect of the duty would be to reduce the returns to the Argentinian or American wheat grower. Lower prices for wheat would constitute an incentive for them to shift their production into other crops. This in the course of time would lead to the same general result as the other alternative. Canada would tend in the long run to maintain the volume of her export trade in wheat in the face of a declining international demand by replacing to some degree the United States and Argentina in the British market.

It will be observed that the preference did not hold out any promise of raising the price of wheat to the Canadian producer. Canadian wheat would continue to be offered freely on a parity basis to British and to continental buyers. If the British Government, instead of granting a preference, had agreed to buy annually a given quota of Canadian wheat at market prices, the effect would have been practically the same. In so far, however, as the preference might lead to a reduction in wheat acreage in such exporting countries as the United States or Argentina, the effect would be to reduce the amount of wheat offered on the world's market for export and thus indirectly tend to raise prices.

An incidental effect of the British preference was to divert to Canadian ports that part of the flow of wheat that had previously gone to Great Britain from the Canadian West via American ports. This was caused by the customs regulations of the British Government. These require that when a preference is granted to the exports of a country, these exports must move from the country of origin to Great Britain by direct voyage. Until the granting of the preference a considerable proportion of Canadian wheat had been shipped to Great Britain from Fort William and Port Arthur by way of Buffalo or other American lake ports and thence to the Atlantic seaboard. Important export interests handling Canadian grain had grown up around this route. They attempted to remedy the situation created by the customs ruling, but without much success. The difficulty lay in the fact that while Canadian grain passed through the United States in bond, it was shipped in bulk, and often remained for a time in Buffalo or the other points in the transfer elevators awaiting a purchaser. It was practically impossible to satisfy the British customs that parcels of Canadian wheat reaching Great Britain from an American port under these conditions conformed to the requirements of·being conveyed to Great Britain by direct voyage. Hence, while Canadian grain exports to countries other than Great Britain continued to move by the American route, more Canadian wheat destined for Great Britain was shipped through Canadian maritime ports. This inconvenience undoubtedly hampered certain exporters in making trades with Great Britain, but on the other hand, it brought additional traffic, particularly to Saint John and Halifax. These ports have always been jealous of the Canadian traffic enjoyed by their American rivals and welcomed the preference.

While the preference had a measurable influence in inducing British millers to use a greater proportion of Canadian wheat in their mix, the general effect on the Canadian situation was not noticeable, for a variety of reasons. The whole international wheat situation was in a condition of chronic crisis because of excessive production. Even certain European countries were prepared to subsidize export shipments in order to get rid quickly of their surplus stocks. Moreover, the pegging of wheat prices on the Winnipeg Grain Exchange and Mr. McFarland's policy of supporting wheat prices in the Exchange meant that from time to time Canadian wheat was being held at prices above the world level. In so far as this occurred the advantage of the preference disappeared. Certain foreign exporters, such as Argentina, at the outset discounted the preference in the price to British buyers. This meant a loss to the Argentinian producer, but actually the preference did not remain in effect for a long enough period for this loss to have any important influence upon Argentinian wheat production. Exporters from Argentina and from the United States found the preference an obstacle to promoting sales of wheat in Great Britain and wished it removed. Hence the elimination of the preference became one of the important objects sought for in the negotiation of the trade agreement of 1938 between Canada and the United States. In return for concession granted by the United States in other fields, Canada relinquished her preference on wheat in the British market. Thus while the preference was never highly valued by the Canadian wheat producer, because it was disliked by the United States it became a bargaining factor of considerable importance in settling the terms of the 1938 agreement. By its disappearance the preference helped to secure wider markets for other Canadian products in the United States.

The continued low price of wheat and the accumulation of carry-overs from 1930 on acted as a constant incentive to the federal Government to take further action on behalf of the Canadian wheat grower. Although the world's wheat problem was not set down for consideration by the Monetary and Economic Conference held in London in June and July of 1933, Premier Bennett, who headed the Canadian delegation, raised the question and urged the conference to give consideration to the wheat problem.[9] As a result, on the invitation of the governments of Argentina, Australia, Canada, and the United States, which were all deeply concerned over the wheat situation, a conference was convened on August 21 of 1933 after the close of the Monetary and Economic Conference. This conference included eighteen European countries, as well as the above-mentioned overseas exporting countries. Premier Bennett was made chairman and presided over the meetings which lasted four days.

The aims of the conference were stated to be, (1) to arrive at an international agreement for the adjustment of exports to effective demand, with the object of eliminating the abnormal carryover which had been depressing the market for more than four years; and (2) to increase and stabilize the price of wheat to a level which would be remunerative to the farmers and fair to the consumers of bread-stuffs. Certain obstacles stood in the way of achieving these objectives. There was the purely technical problem of drafting an arrangement of sufficient flexibility to provide for the great variations in yield of wheat from year to year occurring in the chief exporting countries. It was foreseen that too rigid an agreement would almost certainly lead to its breaking down even if accepted at the time it was formulated. Secondly, there was the delicate problem of allocating the proportions of exports entering into international trade between the various countries producing wheat for export. Finally, there was the underlying difficulty of reconciling the interests of those countries which were large importers of wheat and, therefore, naturally would find it advantageous to maintain wheat prices at a relatively low level, with the interests of the great wheat-exporting countries which were keenly desirous of raising wheat prices to a solidly remunerative basis. All these difficulties were believed to be surmounted, and a wheat agreement was signed on August 25, 1933 by twenty-two nations, three of whom signed *ad referendum*.

[9]Before leaving for England Mr. Bennett had discussed the wheat situation with the premiers of the Prairie Provinces.

The terms of the agreement covered the crop years of 1933-34 and 1934-35 and were based on the assumption that the world import demand for the crop year 1933-34 would amount to 560,000,000 bushels. The quotas subsequently established for the different exporting countries gave Argentina 110,000,000 bushels, Australia 105,000,000 bushels, Canada 200,000,000 bushels, the Danubian countries 50,000,000 bushels, the United States 47,000,000 bushels, and the other countries, including Russia, 48,000,000 bushels. For the crop year of 1934-35 the governments of Argentina, Australia, Canada, and the United States agreed to limit their exports, after deducting normal domestic requirements, to maximum amounts of 15 per cent less, in the case of each country, than the average outturn on the average acreage during the period of 1931-33 inclusive. The difference between the effective world demand for wheat in the crop year of 1934-35 and the quantity of new wheat from the 1934 crop available for export was to be shared between Canada and the United States as a supplementary export allocation with a view to a proportionate reduction of their respective carryovers. It was estimated that the basis of allocating quotas for the crop year of 1934-35 would give Canada an export outlet for at least 263,000,000 bushels of wheat plus whatever might be gained under the supplementary export allocation.[10]

The engagements entered into with a view to increasing and stabilizing the price of wheat lacked the definiteness of those covering wheat exports. Indeed, it might be said with some truth that they merely registered good intentions. The governments of the wheat-importing countries agreed that they would not encourage any extension of the areas sown to wheat and that, when the international price of wheat reached and maintained an average gold price to be fixed upon, they would make a downward adjustment of tariffs accompanied by a relaxation of the general régime of quantitative restrictions upon wheat imports. The price agreed upon was 63.02 gold cents per bushel, and the period this price must be maintained was set at sixteen weeks. This general undertaking was modified by various saving phrases which had the effect of rendering it almost nugatory if any country desired to ignore it. The conference itself seemed to be aware of this weakness, for it summed up its purport in the following declaration: "The intention of this agreement is nevertheless that the importing countries will not take advantage of a voluntary reduction of exports

---

[10]D. A. MacGibbon, "The Wheat Problem," *University of Toronto Quarterly*, vol. III, no. 2, Jan., 1934, pp. 228-44.

on the part of the exporting countries by developing their domestic
policies in such a way as to frustrate the efforts which the exporting
countries are making, in the common interest, to restore the price of
wheat to a remunerative level."

Finally, a Wheat Advisory Committee composed of representatives
of the wheat-exporting and wheat-importing countries, with an adequate secretariat, was constituted with headquarters at London. The
function of this committee was to watch over the working and applications of the agreement. The secretariat was charged with the duty of
supplying regularly the various governments adhering to the agreement with indices of the international price of wheat. The index was
to be based on the average price of all parcels of imported wheat of
all grades sold during each week in all the parts of Great Britain. This
was considered to be a fair basis to fulfil the intentions of the draft
agreement.

The Wheat Advisory Committee met from time to time and made
various recommendations to the signatories of the agreement. In April
1934 it approved of a proposal to establish a minimum price for wheat
among the exporting countries which would represent an increase of
about 10 per cent over current prices. This proposal, however, did
not prove acceptable to the governments concerned. In May of the
same year it had before it the fact that Argentina had failed to observe
the agreement for 1933-34 by exceeding its quota of exports by
40,000,000 bushels, but in dealing with this default the committee did
not seem to be able to take effective action. During the summer unfavourable weather conditions led to greatly reduced yields in Canada
and the United States. This induced the optimistic view that the
situation was in process of curing itself. In September Mr. McFarland
expressed the opinion that the period of burdensome surpluses was
temporarily at an end.[11]

However, when the Advisory Committee met in Budapest in
November 1934 it was apparent that the hope of carryovers quickly
disappearing in the overseas grain-exporting countries was premature.
With good crops in Europe there were small prospects of an increase
of imports from the New World. Undaunted, the committee wrestled
with the problem of controlling the 1935 crop. At the Budapest meeting Argentina refused to be bound further by the 1933 wheat pact.
Finally, in March of 1935, attempts were made to reach further
agreement on acreage limitations, but these failed in the light of

[11]*Canadian Annual Review* (Toronto, 1934), p. 420.

Argentina's refusal to accept the basis suggested for that country. For the same reason the proposed export quotas also failed. Thus the agreement expired with the committee in deadlock. A further meeting of the four overseas exporting countries made no progress, and their negotiations on this occasion marked the downfall of the whole scheme. The Wheat Advisory Committee and its secretariat continued to exist, but did not appear to exert any decisive influence upon the world's wheat situation. Early in 1939 a meeting in London made a renewed attempt to secure an agreement, and had brought a draft nearly to the point of adoption by the exporting countries when these discussions terminated with the outbreak of war.

Commenting upon the agreement at the time it was made, the London *Economist* remarked that instead of providing an interim solution it merely sounded a call for an armistice.[12] As it worked out, those who expected great results from it were disappointed. After it failed it was said that valuable experience had been gained, but it could not be claimed that this experience demonstrated the feasibility of contriving and bringing about an agreement that would genuinely reconcile all the conflicting interests involved and stabilize wheat growing. On the technical side, the agreement revealed a lack of sufficient flexibility to cover all contingencies. When Argentina had a bumper crop in 1933 she felt obliged to disregard her obligations to other exporting countries. Thus the problem of how to cope with great variations in yield in different parts of the world without disturbing the even flow of exports remained unsolved. The attempt on the part of the overseas exporting countries to raise prices by agreement was

TABLE IV

ACREAGE STATISTICS DURING INTERNATIONAL WHEAT AGREEMENT
(Millions of acres)

		1933	1934	1935
Canada		26.03	24.19	24.22
Argentina		19.66	18.81	14.21
United States		68.49	63.56	69.21
Australia		14.90	12.54	11.96
	Total	129.08	119.10	119.60
Russia		82.0	87.2	91.7
Hungary		3.92	3.80	4.14
Rumania		7.70	7.61	8.50
Yugoslavia		5.14	5.00	5.31
Bulgaria		3.10	3.11	2.73
	Total	19.86	19.52	20.68

[12]*Economist*, Sept. 2, 1933.

rejected.   In the event the crucial question whether nations could successfully and concertedly enforce acreage reductions if this became desirable was really not answered.

While acreage statistics during the life of the agreement revealed a moderate reduction in the area devoted to wheat in the overseas exporting countries, this was not true everywhere. In Russia, a rather uncertain element during the course of negotiations, acreage increases continued. In the Danubian countries there was practically no change. Although the wheat-importing countries had gone no farther than to agree not to encourage the extension of wheat growing, the acreage trend in these countries was upward.

The impasse created by overflowing wheat warehouses and low prices was finally resolved by a sequence of short crops which came to an end in 1937. During this period surpluses disappeared. The world carryover, which had reached an estimated figure of 1,189,400,000 bushels in 1934, had fallen to 566,000,000 bushels in 1937. In Canada, the surplus at the end of the crop year of 1937-38 had shrunk to only 24,000,000 bushels, or much below a "normal" carryover of from 40,000,000 to 50,000,000 bushels. The disappearance of excess supplies naturally was reflected in Canadian prices. For the crop year of 1936-37 the average cash price of No. 1 Northern wheat basis Fort William and Port Arthur was $1.225 per bushel. In 1937-38 it had risen to $1.314 per bushel. For the time being, but only for the time being, as the large crop of 1939 indicated, the emergency had disappeared.

One Canadian problem arising out of the International Wheat Agreement remains to be touched upon—the domestic situation created in the western provinces by Canada's undertaking to restrict exports. While the agreement did not specify that the overseas exporting countries were to reduce wheat acreage, the undertaking of these countries for the crop year of 1934-35, to limit exports to maximum amounts of 15 per cent less than the average outturn on the average acreage during the period of 1931-33 inclusive, implied permanent reduction in the acreage devoted to wheat. It was considered that a moderate reduction would stabilize the situation created by reduced exports by leaving the overseas countries with sufficient acreage to provide for their domestic supplies and their quotas of exports without the danger of again building up excessive carryovers.

When the wheat agreement was under debate in Parliament Premier Bennett read a telegram from the premiers of the Prairie Provinces which he had received while on his way to London, asking him to work for a reduction of world wheat acreage. This appeared to suggest a willingness by the governments of the western provinces to take formal steps, if found necessary, to enforce reduced wheat acreage in the Canadian West. In June of 1933 Premier Bracken of Manitoba, in a considered statement given to the press, referred to the representations made by the three premiers to Mr. Bennett. These included the statement that "the Governments of Manitoba, Saskatchewan and Alberta pledge the support of their respective Provincial Governments to the principle of such curtailment of wheat production or control of exports and offer to co-operate with the Federal Government in formulating plans to carry the principle into operation in Canada." Premier Bracken said: "A general plan to restrict wheat acreage among the chief exporting countries appears to be the first and most important step toward the elimination of price-ruining wheat carryovers. The details of putting such a plan into effect will present difficulties, of course. But those difficulties are ones which can be overcome if general agreement on the principle is once achieved."[13]

The terms of the wheat agreement, implying a reduction in wheat acreage, did not receive a favourable reception from producers in Western Canada, and the attitude of the provincial premiers appeared to change in response to public opinion. In February of 1934 Premier Bracken, in reply to a question in the legislature, denied that he had come to an agreement with the other premiers of the Prairie Provinces on contracting or reducing wheat acreage. He said that in consultation with representatives of the other provinces it was "the unanimous thought to consider the possibility of bringing in legislation, not to reduce acreage, but to provide an orderly and equitable method of carrying out the agreement in case the crop should be normal or greater than normal proportions."[14] An arrangement was agreed upon by the federal and the prairie governments, but in the event action by the latter went no farther than to put through measures, substantially the same in content, giving the governments power through an appropriate organization to control the marketing of wheat.[15] The legislation would control the movement of wheat in each province for the crop year of 1934-35. Emergency wheat control boards were to be set up which would work in conjunction with a board being established

[13]*Winnipeg Free Press,* June 10, 1933.
[14]*Ibid.,* Feb. 27, 1934.
[15]E.g., the Emergency Wheat Control Act, Statutes of Manitoba, 1934, c. 48.

by the federal Government under an act for the marketing of natural products. No mention was made of curtailing wheat acreage, although the power of these provincial emergency boards generally was stated to be that of carrying out Canada's undertaking under the International Wheat Agreement. The method outlined was entirely one of controlling the volume of sales of wheat made by the producers. By limiting the volume of sales, the board or joint board would be able to bring indirect pressure on the producers to limit their acreage.

By this cautious and reluctant approach the possible necessity of acreage reduction was placed before the western wheat grower. Compulsion to reduce acreage was not liked by the western grain grower, and therefore, as the measures taken reveal, was handled very gingerly by the provincial politicians of Western Canada. The directors of the Canadian Co-operative Wheat Producers Limited (the Pools) in their report for the crop year 1933-34 "registered their unanimous opposition to any proposal of compulsory legislation to restrict acreage."[16] Premier Bracken said the consensus of opinion among the western provincial representatives was that "natural causes would probably accomplish the results the agreement seeks."[17]

Just as short crops for a time eliminated the problem for the world at large, the severe reduction in the Canadian yield which had set in in 1933 did relieve the provincial governments from any implied obligation to control production. As a matter of record, Canadian exports in both the crop years of 1933-34 and 1934-35 were below the quotas allowed Canada under the International Wheat Agreement. What was becoming apparent, however, was that governmental intervention in wheat with a view to protecting the living standards of the wheat producer was leading to government control of wheat production. This was something that the western producer hated to contemplate. He wanted protection in prices, he favoured a government marketing board, but at the same time he resented the idea of any control being exercised over the volume of wheat that he might choose to produce. As yet he was not ready to accept the proposition that this might be a logical sequence to government administered prices. The Dominion Government, on its part, while beset with the manifold problems arising out of the depression, was trying out various expedients to alleviate the position of the wheat grower without considering too deeply the long-run implications of its actions.

[16]*Canadian Annual Review,* 1934, p. 424.
[17]*Winnipeg Free Press,* Feb. 17, 1934.

3

The establishment of the
Canadian Wheat Board:
The Turgeon Commission

WHEN Mr. McFarland became General Manager of the Pools' central selling agency, current wheat stocks were owned about equally by the Pools and the private trade,[1] but with this difference, that a large proportion of the stocks owned by the private trade was hedged. Mr. McFarland's task was to liquidate the Pool stocks with as little disturbance and loss as possible and allow the wheat trade to return to its customary channels. But as the price of wheat fell month by month, disposal of the surplus became progressively more difficult. Falling prices, moreover, increased the pressure upon the federal Government to relieve the plight of the wheat farmers generally, Pool and non-Pool farmers alike. Mr. McFarland was thus led to broaden his operations.

With a view to checking the decline in price Mr. McFarland adopted the policy of withholding wheat owned by the Pools from the market. Futures taken back as a result of sales of cash wheat were also spread forward to future delivery months. In themselves these measures did not prove sufficient to stabilize the market. His next move, therefore, was to purchase wheat futures as they were offered while retaining the cash wheat. The exact date of the initiation of the policy is not definitely established, but by July 1931, six months after Mr. McFarland entered the picture, the situation was sufficiently intricate to require clarification. At this time the provincial Pools were divorced from what had hitherto been their central selling agency, and thenceforth marketed substantially all their current wheat by the

[1]*Winnipeg Free Press*, March 23, 1934.

same general methods as those employed by the private trade. The central selling agency, on the other hand, continued to be the vehicle through which Mr. McFarland operated to dispose of the Pool surplus and whatever additional stocks he had accumulated as a result of his stabilizing policy. This arrangement carried with it the approval and guarantee of the federal Government, which, however, put a credit limit on the extent to which Mr. McFarland could draw upon the banks for support. The holdings of the central selling agency in cash wheat and in futures in November of 1930 when Mr. McFarland originally took over were 36,935,000 bushels. But as a result of his stabilizing operations this amount had increased to 75,164,000 bushels by the end of July 1931.[2]

At the outset the federal Government had guaranteed the banks against loss only upon the wheat held by the central selling agency, that is, by the Pools, but this guarantee was subsequently extended to cover wheat purchased by Mr. McFarland in order to support the market. This change represented an assumption by the federal Government of wider responsibilities; in effect, it admitted an obligation to all western wheat growers to hold wheat prices at a level that would protect them against excessive loss. Mr. McFarland's action in acquiring wheat with the object of stabilizing prices on the Exchange came under strong attacks dictated partly by purely political considerations and partly by considerations of commercial policy. As his holdings increased from one year to another the wisdom of his policy, which had the backing of the federal Government, was challenged on the ground that Canadian export markets were being lost because Canadian wheat was being held at too high a price, and that the Canadian carryover, instead of being reduced to manageable size, was increasing to alarming dimensions. Meanwhile, in Western Canada, the Pool organizations were conducting a strong agitation in favour of the creation of a wheat board to market the entire crop. Moreover, the very slow pick-up in wheat prices continued to aggravate dissatisfaction and develop pessimism in the country. It had become quite clear that the problem of marketing Canada's wheat surplus was not going to be disposed of quickly. It was under these circumstances that the federal Government felt itself compelled to regularize the situation by taking a further step which identified it still more closely with the business of selling wheat. This was the creation of the Canadian Wheat Board.

[2]T. W. Grindley, in *Canada Year Book*, 1939, p. 571.

When the bill to create a wheat board was submitted to Parliament in 1935, it was observed with surprise that the Government had gone much farther than was necessary to put Mr. McFarland's operation on a statutory basis. The bill provided for a Canadian grain board with power to take over all elevators in the Prairie Provinces and with exclusive control over export and inter-provincial grain movements. The scheme contemplated in effect a compulsory grain pool which would operate on lines similar to those followed previously on a voluntary basis by the Wheat Pools. The terms of the bill implied that the board was to be a permanent body and that all other agencies of purchase and sale would be eliminated. In brief, in sponsoring this legislation, the federal Government moved from the position of giving temporary aid to a distressed industry to that of establishing a government monopoly to administer the handling and sale of the grain crop of Western Canada. This was a long step in the direction of state socialism for a Conservative government.

What were the reasons for this swing to the left? Newspaper reports suggested that an important influence was the powerful pressure exerted on the Government by the representatives of the western Wheat Pools.[3] This was probably one factor in the situation. A Dominion election was approaching, and the Wheat Pools, with their local committees all over the West, were in a position to have considerable influence on the result. For some time they had been demanding a national grain board to market Canadian grain, and it might be expected that the concession of such a board would line up their organizations behind the Government when the Government went to the country. An added factor, undoubtedly, was the resentment felt by Mr. McFarland against the private trade, with which he had come into conflict in enforcing his policy of holding wheat. Holding wheat involved the payment of carrying charges to the elevator companies, and sharp differences of opinion occurred between him and the trade over what the effective storage rate should be. One cause of difference led to another, and Mr. McFarland seemed to feel that members of the trade were "unco-operative" and should not receive any special consideration. Although originally a strong defender of the open market system of trading, Mr. McFarland's task had brought him into close contact with the Pools. This and the general problem with which he had to deal gradually undermined his original point of view until he became an outright defender, as

[3] *Winnipeg Free Press*, June 10, 1935.

an emergency measure, of the Government's policy of centralized marketing.

The country as a whole was not at this time prepared for a national grain board and all that this implied in the organization of the grain trade. Objections to a compulsory grain board came at once from the official Opposition in Parliament. The Liberals favoured temporary assistance but were not ready to go much beyond that position. Members of the private grain trade had suggested the establishment of a floor price but both they and the Winnipeg Grain Exchange were up in arms at the Government's proposed legislation. The Exchange maintained that under the terms of the proposed legislation it would cease to function, and there would be an end to the futures market which only recently had been commended by the Stamp Commission as advantageous to the farmer. The elevator companies claimed they would be forced to become merely the agents of the new board. In fact, apart from the members of the Wheat Pool organizations, there was a noticeable lack of warmth all over Canada towards this radical swing to state socialism. The project was also received critically by leaders of the grain trade in the United Kingdom, Canada's best customer.

The opposition to the measure grew, and as a result, when the bill was in committee, the Government, while insisting upon a board, executed a strategic retreat by abandoning in effect the compulsory features. These ceased to be mandatory but could be brought into force by proclamation. They remained in the Act as a big stick which could, if desired, be flourished over the trade. Instead of the pool system of payment, the principle of a fixed minimum initial price was adopted. This was to be supplemented by an issue of certificates which would enable the producers to participate in any surplus of profits which might accrue over the minimum price as a result of the operations of the board in disposing of the wheat of a given crop. The scope of the board was limited to wheat, and it became the Canadian Wheat Board instead of the Canadian Grain Board, as originally contemplated. By this change the coarse grains remained outside of government control.

The Wheat Board Act, when it finally passed Parliament, bore all the marks of a compromise measure. The Canadian Wheat Board became part of the federal Government's institutional organization for dealing with the problems arising out of the sale of stocks of surplus wheat. The Wheat Board, however, was not looked upon yet as a permanent body, but was to disappear when the situation became "normal."

The Bennett administration was defeated at the polls in October, and in December Mr. McFarland and the other two members of the Canadian Wheat Board were compulsorily retired and a new Board appointed headed by Mr. James R. Murray. The reason given for the change was that Mr. McFarland's policy had led to antagonism towards him and his Board in the world's markets which was affecting the sale of Canadian wheat. To initiate a new policy of selling wheat more freely it was held desirable to have a new Board. Apart from considerations of this nature, it is undoubtedly true that Mr. McFarland's very close relationships with Mr. Bennett would have probably made it difficult for him to work sympathetically with a Liberal Government, but it is also a fact that Mr. McFarland assumed most unwillingly a very difficult task, and was dismissed from the Board at a time when his policy of holding wheat until natural demand increased was on the eve of being vindicated.

The task of liquidating the surplus, with increased demand developing, was capably accomplished by the new Board. Because of crop failures in the United States and Argentina, in the fall of 1935 Canada was able to secure a large proportion of the world's trade in wheat. At the end of November 1935, the total holdings of the Board were 295,376,167 bushels; they were reduced to 84,698,654 bushels at the end of the crop year on July 31, 1936. In 1936 there were short crops in both the United States and Canada. As a result, during the course of the crop year of 1936-37, the Wheat Board was able to dispose of the balance of its stocks with the exception of 6,964,000 bushels held as futures. This remainder it could easily have sold, but the particularly severe drought in Saskatchewan led the federal Government to sanction holding these futures with a view to exchanging them for cash wheat for seed purposes in Saskatchewan for the 1938 crop. The net result of the Board's operations up to July 31, 1937 was a loss of $2,278,797.95. But this represented net profits of $9,628,881.61 on its transactions up to December 2, 1935 in respect to the surplus with deductions for losses, particularly in marketing the 1935 crop.[4]

In the meantime, the Canadian carryover of wheat had fallen to 32,937,991 bushels and no longer constituted a problem. Logically, it would appear that the Canadian Wheat Board had completed the job for which it had been established and might now be allowed to

[4]Canadian Wheat Board, Report, crop years 1935-36, 1936-37.

disappear. But although the 1937 wheat crop was handled through the ordinary channels of the grain trade, the Wheat Board was not promptly dissolved but continued to exist. It acted as agent for the Saskatchewan Government in purchasing seed wheat for that province; it co-operated with the Board of Grain Commissioners in introducing Thatcher wheat to the millers of the United Kingdom, and organized a publicity campaign in the Old Land to promote increased sales of Canadian wheat. All told, however, it was rather hard put to keep itself busy; these activities were minor compared with its previous operations. The real reason why the federal Government retained the Board at this time was that another royal commission was currently conducting an investigation into the problem of what were the best methods for Canada to employ in selling wheat, and the federal Government could hardly commit itself to a definitive policy until it had the Commissioner's recommendations before it. When in 1938, with a large crop, the situation reverted to that of surplus conditions and falling prices, the Board again became important to the federal Government in marketing the Canadian wheat crop. To protect the wheat grower the Government fixed a minimum price for wheat of 80 cents per bushel when delivered to the Board. This price was higher than that ruling on the open market. Consequently, the growers delivered their wheat to the Wheat Board and it became once more the principal agency through which Canadian exports of wheat were channelled to market. Obviously the Canadian Wheat Board was gradually establishing itself in the western mind as an indispensable part of the wheat marketing machinery of Canada. Theoretically, the federal Government had not accepted this position, but actually that was what was taking place. This will become more apparent when we study the outcome of the recommendations made by the Royal Commission under Mr. Justice Turgeon, which began its labours in June 1936.

The genesis of this commission is interesting. From the time that Mr. McFarland assumed responsibility for disposing of the Wheat Pools' surplus, his operations, with which the federal Government was necessarily identified, were under almost continuous parliamentary review. When the Wheat Board Act, 1935, was before the House of Commons it was referred to a special committee under the chairmanship of the Prime Minister, Mr. Bennett. On this occasion Mr. McFarland and other members of his organization were examined at length by members of this committee. The Government and the

Opposition treated the problem as a political issue. The Government was anxious to establish that the best possible course had been followed and the Liberal Opposition was equally intent on proving that Mr. McFarland's policy of holding wheat was fraught with danger for the future, would, in fact, reduce Canada's share in the international market. The Liberals advocated the continuous sale of Canadian wheat abroad.

Incidental to the discussions of the committee was the fight between the Pools, which supported Mr. McFarland and the Wheat Board, and the private trade, which was anxious to see the Government out of the wheat-marketing field. For the rural electorate of Western Canada there is no question that has greater political significance than the federal Government's wheat policy; hence the discussions of the committee were important from the standpoint of party fortunes at the polls. The defeat of the Conservatives in 1935 appeared to be a setback for the policy of marketing wheat through a government board. As we have seen, Mr. McFarland ceased to be Chairman of the Canadian Wheat Board, and his successor was given the job of disposing of the wheat surplus as rapidly as possible.

In 1936 Mr. Bennett, now in opposition, declared that the appointment of the new Board with James R. Murray at its head was conceived by the Liberal ministry as a body blow to the Wheat Pools and to the whole conception of marketing held by the previous Government and practised by Mr. McFarland.[5] So heated grew the interchanges between the Government and the Opposition that a special committee of the House of Commons was once more set up to review the operations of the Wheat Board. On this occasion Mr. Murray, the Chief Commissioner, bore the brunt of the investigation, with Mr. Bennett as chief examiner. Mr. Murray declared that the Board had taken a long-range view of the situation in disposing rapidly of the Canadian wheat surplus. He referred to the reduced markets for wheat in Europe and said that the Canadian problem for years to come would be to find the best method of placing Canada's wheat surplus on the foreign market. In this connection, he recommended the appointment of a commission to examine the problem in all its aspects at home and abroad. It will be noted that the problem was still considered to be one of marketing rather than one of the world-wide over-production of wheat. Mr. Murray's recommendation was endorsed by the committee and accepted by the Government.

[5]*Winnipeg Free Press*, Feb. 11, 1936.

Hon. Mr. Justice Turgeon of Saskatchewan was selected to conduct the investigation.[6] He possessed wide experience as an investigator, having served on a large number of royal commissions. As Chairman of the Royal Grain Inquiry Commission of 1925 he was intimately acquainted with the problems involved in wheat marketing. His new commission contained instructions to inquire into and to report upon the methods employed in marketing Canadian wheat abroad, including government grain boards, pool marketing, price stabilization measures, and the open market or competitive system, and the effect of these various methods upon Canada's markets. He was also called upon to report on the causes of the decrease in Canadian grain exports and to recommend what measures should be taken to retain and to extend markets abroad for Canadian wheat and coarse grains.

These were to be the main objects of his inquiry, but in addition certain questions, which had become the subject of political controversy, were referred to him for consideration. He was to make an investigation into the handling of grain for relief and seeding purposes since 1930 in the provinces of Alberta, Saskatchewan, and Manitoba; an inquiry into whether the Canadian Wheat Board had protected speculative short interests in the Winnipeg Grain Exchange in December of 1935; and a study of the effect of the practice of mixing and of the selection of grain for high protein content by millers and exporters.

Although the Order-in-Council recommended to the Commissioner that he make his report "as speedily as possible," it was not until 1938, after an interval of nearly two years, that the Commissioner reported his findings. This delay was partly due to his being concurrently engaged in conducting an inquiry into the textile industry for the Dominion Government, which involved lengthy adjournments of the grain inquiry, and partly due to the wide scope of his investigation. In all, 122 days were devoted to public hearings, 260 witnesses were heard, and 715 exhibits filed. In addition to the sittings held in Canada and one held in Chicago, the Commissioner visited Europe and met representatives of the grain trade and of the millers in Great Britain, France, Belgium, and Holland.[7]

In line with the terms of reference the Commissioner's report revealed a preoccupation with the problems of marketing rather than

[6]P.C. 1577, 1936.
[7]*Report of the Royal Grain Inquiry Commission, 1938* (Ottawa, 1938), p. 13.

with the deeper long-run economic forces which have made wheat a world problem. "In the course of time," he observed, "our producers may find it to their advantage to devote their activities in a larger degree than at present to some other form of agricultural production. But our present problem is to find markets for the whole of the wheat surplus we are producing and are likely to continue to produce for a long period of years."[8] The narrowed export market for wheat he found to be due to the heightened protective policies employed by the European governments in the interests of their own agriculturalists. These policies involved the use of such new devices as fixing milling quotas and setting out the amount of domestic wheat to be used in manufacturing flour. He pointed out that apart from the general purpose of ensuring a prosperous farm population through the media of higher prices and a wider market, other considerations were also effective in Europe, such as the desire of various countries to protect their currencies by reducing imports, and the fear of war with the inadvisability of depending upon foreign supplies of food in that contingency.

The reduction of Canada's share in this reduced overseas market he attributed to several factors: a succession of short crops in Canada; the Canadian tariff policy which, by limiting the market in Canada for manufactured goods from Europe, caused a shrinkage in the amount of wheat European nations could buy from Canada; and, in general, the announcement by the leaders of the Canadian Pools that they were looking forward to the formation of an international selling organization able to enforce a rise in wheat prices, which could only be procured at the expense of the European consumer.[9] In connection with the latter factor, he cited the Wheat Pools' policy of withholding supplies from the market during the crop year of 1929-30 and the stabilization measures employed by Mr. McFarland, particularly in 1934-35. "If ever again circumstances should induce the Government of Canada to intervene in wheat marketing by paying the producer a price in excess of world prices," he observed, "no attempt should be made to enforce that excessive price overseas, that is, to pass the burden of our relief to the producer on to the overseas buyer. He will not accept the burden. And in the long run all attempts to pass it on, by withholding supplies or otherwise, will prove detrimental to the producers themselves, because it will again indispose buyers towards Candian wheat."[10]

[8]*Ibid.*, p. 139.   [9]*Ibid.*, p. 141.   [10]*Ibid.*, p. 158.

The possibility of an international agreement to reduce wheat acreage and to ensure fair prices to the producer, such as was attempted by the International Wheat Agreement in 1933, apparently was not examined by the Commissioner. At any rate, arrangements of this sort and their limitations, if considered, were not deemed to be of sufficient significance by him to become part of his report. Substantially, the inquiry concentrated upon the problem of disposing of Canada's exportable grain surplus within the existing framework of governmental policies. Accordingly, as one would expect, the stress was laid on marketing techniques and marketing policy.

In this field the old controversies between the Winnipeg Grain Exchange and the producers' organizations were again rehearsed. All the old arguments on the merits of a futures market versus direct selling by a government board or compulsory pool were threshed out once more. The Commissioner heard a great deal of evidence and wearisome argument on this threadbare topic both in Canada and abroad, but the inquiry did not uncover any essentially new points of view. Mr. Justice Turgeon's conclusions were substantially in accord with those reached by the Stamp Commission in 1931. "I am convinced," he said, "from all the knowledge I have been able to acquire on the subject, that the futures trading system, despite its imperfections, is the one best qualified to look after the interests of our producers, at home and abroad."[11]

With respect to charges that the futures market made possible price manipulations that were detrimental to the welfare of the producers he said that he found himself "back again to the position expressed by the Stamp Commission . . . 'Nothing was given in evidence of a practical or satisfactory character as to what is done or how it is done,'" but there was no conclusive satisfactory proof "'as to the impossibility of such practices existing.'"[12]

The Commissioner's finding in favour of the maintenance of the free marketing system involved, as he recognized, the rejection of the "one alternative": ". . . a national marketing board, created and supported financially by the Government of Canada, charged with the duty of disposing of the whole of the western wheat crop." Of this alternative he said: "This proposal of a compulsory Government Board

[11]Ibid., p. 183.
[12]Ibid., p. 53. Commissioner Turgeon went further than the Stamp Commission in recommending supervision of the trading activities of the Exchange. See above, p. 20.

has preoccupied me more than anything else since the beginning of this inquiry. It was asked for by nearly all farmers' organizations; and by a great many individual farmers who appeared before me."[13]

While admitting the attractiveness of a government board, the Commissioner expressed the opinion that it was not practicable. At the present time a Canadian grain board would be regarded abroad as a further restriction upon the freedom of trade and commerce. Within the grain trade itself it would meet with "antagonism, at least passive and perhaps even active in some places." Canada, consequently, would be going into a field of diminished markets, with many free competitors, under a great handicap. The technical position of such a board, because of its great volume of holdings, would be most delicate, and its action in time of uncertainty would have a magnified effect upon the market. There would be no bargaining in Canadian wheat as there is under open market conditions and as there would continue to be in respect of the wheats of other countries. Earlier in his report the Commissioner had remarked with reference to the abnormal conditions of 1919 that the experience of the Wheat Board of that time could be no guide to the potential success of a board doing business in world markets in the midst of buyers and sellers in active competition. In 1919 there was no marketing problem, there were only a few overseas customers, and these all government boards themselves. They were operating while futures markets were closed in Great Britain and Canada.[14]

The situation in Canada under a government board, in his opinion, would also be disadvantageous to the producer. Mr. Justice Turgeon cited the evidence of Mr. McFarland and of Mr. Murray, both of whom had had experience in operating the Canadian Wheat Board, as favouring supervised futures trading. Mr. McFarland had qualified his evidence with the view that in a time of crisis a government board as an emergency organization would be necessary. Referring to the fear of criticism from their members by Pool officials, the Commissioner pointed out that "any group of men endeavouring with the best intentions in the world to make a success of selling wheat would be exposed to a great deal of criticism." This, he said, would apply with even greater force to a government board. The members of a compulsory government board would be answerable not only to the producers who believed in the board, but those who did not believe in it, and who would protest against what they considered to be high-

[13]*Ibid.*, p. 185.   [14]*Ibid.*, p. 63.

handed interference. In the light of past experience, one could conclude that as time went on such a board would suffer more and more from the atmosphere of political controversy that would surround it.

For all these reasons Commissioner Turgeon held that, under what might be called normal conditions, the Canadian Government should remain out of the grain trade and said he could not recommend compulsory marketing of all Canadian wheat by a government board, at least as long as there was free, open marketing in the United Kingdom.[15]

Nevertheless, despite the considerations against a compulsory wheat board, the Commissioner said he did not feel he could suggest the immediate dissolution of the Canadian Wheat Board since there appeared to be a strong possibility that conditions might develop which would require a measure of assistance in the marketing of the 1938 crop. While he was not in favour of a compulsory board, Commissioner Turgeon expressed approval of the form of producers' organization that had been adopted by the Australian Pools. These operated on a flexible basis, selling in line with marketing conditions, and conducting their business through regular trade channels.

The results of Commissioner Turgeon's wide and intensive survey were given in his recommendations (1), that the Government should remain out of the grain trade; (2), that Canadian wheat should be marketed by means of the futures market system; (3), that the Winnipeg Grain Exchange should be placed under proper supervision, (4), that encouragement should be given to the creation of co-operative marketing associations or pools on the Australian model. Taken all in all his report constituted a searching analysis of the difficulties and disadvantages under ordinary competitive conditions of a government embarking upon a course of commercial trading in a highly competitive business, but it must be said that the restriction of his conclusion to "what may be called normal conditions" made it unrealistic. This was tacitly recognized in the suggestion that the Canadian Wheat Board should for the time being be retained. One could only conclude that the sickness of the wheat industry was not caused by the methods of marketing employed but by a fundamental disequilibrium between supply and demand.[16]

[15]*Ibid.*, p. 188.
[16]The Commissioner found that the Canadian Wheat Board did not protect speculative short interests in the Winnipeg wheat market in December, 1935. *Report of the Royal Grain Inquiry Commission, 1938*, p. 206.

Commissioner Turgeon's report was received in Western Canada without any marked expression of public opinion except from those organizations directly affected. The Wheat Pools were disappointed that a compulsory wheat board was not recommended, while private trading interests were pleased over one more "vindication" of the system of free marketing. To the general public it looked as if the situation had been left very much as it had been. The course of events seemed to confirm this view. Despite the fact that short crops had cleaned up previous excessive carryovers and average wheat prices had risen in 1936 and 1937 until they had reached over $1.00 per bushel, when larger crops in 1938 led to another sharp decline in prices the federal Government again felt itself forced to intervene. By fixing a farmer's delivery price of 80 cents per bushel on wheat delivered to the Board, the Government in effect took the marketing of this crop into its hands, since this price was in excess of that ruling on the open market.

The federal Government's substantial acceptance of Commissioner Turgeon's recommendations, however, became apparent in 1939 when it announced a new policy designed (1) to implement his principal recommendations and (2) to establish a more equitable method of distributing aid from the federal treasury to the western grain producer.

It indicated that it proposed to abandon the Canadian Wheat Board, with its fixed minimum delivery prices, and to rely on the futures market system for the marketing of Canadian Wheat. To meet the strongest of the objections of the wheat growers to this system the Government announced that the Winnipeg Grain Exchange would be placed under proper supervision. This was in accord with Commissioner Turgeon's agreement with the conclusions of the Stamp Commission of 1931 and his own recommendation, set out in more explicit terms, that the Government adopt this course. After a lapse of eight years from the time the original recommendation was made the Government took the first steps in this direction. The Grain Futures Act was passed in May of 1939, and proclaimed in July of the same year.[17] This Act provided for the appointment of an official who was to serve under the Board of Grain Commissioners for Canada as a supervisor of the Winnipeg Grain Exchange. The Board of Grain Commissioners were empowered, whenever they were of the opinion that transactions in grain futures were causing or threatening to cause

[17]Statutes of Canada, 1939, c. 31.

sudden or undue fluctuations in the price of any kind of grain, to fix minimum margins, to fix the amount of any kind of grain which could be traded in by any person, and to suspend from trading privileges any member of the Exchange guilty of a breach of the Grain Futures Act or orders or regulations made thereunder. This measure, however, never became operative.

The failure to make supervision effective is understood to have been partly because of objections raised by the Canadian Wheat Board. The Board was at this time an important factor in the marketing situation and no doubt felt that it had the market under sufficient control to protect the public interest. Moreover, it is likely that it did not desire to have its day-to-day pit operations placed under the surveillance of another government department. The outbreak of war strengthened these objections and diverted attention to other aspects of the grain marketing problem.

In the interest of producers who wished to dispose of their wheat by the pooling method, a second measure, the Wheat Co-operative Marketing Act,[18] provided for the establishment of co-operatives of the Australian type. Producers who elected to adopt this method of marketing would receive from the Government a guarantee of a minimum price of 60 cents per bushel. In the outcome this method of marketing received little support from the producers. Co-operatives established under this Act were of almost no significance and disappeared when the Government closed the futures market in 1943.

Finally, to meet situations where farmers in certain districts might suffer widespread losses of crops on account of drought or from other causes, the Government announced the establishment of an acreage bonus scheme providing for payments to those who suffered on the basis of the acreage sown to wheat. This measure, destined to become an important feature of the western farm economy, was embodied in the Prairie Farm Assistance Act.[19] The terms of this Act will receive consideration in the next chapter.

When the Government disclosed its policy public attention concentrated on its rejection of state marketing. While the Prairie Farm Assistance Act was welcomed, the Government's intention to dispense with the Wheat Board and to put marketing back where it was in 1929 was not favourably received in the West either generally or by its own western supporters in Parliament. So strong were the objections

[18]*Ibid.*, c. 34.
[19]*Ibid.*, c. 50.

raised by western Liberal members that the Government found itself forced to bow to the storm and to retain the Wheat Board as an organization to which the grain growers could deliver their wheat at a minimum price if the open market price fell below satisfactory levels. Having yielded to this degree the Government, in the face of the strong pressure from western members of the House of Commons to make it higher, refused to set this minimum price at more than 70 cents per bushel for No. 1 Northern wheat in store at Fort William, Port Arthur or Vancouver.

The really significant fact was that the Government had tried to get out of the business of selling wheat and had failed. Its inability to divest itself of the Canadian Wheat Board at this time registered the fact that the Canadian wheat growers were determined that the Government should maintain the Board, if not primarily as a regular vehicle for selling wheat, at least as a stand-by organization that would protect them against drastic downward swings in the market. The producers were firmly convinced that they were entitled to a "fair" price for their product, and if this was not forthcoming on the basis of supply and demand then they looked to the Government to make good the deficiency through the Wheat Board. With the capitulation of the Government to this point of view it was no longer possible to regard the Canadian Wheat Board as a temporary organization established to meet a single emergency, but as a permanent part of the institutional machinery of Canada for dealing with wheat marketing. Henceforth it was clearly apparent that the Canadian wheat growers were not willing to rely upon the processes of an open world market to reward them for their toil no matter how many royal commissions might tell them that in the long run this was the most efficient method of selling wheat. What they were interested in was the immediate present rather than the uncertain and more distant future. It was also apparent that they were able to exert sufficient political pressure at Ottawa to make their view effective with the federal Government.

The shift away from a free trading to a socialistic point of view with respect to marketing among the wheat growers had really begun with the slump in wheat prices that followed the First World War. Unable to secure a continuance of the Wheat Board of 1919 the wheat growers organized the Pools, and the success of these organizations for a time led them to believe that the pooling method of marketing wheat solved the problem of assuring to them at all times a reasonable average price. The disastrous collapse in prices of 1929 made it evident, however, that this position could not always be maintained. Thereafter the wheat growers looked to the federal Government to guarantee them a price for their product that would be satisfactory to them in the face of whatever fluctuations might occur in the international level of wheat values. That the unsatisfactory condition of the international wheat market was caused by the over-production of wheat did not come home to them clearly, but in shifting to a nationalistic viewpoint the Canadian wheat grower was in the broad current of the times. Over-production of wheat was a direct result of the general régime of nationalism and protection that developed in Europe after the First World War. With the onslaught of the depression in 1929, as protective tariffs rose and other restrictive devices appeared in European countries, the situation became aggravated. Canadian wheat growers were only saved from complete disaster through the intervention of the federal Government. But having thus become beneficiaries of the Government's stabilizing policies, the Canadian wheat growers were no longer willing to face without protection the wide downward swings in price that from time to time were an unwelcome feature of unwise production practices. The Canadian Wheat Board became the chosen instrument to meet such a situation.

4

Wheat growing becomes a protected industry

THE final outcome of federal wheat policies between 1929 and 1939 was the retention by the Dominion Government of the Canadian Wheat Board as an agency to protect the wheat growers from the effects of a drastic decline in wheat values such as had occurred at the beginning of the decade. This result represented a compromise in the face of the play of conflicting interests, which on the one hand favoured the establishment of a compulsory wheat board and on the other urged strict adherence to the open market system of trading. As it worked out, the method devised developed into an alternating system of marketing. When the price of wheat was relatively high, that is, above the minimum price fixed for deliveries to the Wheat Board, the wheat growers sold their wheat mainly to the elevator companies, who in turn disposed of their purchases through the open market system of selling. When this occurred the Wheat Board became inactive except in so far as it might have small portions of the crop delivered to it or had stocks on hand from previous deliveries. But when wheat prices fell until the Wheat Board's minimum delivery price was in excess of that obtainable on the open market, the situation quickly changed. The growers then naturally delivered their wheat to the Board. While the elevators continued to handle the crop physically as agents for the Wheat Board, the latter had the responsibility of selling it and of determining settlements to the growers. The growers were now in a strong position; the minimum price they received carried with it, in the form of a participating certificate, the right to share in any profits that might accrue to the Wheat Board from the final disposal of the year's crop; but if the Board's operation resulted in a

49

loss, this loss was absorbed by the Government. Thus western wheat producers could count on being able to share in any upward trend of prices and yet were sheltered from the effects of an excessive decline.

What they were not protected against was the natural hazards of production, and these constitute a serious problem in Western Canada. It will be recalled that when the Government announced its 1939 policy, a scheme of payments to wheat producers in the event of light crops or crop failures was included.[1] At the time that this policy was put forward by the Government it was offered largely as a substitute for the guaranteed minimum delivery price provided for under the Wheat Board. But although forced to retain the Wheat Board by public opinion and its western supporters, the Government did not relinquish this measure, the explanation being that the western wheat grower naturally wanted to have both.

The criticism had frequently been urged against the guaranteed minimum delivery price, as a method of relieving the distress of the prairie wheat grower, that while it aided the farmer who had produced a crop, it gave no assistance to the one who suffered from a crop failure. Moreover, a minimum delivery price was relatively of less benefit to a farmer with a light crop, who presumably needed the most help, than to a farmer with a heavy yield. Hon. J. G. Gardiner, Dominion Minister of Agriculture, made this point in a statement before Parliament. In the crop year of 1938-39 it was calculated, he said, on the basis of export prices realized by the Wheat Board on its sales, that the minimum delivery price of 80 cents per bushel which the wheat grower received on his deliveries for that year represented a bonus of approximately 20 cents over open market prices on each bushel delivered to the Board. Mr. Gardiner estimated that this bonus involved a total subsidy to prairie wheat growers of $48,000,000. Of this sum Saskatchewan, his own province, where the crops were lightest, would receive only $18,000,000, while $22,800,000 would go to the wheat growers of Alberta. "The Province where the greatest difficulties were experienced and which had the greatest acreage, received only $18,000,000 out of $48,000,000 paid out under the fixed price."[2]

The Prairie Farm Assistance Act was designed to meet such a situation and to distribute a subsidy more fairly when one was being given. It provided that any crop year in which the average price of No. 1 Northern wheat in store at Fort William or Port Arthur was

[1]The Prairie Farm Assistance Act, Statutes of Canada, 1939, c. 50.
[2]Hon. J. G. Gardiner, House of Commons, Feb. 16, 1939.

less than 80 cents per bushel might be declared by the Governor-in-Council an "emergency year" under the Act. In that event, if large areas were affected, certain specified amounts were to be paid to the producers in Western Canada. These payments were to be based on the average yield per acre in each individual township. If the yield were more than 8 bushels per acre and not more than 12 the award was to be 10 cents per acre of the cultivated land of the farmer for each cent or fraction of a cent, not exceeding 10 cents, by which the average price was less than 80 cents per bushel. If the average yield was between 4 and 8 bushels per acre, the payment was to be $1.50 per acre. If not over 4 bushels per acre, the payment rose to $2 per acre. Payments were limited to one-half of the cultivated land of the farmer, with a maximum acreage upon which payments could be made of 200 acres. This provision was designed, essentially, to aid those farmers who had not only to face low prices but also a poor crop. In 1942 the requirement that wheat must fall below 80 cents per bushel was deleted and the Governor-in-Council was empowered to declare any year an emergency year.[3]

Whenever the Minister of Agriculture found that the average yield of wheat, as a result of anything other than hail, was 5 bushels per acre or less in each of not less than 135 townships in Saskatchewan or 100 in Alberta or Manitoba, the Governor-in-Council could declare such a provincial area to be a crop failure area. The Minister of Agriculture was authorized when this occurred to make payments by way of assistance to each farmer in the area of a sum of $200 or, if greater, a sum not exceeding $2.50 per acre on one-half of the cultivated acreage of the farmer not to exceed 200 acres. In 1940 the Act was amended by instituting a board of review to determine the average yield per acre in any township seeking assistance. The number of townships per province needed for the declaration of a crop failure area was increased in Saskatchewan to 171 and reduced in Alberta to 90 and in Manitoba to 54. In 1947 this section of the Act was repealed; applications for assistance could henceforth be made on a township basis. The necessity for declaring any year to be an emergency year was thus eliminated and this requirement under the Act also disappeared.[4]

The granting of this assistance was made more acceptable to the taxpayers of Canada by a requirement that a levy of 1 per cent should

---

[3]Statutes of Canada, 1942, c. 5.
[4]*Ibid.*, 1940, c. 38; 1947, c. 43.

be deducted from the purchase price of all grain sold to licensees of the Board of Grain Commissioners. This requirement brought within the scope of the levy substantially all grain entering into commerce in Western Canada. The amount collected by this levy was to be paid into a special account of the Consolidated Revenue Fund of Canada, called the Prairie Farm Emergency Fund, by the Board of Grain Commissioners, which was made the collecting agency. The imposition of this levy in effect incorporated into this legislation the idea of crop-loss insurance, but the rate of levy quite obviously would not yield a return which would prove sufficient to cover the amounts paid out as bonuses.[5]

A secondary effect of price and acreage subsidies was to encourage the production of wheat. The probability of this had been pointed out by the Minister of Agriculture for Alberta in discussing the Government's programme. He said that the plan would "encourage the growing of more wheat" and would "offer no inducement to growers of any other grains."[6] Indeed, no other group of farmers in Canada was placed in an equally privileged position. In announcing the Government's programme to Parliament the Minister of Agriculture, Mr. Gardiner, said the objective of the Government was to "set up as many homes as can possibly be maintained in the prairie section of Western Canada."[7] That this end might be achieved by a more balanced method of agriculture was still not within the purview of federal policy. In the face of a strong trend throughout the world towards the over-production of wheat, which led to recurring surpluses and price difficulties, there was no hint at this time that the Canadian Government or the grain growers themselves recognized any necessity to restrict wheat production in Canada to within the limits set by home consumption and the amount that the export markets ordinarily would absorb. The emphasis was still on expansion.

Nevertheless, for years the hard core of the Canadian wheat problem had been that the world was growing too much wheat relative to effective demand, and that the prairie farmers specialized on an enormous scale in this production. In 1930 sown acreage in the western provinces was estimated at 23,960,000 acres. In 1935, after five years of low prices, there had occurred no substantial reduction in acreage. In 1936, with better prices, wheat acreage had increased to 24,838,000

[5]See below, p. 219.
[6]*Winnipeg Free Press*, Feb. 18, 1939.
[7]*Canada, House of Commons Debates*, Feb. 16, 1939.

acres. The legislation of 1939 began at once to bear the fruit that might logically be expected from it. In 1939 Canadian wheat growers increased their acreage by approximately 1,000,000 acres. In 1940 there followed another increase of 2,000,000 acres, Canadian wheat acreage in that year reaching the peak figure of 27,750,000 acres. Undoubtedly, the expectation that the war would increase the demand for wheat was also a factor in this expansion.

It was the combination of relatively high yields and expanded acreage in 1939 and 1940 that finally forced the Government into a policy of restricting the production of wheat. Production of wheat was increasing at such a rate in Canada that, lacking wider markets, it was threatening to go beyond the physical possibilities of storage. Even with increased exports in 1940 the carryover at the end of the crop year, July 31, 1941, reached the enormous total of 480,129,000 bushels. Before that date, however, the Government acted. The probability of a carryover of this order of magnitude was so plainly apparent in the winter of 1941 that, however reluctant to act, the federal Government had to face the situation. The only feasible solution was one that involved a reduction in acreage.

The effort to solve the wheat problem by reduced production was a belated recognition of the fact that the cause of low prices and the wheat growers' difficulties lay deeper than the methods of marketing employed. This occurred gradually and, in so far as it happened, represented a notable change in view. All the royal commissions that had investigated the grain trade had proceeded upon the premise that with suitable marketing organization the western wheat grower's problem of disposing of his product at a remunerative price would be solved. Mr. Justice Turgeon's Commission of 1938 began its investigation with some consideration of fundamental world conditions, but it soon bogged down in the question of competing theories of marketing, namely, a compulsory wheat board versus free enterprise. The Commissioner's views seemed to centre around the inadequacies of markets; he apparently did not come to any conclusion about whether Canada was producing a quantity of wheat beyond the normal capacity of its foreign markets. While he pointed out the uncertainties of the international situation, he placed his emphasis upon the necessity of Canadian wheat being of high quality and being offered at a reasonable price rather than upon sheer quantity produced.[8] One man who had early seen the necessity of acreage reduction was John I.

[8]Report of the Royal Grain Inquiry Commission, 1938 (Ottawa, 1938), p. 157.

McFarland; throughout his period of public office he had repeatedly urged the importance of such a policy. But neither western wheat producers nor provincial farm leaders were disposed to admit such a necessity. It was only the emergence of the difficulties of storing excess supplies under wartime conditions that forced the federal Government finally to devise measures that would tend to restrict acreage. Although western farmers did not like the prospect, the force of events was compelling them to accept reluctantly the idea that wheat acreage in Western Canada would have to be reduced. The practical problem they faced was what to do with the land that they would be forced to take out of wheat; how were they to maintain farm income? This was the problem the federal Government had to solve when it undertook to cut down wheat production.

On March 12, 1941, an interlocking programme was announced to Parliament by the Ministers of Agriculture and of Trade and Commerce; it called for a substantial reduction in the farm acreage sown to wheat and limited the wheat deliveries that could be made to the market. While the Minister of Trade and Commerce announced that Canadian wheat growers would be limited in their market deliveries to 230,000,000 bushels, the Minister of Agriculture made public a scheme of compensation whereby grain growers who reduced their wheat acreage in 1941 would receive payments from the Government. The Departments of Trade and Commerce and of Agriculture were linked together in the Dominion Government's wheat programme of 1941 because of the division of function that exists between these two Departments with respect to agricultural products. Upon the Department of Trade and Commerce devolves the duty of promoting the sale of Canada's products abroad, and for this reason the problem of marketing Canadian wheat under the best conditions has always been a major responsibility of the Minister of Trade and Commerce. For the same reason the Board of Grain Commissioners, which is responsible for the official weighing and grading of Canadian grains, is under this Minister. The Department of Agriculture concerns itself with the problems of production. With respect to wheat production it has achieved some really great successes. The development of improved varieties of early maturing wheat expanded the wheat-growing area in Western Canada, while the breeding of rust and drought-resistant varieties increased the yield per acre. The whole emphasis of the Department has always been upon the greater production of high quality wheat in Western Canada. The larger and larger harvests that were garnered on the prairies were a tribute to the success that crowned its efforts. Hence, when a situation arose that required limitations upon wheat production, this problem also became one for the Department of Agriculture. The 1941 programme recognized that the wheat problem was no longer one merely of marketing methods, but also one of production.

Since the Government's policy was not announced until nearly the middle of March, prompt action was necessary with respect to both measures in order that the farmers might know where they stood when sowing their crops for the season of 1941. For this reason, while its proposals were freely debated in the House of Commons, the Government did not proceed with them by way of legislation but took advantage of its powers under war conditions to make them effective by other methods. Acting through the Canadian Wheat Board the Government authorized the Board to accept for the coming crop year the limited quantity of 230,000,000 bushels of wheat, of which 223,000,000 bushels were to come from Western Canada.[9] Payments as compensation for a reduction in the acreage sown to wheat were authorized to be made to the wheat producers by an Order-in-Council passed on April 30, 1941.[10] By these short cuts the Government's programme was made clear to the wheat growers in time to affect their decisions governing the crop of 1941. The principles embodied in the payment of compensation for acreage reduction in 1941 were subsequently given statutory form by the Wheat Acreage Reduction Act of 1942, and continued for that year.

The execution of the 1941 programme involved at the outset the collection of a vast amount of statistics both by the Canadian Wheat Board and by the organization established in the Department of Agriculture to administer the Prairie Farm Assistance measure, the latter organization being given the additional task of making the payments authorized for reductions in wheat acreages. The base upon which individual marketing quotas and compensatory payments rested was the declared acreage in wheat on each farm in the year 1940. The collection of data was made independently by both organizations. They served as a check upon each other, for in the event of a marked discrepancy between the figures submitted by the two bodies, an investigation was conducted by the federal treasury before money was paid out.

[9]Canadian Wheat Board, *Instructions to the Trade*, no. 200, April 30, 1941.
[10]P.C. 3047 amended by P.C. 3231.

The Canadian Wheat Board was fortunate in that part of the work required had been done by it already. In 1940, when limited storage space had made it necessary to regulate deliveries at country points, in order to divide the available space fairly between all, the Wheat Board, under the authority of an Order-in-Council,[11] had instituted the requirement that no wheat, oats, or barley could be delivered at a country shipping point without a permit from the Wheat Board. Farmers were to share in the deliveries possible on the basis of acreage in crop, and in order to carry out this principle permit books were validated for each farmer. These permit books contained a sworn declaration by the holder, stating the number of acres in each farm and the seeded acreage of wheat, oats, and barley, and provided a record of deliveries made. When it became necessary in 1941 to restrict marketings, the information contained in these permit books was on file with the Wheat Board. In April of 1941 the Wheat Board announced that it had worked out the principles of a quota plan by which wheat producers would be permitted to base their deliveries of wheat during 1941-42 on 65 per cent of their 1940 wheat acreage.

The Board pointed out that it was not possible to forecast the crop in advance nor to foresee the distribution of high and low yields between different parts of the wheat-growing area. Nevertheless, a basis of 65 per cent of the wheat acreage sown in 1940 would give the growers a rough idea of what reduction in acreage would be required to bring the total yield into reasonable conformity with the amount that could be marketed. Because of the restrictions announced upon marketings and the compensating features of the programme, appeals to the growers to reduce acreage were relatively effective. In 1941 the acreage sown to wheat fell from 27,750,000 acres to 21,140,000 acres, a reduction of 6,610,000 acres or approximately 24 per cent under the 1940 acreage. While the actual reduction made by the producers was not as drastic as the calculations of the Wheat Board had indicated as desirable, it proved sufficient to ease the situation because of a relatively low yield. The yield per acre in 1941 was 14.0 bushels per acre, compared with 18.5 bushels in 1940. On the reduced acreage this meant a total production of 296,000,000 bushels, or less than ordinary exports plus domestic disappearance. As a result, the carryover on July 31, 1942 was estimated at approximately 424,000,000 bushels or a reduction of 56,000,000 bushels over the carryover for the previous year.

[11]P.C. 3750, Aug. 7, 1940.

For the purpose of making the compensatory payments, reductions in wheat acreage were computed by deducting the number of acres sown to wheat on each farm in 1941 from the number of acres sown to wheat on the same farm in 1940. This was the general basis, but provision was made to cover various special circumstances such as on farms where no land had been sown to wheat in 1940, or where land had been newly broken. Basic acreages for each farm were also determined for summer-fallow, coarse grains, and grass.

The scale of payments established in 1941 under the Order-in-Council was as follows: $4 for each acre summer-fallowed in 1941 in excess of the number of acres computed for the year 1940 as being in summer-fallow; $2 for each acre sown to coarse grains or grass before July 31, 1941, in excess of the number of acres computed to be in coarse grains or grass in 1940; and $2 for each acre sown to rye or grass before July 31, 1941. Further, a payment of an additional $2 per acre was authorized to be made for each acre sown to rye or grass in 1941, and which continued to be kept in rye or grass on July 31, 1942, provided that the acreage in grass in 1942 was additional to the basic acreage computed to be in grass on July 1, 1940.[12]

The Wheat Acreage Reduction Act of 1942 reduced the payment on land in summer-fallow from $4 to $2 per acre, but apart from clarifying various sections of the regulations, made no substantial change in the provisions set forth in the original Order-in-Council of 1941.[13] The reduction in payments for land in summer-fallow followed an increased demand for coarse grains and a rise in their price. Payments for summer-fallow had been justified on the ground that it tended to conserve the qualities of the soil. By reducing this payment the emphasis was shifted to putting a greater part of the land to alternative uses. An appreciable increase in acreage devoted to oats and barley followed the initiation of the 1941 programme, but it is impossible to determine what part of this increase was due to the acreage payments and what part to more favourable prices for coarse grains. Payments for summer-fallow were discontinued after 1943.[14]

The reduction in wheat acreage contemplated in the 1941 programme was based on the assumption that normal physical conditions of production would prevail in the West. In 1941, as we have seen, this did not turn out to be the fact. Drought, excessively hot weather,

[12]P.C. 3047 and P.C. 3231, 1941.
[13]Statutes of Canada, 1942, c. 10.
[14]Ibid., 1943-44, c. 12.

and the ravages of the sawfly reduced the yield per acre. When the effect of these conditions was combined with the reduction in acreage, the result was a wheat harvest in the West of less than 300,000,000 bushels, the smallest crop in four years. While this relatively short crop relieved the strain upon storage facilities, the large amount of wheat carried over from 1940 and the big crop of 1942 overhung the market and tended to keep wheat prices down. This involved a sharp reduction in income for the wheat growers, and soon a widespread agitation developed among them for an increase in the price they should receive. It was alleged that the current returns from wheat and other grains would not yield an income sufficient to maintain them under prevailing conditions of livelihood. Recognizing the possibility of hardship arising out of the short crop and the marketing controls imposed, the Prime Minister, Mr. King, announced that the Government would supplement the growers' income by providing approximately $20,000,000 as a straight subsidy based on cultivated acreage. Payments were to be at the rate of 75 cents per acre on one-half of the cultivated acreage on each farm with a minimum payment of $150 per farm.[15] This subsidy was distributed by the organization handling the payments that were made under the Prairie Farm Assistance Act.

There were thus for a time three different federal measures under which the prairie wheat grower might derive assistance, and the sums paid out by the Dominion Government were therefore substantial. In the three years 1941, 1942, and 1943 total payments approximated $122,000,000. Of this sum the payments made under Prairie Farm Assistance amounted to $21,057,927; payments to augment prairie farm income accounted for $18,898,000; and payments for wheat acreage reduction totalled $82,000,000.[16] Earlier, the losses absorbed by the federal treasury by reason of the operations of the Canadian Wheat Board in buying wheat from the wheat grower at a higher price than that at which it could be finally marketed had constituted a concealed subsidy from which the wheat grower benefited in certain years before 1941. The record down to the operations covering the crop of 1939 shows that total payments made up to that date by the Dominion Government to cover Wheat Board deficits in this account amounted to approximately $65,000,000.[17]

[15]P.C. 8162, Oct. 22, 1941.

[16]*Winnipeg Free Press*, June 14, 1944.

[17]Canadian Wheat Board, *Report*, 1941-42, p. 23; also *ibid.*, 1943-44, Exhibit VI.

While the initial delivery payments were designed originally to put a floor under the wheat growers' income on a reasonable basis, as the war progressed other considerations also became of importance. The general policy of the Government was to keep down the price of food while maintaining Canadian production at as high a level as possible. There was also an attempt to direct agricultural effort generally along those lines that would yield the greatest advantage in the prosecution of the war. In accord with this policy substantial subsidies were paid to encourage the production of dairy products and of bacon and other animal products. These subsidies, of course, were not limited to the West, but applied to agriculture in other parts of Canada as well. In the seven years from 1939 to 1945 inclusive the Canadian Government disbursed to the farmers of Canada over $400,000,000 in subsidies.[18]

In so far as the West was concerned, the general effect of this policy was to lead for a time to a broader diversification of agriculture. This was a development of great advantage to the country. The hazards of one-crop farming have always been recognized as a weakness in the agricultural economy of the West, and any policy that tended to divert from wheat production areas capable of being used economically for stock or dairy farming was clearly a move in a desirable direction. The 1941 programme of the federal Government had this especial merit, that it endeavoured to accomplish a reduction in wheat acreage that would tend to bring annual wheat production down to the limits measured by the annual disappearance of stocks by home consumption and what experience had demonstrated Canada could sell ordinarily in competition with other wheat-producing countries abroad.

Notwithstanding the advantages of the Government's policy, on the whole it was received by the grain growers with evidence of discontent or resignation rather than with active approval.[19] The western wheat producer wanted to grow wheat, and disliked a government policy that tended to compel him to give some attention to stock feeding and the production of dairy products. This attitude led to continued agitation by the wheat growers for the Government to fix higher wheat prices. With the assistance of the Saskatchewan Pool this agitation expressed itself in the organization of an excursion of

[18]See the *Alberta Wheat Pool Budget,* May 3, 1946, for details.
[19]See the submission to the Dominion Government in support of the Saskatchewan Agricultural Petition, Feb. 2, 1942.

over four hundred Saskatchewan wheat growers and their supporters who descended upon Ottawa in February of 1942 to lay their demands before the Government. They presented a petition bearing 185,000 names which demanded that the initial price of wheat paid by the Wheat Board should not be less than $1.00 per bushel. While there had been general agreement that increasing costs of production warranted some increase over 70 cents per bushel, the Government was reluctant to place such a heavy additional burden upon the taxpayers of Canada as an increase from 70 cents per bushel to $1.00 per bushel involved. It finally compromised with the demand by fixing the initial price for the year 1942 at 90 cents per bushel basis No. 1 Northern delivered at Fort William or Port Arthur, with marketing limited to 280,000,000 bushels for the West.[20] An Order-in-Council gave the Wheat Board power to adjust wheat futures to the new price levels, thereby preventing speculative profits from accruing as a result of the Government's decision to increase the initial price. To counteract any tendency for the grain growers to shift back into wheat from the coarse grains as a result of this increase in wheat prices, the Government also established minimum prices for barley, oats, and flax.[21] These prices were designed to maintain substantial equality in the price relationships between these various grains.

The response of the western farm leaders to the Government's decision was one of criticism. J. H. Wesson, President of the Saskatchewan Pool, in expressing disappointment that a higher price had not been established, said the Ottawa delegation's demand for "$1.00 wheat" represented the minimum requirement and was "in no sense submitted as a basis for bargaining."[22] Robert Gardiner, President of the United Farmers of Alberta, declared: "We are still not satisfied, although we are appreciative of the increase that has been granted."[23] This reaction illustrates one of the difficulties that faces a government in a democracy when confronted with a demand from a powerfully organized economic group for it to fix prices by ministerial fiat instead of allowing them to be determined by the impersonal valuation of the market. In this instance there is reason to believe that if the demand for wheat at $1.00 per bushel had been acceded to, the next move would have been a demand for a further increase. The petition

[20]P.C. 1802, March 9, 1942; Statutes of Canada, 1942-43, c. 4.
[21]P.C. 1801, 1942.
[22]*Winnipeg Free Press,* March 7, 1942.
[23]*Ibid.,* March 9, 1942.

presented at Ottawa had in fact laid the ground for such a request. It asked the Government to "accept the principle of parity prices for all agricultural products" and mentioned the 1926-29 price level for wheat as the basis. This would mean that the Government would be expected to fix a minimum price for wheat at approximately $1.40 per bushel, a price distinctly out of line at the time with the general controlled price structure of the country.

The next step in the evolution of the marketing structure for Canadian wheat occurred in September of 1943. The third year of the war found wheat-exporting countries still struggling with the problem of surplus supplies. In Canada the upward trend in wheat stocks had been only temporarily checked by the small crop produced in 1941, the carryover at July 31, 1942 being 424,000,000 bushels compared with 480,000,000 bushels the year before. In the crop year 1942-43, on top of this carryover there was coming into the market one of the largest crops in the history of the West. The total yield in 1942 in Western Canada was estimated at 529,000,000 bushels. Thus the situation in the autumn of 1942 was that Canada was holding a larger total supply of wheat than she had ever held in the past. Marketing prospects were only moderately favourable. Making due allowance for expected export sales and domestic disappearance, wheat stocks promised to reach an excessively high level when the crop of 1943 would become available. It thus seemed desirable that the 1943 crop should be kept down to moderate limits.

In the light of this situation, in January of 1943 the Minister of Trade and Commerce announced that farmers' deliveries of wheat to the Wheat Board for the crop year of 1943-44 would be limited to 14 bushels per authorized acre based roughly on the acreage of 1940.[24] It was estimated that this would limit the amount that would be available for market to 280,000,000 bushels. The initial price was to remain at 90 cents per bushel. At this time, therefore, the Government contemplated no change in its wheat policy, but apparently hoped that restriction on wheat marketing would lead to further reduction in wheat acreage and to an increase in the production of the feed grains which were needed in connection with the Government's livestock production programme.

The circumstances that forced a change in this policy were a partial failure in feed crops in large parts of the United States and in Eastern Canada for 1943, combined with entirely unexpected heavy

[24]*Ibid.*, Jan. 30, 1943. This limitation was withdrawn at the end of May, 1944. *Ibid.*, May 30, 1944.

disappearances of reserve stocks of wheat in the United States resulting from consumers' demands and from wheat being used for industrial
purposes. Shortages of feed grains in the United States led to the
release of wheat to augment feed supplies in the United States. Meantime, as a result of the change in prospects, wheat prices in Canada
from March of 1943 began steadily to advance.   As the price rose
until it was in excess of the 90-cent minimum payable on wheat
delivered to the Wheat Board, the bulk of the wheat marketed by
producers was being sold to the independent grain trade rather than
being turned over to the Government agency. As late as March 30,
1943, when No. 1 Northern wheat was selling at over $1.00 a bushel
"spot," the Government apparently had no idea that it might be
necessary for it to make a change in its policy. On that date it used
its majority in the House of Commons to defeat a motion that steps
should be taken to abolish trading in futures in the Winnipeg Grain
Exchange.[25]

Events, however, were sufficiently compelling to force the Government's hand. Heavy losses in the winter and spring wheat areas of
the United States, by reducing the expected crop for 1943, made it
evident that the United States would have to look to Canada for
help in making up an approaching deficiency. On April 30, 1943, the
United States removed quota restrictions on wheat shipments for
feeding purposes from Canada into the United States. This opened
the door to a very large market for Canadian wheat of the lower
grades. American wheat reserves were disappearing rapidly. In January
of 1943 it had been estimated that the American carryover of wheat
on June 30 of 1943 would be around 707,000,000 bushels, but as a
result of the demand in the ensuing six months the carryover on the
later date was estimated at 590,000,000 bushels, and it was considered
likely that before another crop could replenish wheat supplies
American surplus stocks would disappear altogether. In Canada crop
conditions had not been favourable during the growing period and a
large yield was not expected. This factor, combined with the acreage
reductions, led to the view that Canada would harvest the smallest
wheat crop in six years. All the indications were that the Canadian
carryover would be sharply reduced. In line with this view wheat
prices continued to advance and practically all deliveries were being
made outside the Wheat Board, since by this time the prices on the
open market were much higher than the Board's initial fixed price.

[25]*Ibid.*, March 31, 1943.

On September 27, when the Government took action, they had reached a level of $1.23¼ for No. 1 Northern wheat. At that time it was announced that the Dominion Government would acquire all stocks of unsold cash wheat in Canada at the then market price, and that trading in wheat on the Winnipeg Grain Exchange would be suspended. This meant that the Government had finally placed the Wheat Board, as its administrative agent, in sole charge of marketing Canadian wheat.

Several reasons undoubtedly weighed with the Government in deciding to assume complete control over marketing Canadian wheat supplies. One factor was Canadian commitments abroad. The British Government had centralized its purchases of wheat under the Cereal Imports Committee, which purchased supplies from Canada with the Wheat Board as its opposite number. Now, in order to sell in large quantities to Britain, it seemed necessary for the Wheat Board to have control over a large supply of wheat in Canada. As the Canadian surplus declined it became apparent that a situation might arise where the Wheat Board would either be unable to negotiate large sales with the Cereals Import Committee or, if it did make sales, might have to purchase the wheat at disastrously high prices from the trade in the open market. This would probably precipitate a runaway market not unlike that which occurred during the First World War and led to the closing of the futures market at that time. Naturally, the Dominion Government did not wish the Canadian Wheat Board in its negotiations with Great Britain over wheat sales to be hampered by uncertainties of this nature. Another element in the situation was that Canada had entered into certain mutual aid agreements with other countries which involved the shipment of wheat abroad. In this instance, also, if the wheat were not acquired by it directly from the producer, the Wheat Board might find itself in a difficult position by having to go into the open market to obtain the quantities it required to fulfil Canadian commitments. Purchasing wheat in this way in the open market would tend to raise the price still further, and also to increase the cost of the mutual aid being given by Canada. Finally, and this element was very important, the rapidly advancing price of wheat threatened to affect the general price structure of the Dominion, which was now being kept under strict control. Increased prices for wheat would also increase the amount of the subsidies that the Dominion Government would be required to pay to the flour millers if the general cost of living to the public was to be prevented from rising unduly.

All of these reasons combined to force the hand of the Government. Although up to this time the Liberal administration had consistently displayed a theoretical bias in favour of the open market system of selling wheat, it found itself at length compelled to go the whole distance and to place sole responsibility upon the Canadian Wheat Board for disposing of Canada's wheat crop. A combination of causes had finally driven it into this position, rather than a tardy conversion to the belief that a national wheat board was the most desirable method of marketing the Canadian crop. The earlier theory had been that compulsory marketing would bring higher prices, but when · compulsory marketing was actually established it was to keep prices under control.

The price at which the Wheat Board acquired the accumulated stocks of wheat was $1.23¾ per bushel; the initial delivery price for wheat producers on further deliveries was $1.25 per bushel for No. 1 Northern wheat basis in store at Fort William. This price replaced the initial delivery price of 90 cents per bushel which had been in effect since March of 1942. The new price thus represented a marked increase over what the Government hitherto had been willing to guarantee. Of more practical significance was the fact that it was slightly higher than the closing prices on the Winnipeg Grain Exchange on the last trading day before the Government's decision was announced. This price had the political advantage, therefore, of eliminating for the time being any complaints from the producers that they were being deprived of income they might have obtained by delivering their wheat to the independent trade. At the same time it allowed accumulated stocks to be closed out and acquired by the Board at prices corresponding substantially to international wheat values. As the price was an initial delivery price, it assured wheat growers that if world wheat prices continued to advance they would be able to share in the benefits therefrom through payments made on their participation certificates.

The policy initiated in September of 1943 has been continued. With the downfall of Germany in the spring of 1945, the Canadian authorities found an overseas demand for Canadian wheat which made it possible to dispose of the large Canadian surplus still existing in the country as rapidly as it could be moved. Export shipments increased in magnitude during the summer and seemed to be limited only by transportation facilities. At the outset no change in marketing restrictions for the crop of 1945 was indicated but the 1945 wheat crop was small and the Dominion Government authorized the Wheat Board to accept all deliveries. Nevertheless, with a reduced Canadian crop a certainty, Canada, in negotiating sales with Great Britain, clearly did not endeavour to exact the highest price that might have been forced from a necessitous customer. Prior to July 31, 1945, wheat was being moved to the United Kingdom under an agreement with Canada that the price should be $1.46 per bushel for No. 1 Northern. Subsequently, the Wheat Board, as administrative agent for the Dominion Government, announced that prices fixed on wheat shipped from August 1, 1945 would be $1.55 per bushel. This price was well below current world values.[26] That sales to Great Britain were being negotiated really on a credit basis, and that in the last analysis this wheat would probably be paid for by the Canadian taxpayer, was probably one reason for this moderation.

To meet any objections that this forbearance was being exercised at the expense of the western wheat producer, the Government, by way of an equivalent, in September of 1945 announced that it would put a "floor" under wheat prices of not less than $1 a bushel for a five-year period, that is, up to July 31, 1950. This represented a major decision of post-war policy, although all of its consequences may not have been apprehended at the time. Clearly it foreshadowed a continuance of the Wheat Board, presumably after emergency conditions had disappeared, but with what powers was left unexplained. When the Minister of Trade and Commerce was queried in the House of Commons about the future of the Wheat Board, all that could be drawn from him was the statement: "I anticipate that the Government anticipates the Wheat Board will continue indefinitely."[27]

At the close of the Second World War there seemed to be no large body of public opinion in favour of abolishing the Canadian Wheat Board, while it was evident that there would be decided opposition from the wheat producers to a return to the open market system of trading without some guarantee of a "floor" price. Thus, partly as a result of the experiences of the early nineteen-thirties, and partly as a result of the war, Canada appeared to be drifting into a system of state trading for one of its most important export commodities. Wheat was no longer a free article of commerce, but was subject to the policies decided upon by the wheat committee of the Canadian Cabinet, the really effective body in determining

[26]*Ibid.*, Sept. 15, 17, 1945.
[27]*Ibid.*, Sept. 20, 1945.

the course followed by the Wheat Board. This change in marketing method, expanded and worked out under the stress of war conditions, led to the development of various controls that limited the amount the producer could deliver to the market, and also, to a very large degree, the rate at which the railways could be called upon to move wheat forward from country storage points to the terminals. Rigid control of shipments from country elevators indirectly controlled the rate at which the producer could market the quota of wheat he was allowed to deliver. In return, the producer had a fixed minimum delivery price, calculated to stabilize his income, and the knowledge that, should export prices advance, he would benefit from a further payment on his deliveries, through his participation certificates, but that if prices fell below the minimum delivery price the federal treasury would absorb the loss. As this policy worked out, from time to time the Dominion Government, either directly or indirectly, paid out to the wheat producers substantial amounts of money which were in effect federal subsidies.

It should be noted, however, that while the Government's measures were directed towards giving the wheat producers basic protection the general wartime controls instituted to keep down prices applied more severely to wheat than to any other commodity.

5

Wheat politics and the taxation of co-operative profits

THE history of the Pools during the last twenty years briefly is the record of their outstanding recovery from the dark days of 1930 and 1931. All of the indices of expansion, growing strength, and stability are evident. Their membership has increased; their net capital assets have grown greatly in magnitude; they have continued to handle a large proportion of the crop; their annual profits have been large. Most important of all, they have been successful in surmounting the financial difficulties that threatened their existence at the beginning of the period. By prudent management, and under favourable conditions in the later years, they have built up an impressive accumulation of capital with which to carry on their extensive operations. The details of this recovery are set forth in chapter x.

In the realm of public affairs, partly as an aftermath to the débâcle of 1930 and partly because of the incidence of public policy upon their position, the Pools have been almost continuously in the public eye. This was largely a consequence of the dual role Mr. McFarland came to occupy after taking over the task of disposing of the Pool surplus. In order to make the situation clear it is necessary to examine the nature of his appointment, its effect on the Pools' organization, and the sequence of events which brought the Pools into the foreground in the federal election of 1935.

The overpayment to the members on the 1929 crop left the Pools with an aggregate debt of nearly $23,000,000.[1] While the

[1]See D. A. MacGibbon, *The Canadian Grain Trade* (Toronto, 1932), pp. 78-9, 352-4.

provincial governments of Alberta, Saskatchewan, and Manitoba, to avoid the Pools' complete collapse, had come to their rescue at this time and funded the debt on a twenty-year basis, each of the provincial Pools was left with substantial annual payments to make to the provincial governments on the capital sum plus interest payments on the balance outstanding.   The situation did not improve in 1931. Although the initial payment to members on wheat deliveries for the 1930 crop was fixed at the outset at 70 cents per bushel, which was deemed to be a conservative basis, and was later reduced by degrees to 50 cents per bushel, the swift downward plunge of wheat prices during the autumn soon imperilled the 15 per cent margin required by the chartered banks on their loans to the Pools. The banks demanded that their credits should be guaranteed.   The governments of the western provinces were unwilling to assume further burdens and the aid of the Dominion Government was sought. The latter was reluctant to act, but under pressure gave the required guarantee with the condition that the Pools appoint a satisfactory person to be manager of the central selling agency.   Mr. John I. McFarland, who was chosen, was charged with disposing of the Pools' carryover and with their share of the 1930 crop. In effect, this meant that the marketing functions of the Pools, as distinguished from their handling activities, were taken over and placed in the hands of a representative of the Dominion Government. Technically, though, Mr. McFarland was an official of the Pools.

At the end of the crop year, July 31, 1931, an important change occurred which affected each of the three provincial Pools.   The marketing operations of the central selling agency were divorced from those of the provincial organizations.   As liquidator of the Pools' surplus Mr. McFarland continued to act through the central selling agency to dispose of the stocks in hand. In addition, he had been empowered under an Order-in-Council to take what measures he could to stabilize the price of wheat.[2] In this latter capacity he was the agent of the Dominion Government and, as such, in intimate contact with the head of the federal administration.

This division of function permitted the individual Pools to conduct as separate entities their current country elevator and terminal operations. The difficulties caused by their experiences in 1929 and 1930 and by separation from the central selling agency necessitated a change in their method of doing business. Pooling had fallen out

[2]Report of the Royal Grain Inquiry Commission, 1938 (Ottawa, 1938), p. 36.

of favour with many of their members and had practically ceased, although voluntary provincial pools were organized for those members who wished to continue marketing their wheat on this basis and continued to operate for four years between 1931 and 1935. The amount handled in this way was very small and the voluntary pools were discontinued as unnecessary when the Canadian Wheat Board was established.

From the inception of the Pool movement until 1931 the five-year contract, by which the individual Pool members bound themselves to deliver all their saleable wheat to the Pools, had been a characteristic feature, and the contractual basis upon which the Pools conducted their operations. But as the organization got into difficulties because of the continued decline in the price of wheat it became no longer feasible to enforce these contracts rigidly.[3] Hence in 1931, in effect, members of the Pools were relieved by their boards of management of the obligation of dealing only with their own organization. In 1933 when the contracts actually expired no attempt was made to secure renewals. Contract signers were members of the Pools by virtue of their each having been allotted one share of stock, application for which was made when the contract was signed. With no pooling contract any longer in operation, new forms of application were drawn up by which new members might be enrolled and receive one share in the organization of the par value of $1.00. The provincial organizations now bought wheat outright from their members or from non-members and sold it at current prices through the ordinary channels of trade. At the same time the deductions from members' marketings of 2 cents per bushel to provide capital for the construction of elevators and the deduction of 1 per cent of gross sales to provide a commercial reserve were suspended. Interest payments to members on the funds already built up from these deductions were also for the time being suspended. The change in the Pools' methods of operation was destined at a later date to have an important bearing on the legal question of whether their profits were taxable under the Income War Tax Act.[4]

To sum up: the reverses of 1929 and 1930 had forced the Pools to drop the pooling method of marketing and fall back upon the provincial organizations, and to suspend the accumulation of capital by means of deductions from the members' returns, and had left them with

[3] *Report of the Royal Commission on Co-operatives* (Ottawa, 1945), p. 138.
[4] See p. 82.

an enormous debt individually due to their provincial governments. Payments also remained to be made on some of the elevator facilities acquired during the period of prosperity. They had, however, weathered the storm that had nearly swamped them. Moreover, as assets they had reserves amounting to approximately $20,000,000. Their investments included over 1,600 country elevators, and they either owned or had under leases seven terminal elevators at Fort William and Port Arthur with 16,868,000 bushels' capacity; they owned or controlled as well terminal capacity at Vancouver amounting to 8,050,000 bushels. The Saskatchewan Pool had also purchased a transfer elevator at Buffalo, N.Y. In all essential respects their handling organizations remained intact. In addition, they continued to possess a large and loyal group of members, who were determined that their business venture should recover from the serious setback it had suffered. That this was true was demonstrated by the fact that after 1931, employing the ordinary methods of free marketing, the Pools, in competition with the private companies, continued to handle over 40 per cent of the wheat marketed.

While the separation for marketing purposes of the central selling agency from the Pools in 1931 left the latter free to carry on business without government intervention, there remained to be determined what payments, if any, the Pools were ultimately to receive for the wheat taken over from them by Mr. McFarland. When he assumed charge of the central selling agency in November of 1930 there was on hand 36,935,000 bushels of Pool wheat, with deliveries still to come in during the remainer of the crop year. On July 31, 1931, when the separation occurred, there was a carryover of 27,609,000 bushels of cash wheat and 47,555,000 bushels held as futures. This gave a total of 75,164,000 bushels over which Mr. McFarland continued to have control and for which an accounting was ultimately due to the Pools. Obviously, if this wheat had been dumped on the market at the low prices prevailing at the date of the separation of functions, the sale would have further depressed the already disastrously low price of wheat; moreover, the loss would have been so enormous that it would have entailed a heavy payment from the Dominion treasury to make good to the lending banks the guarantee that the Government had given to them.

Shortly after Mr. McFarland assumed the management of the central selling agency, in accord with his mandate from the Dominion Government he entered upon a course of action aimed at raising the price of wheat. This consisted "in holding unusually large quantities of grain out of the cash market for long periods of time and in adding to the Central Selling Agency's cash wheat by the buying of futures."[5] The buying of futures to stabilize or support prices began in July of 1931. It is clear that this policy was designed to serve a double purpose. In so far as it should prove successful in raising the price of wheat it would benefit all the producers of wheat, who at the time were being forced to sell their product at calamity prices; equally important, if the price of wheat could be forced up sufficiently, there was a chance that the ultimate disposal of the Pool carryover might be accomplished without loss to the Dominion treasury arising out of the guarantee the Government had given to the banks. The attempt to achieve this dual purpose is the explanation of the course Mr. McFarland consistently pursued up to the date of his retirement from the Canadian Wheat Board in 1935.

At the outset of his tenure of office, with the great depression increasing in severity, conditions were not favourable to the success of Mr. McFarland's design. The market was in the grip of world forces. The downward trend of wheat prices continued for over a year after he took control. The all-time low figure of 38 cents per bushel for No. 1 Northern wheat spot on the Winnipeg Grain Exchange was reached on December 16, 1932. From this low point the price of wheat slowly and hesitantly rose during the next nine months but the outlook did not become definitely encouraging. With the crop of 1933 coming into the market Mr. McFarland requested the Exchange on August 14, 1933 to prohibit trading in the October future at a price below 70½ cents per bushel. This was an artificial level against the trend of the market. To peg the price at this point Mr. McFarland found it necessary to enter the market and buy heavily in futures. When the peg was removed on September 15, the October future fell in the course of a month to 54¾ cents per bushel despite net stabilizing purchases of 31,756,000 bushels. The following year, in November of 1934, the December future was pegged at 75 cents and the May future at 80 cents per bushel, which entailed further purchases of stabilizing futures. Subsequently, the July future was pegged at 80 cents, and this peg was maintained until the July future expired without the aid of stabilizing purchases.

In spite of all his efforts, however, Mr. McFarland, after nearly five years of struggle, had not managed to dispose of the Pools' carry-

[5]*Report of the Royal Grain Inquiry Commission, 1938*, pp. 36, 95.

over at prices he deemed satisfactory. He finally held 205,187,000 bushels on central selling agency account, of which 53,728,000 bushels was cash wheat with the balance held as futures. The problem still remained, and the necessity of replacing the makeshift arrangements of 1930 by more formal organization was apparent. The Canadian Wheat Board Act of 1935 was passed. Under the Act the newly created Wheat Board was instructed to acquire from the Canadian Co-operative Wheat Producers Limited (the central selling agency of the Pools), upon terms to be approved by the Governor-in-Council, all wheat or contracts to purchase or take delivery of wheat in respect of which the Government of Canada had given a guarantee. The establishment of the Canadian Wheat Board and its acquisition of these holdings by outright purchase would terminate the rather ambiguous relationship of the Government, through Mr. McFarland, with the Wheat Pools. It was obvious that for both parties the terms of the settlement were a matter of high importance. The circumstances surrounding the negotiation of this transaction present one of several illustrations of the close connection that wheat and politics have always had in Western Canada.

At this time the life of Parliament was drawing to a close; after five years in office the Conservative administration under Mr. R. B. Bennett was faced with the necessity of seeking a fresh mandate from the electors. Parliament was dissolved on August 15, 1935 and a general election called for October 14. The responsibility of coping with the difficult problems caused by the great depression of the early 1930's had rested heavily upon Mr. Bennett's administration. While economic conditions in Canada by 1935 were definitely improving it was generally recognized that there was still much discontent in the country arising out of the harsh experiences that the people had suffered during this unprecedented period of hard times. The natural instinct of many people was to hold the Government responsible, and it appeared probable that the Prime Minister and his party would have great difficulty in securing a majority in the new Parliament.

The western grain growers had suffered so severely from low prices, as well as from drought, that they were in no mood to give the Government credit for what it had done in attempting to meet the situation. However, if Mr. Bennett could win the active aid and backing of the Pools with their network of local organizations, there was the possibility that this support might be the decisive factor in many constituencies on the prairies. A settlement satisfactory to the

Pools of their claims against the Government for the wheat which the Government had taken over would be of great importance to them and a probable factor in securing this support. This was the general background to the negotiation of the settlement that was reached.

The Canadian Wheat Board was constituted on August 14, 1935, with Mr. McFarland as Chairman. The exact date on which conversations with the Pools over a settlement began has not transpired, but the fact that negotiations were in progress was not a matter of general knowledge until a few days before the election. On October 8 Mr. L. C. Brouillette, President of the Canadian Co-operative Wheat Producers Limited, exchanged letters with Mr. McFarland, setting forth the terms of an agreement. Mr. Brouillette offered to settle the claims on behalf of the Pools for $8,262,415. This included sums sufficient to give Pool farmers who had delivered their wheat to the Pools in 1930-31 with an initial payment of less than 60 cents per bushel, basis No. 1 Northern delivered in Fort William, an adjustment equal to that figure, and to make an adjustment for members of the coarse-grain pools who had received less than the original initial prices established. It also provided for a sum of $862,487 to reimburse the Pools for their operating expenses in 1930. The Canadian Wheat Board, through Mr. McFarland, accepted these terms. On October 10, four days before the election, an Order-in-Council, signed by four ministers of the Crown, ratified this agreement. Subsequently it was approved by Mr. Bennett, who added the notation that the figures must be confirmed by the auditors.[6]

Rumours of this agreement began to circulate in Western Canada in connection with the electoral campaign some days before it was actually ratified. On October 8 the *Winnipeg Free Press* first published in its weekly edition and thereafter in its daily issue a statement to the effect that for the preceding ten days information had been reaching it that as part of the Conservative election campaign a pre-election distribution on account of Pool claims was to be made. This payment, it was stated, had been planned for the week before, but some hitch in the arrangements had occurred. Added to this information was the assertion that cheques had already been written in the Pool offices in Winnipeg and Regina, in anticipation of instructions for their release from Ottawa.[7] It may be noted that Mr. Bennett's stipulation that the figures must be audited would entail a delay in making the payments.

[6]P.C. 3199, 1935. *Winnipeg Free Press,* Dec. 6, 1935.
[7]*Winnipeg Free Press,* Oct. 11, 12, 16, 1935.

Government sources kept silent and on October 9 a prominent Pool official told the *Free Press* that there was no truth whatever in the report that a payment would be made.

On October 10, however, Mr. Brouillette announced that negotiations between the Pools and the Canadian Wheat Board had been completed, and that it was now possible to provide for the adjustment to Pool members who had received for their wheat an initial payment of less than 60 cents per bushel, basis No. 1 Northern delivered Fort William, and to members of the coarse-grain pools who had received less than the prices initially established. This statement was confirmed by the Manager of the Alberta Wheat Pool who said in a radio address that Mr. Bennett had "seen fit to settle the issue," and that "the Alberta Wheat Pool would be lacking in spirit and common gratitude if it failed to express on behalf of the 27,000 Alberta wheat growers its appreciation of the action of Premier Bennett and the Canadian Wheat Board in definitely settling this vexed question in a manner reasonably satisfactory to all."[8] In this instance it was announced that "cheques covering this distribution will go forward from the head office of the Alberta Wheat Pool to interested Alberta members just as soon as it is humanly possible for the clerical staff to do the necessary work." It was intimated that this would likely involve a period of 30 days.

The reaction of the Liberal party to these developments was immediate. Mr. Mackenzie King, leading the campaign against Mr. Bennett, said that the proposed payment was an attempt to bribe the farmers with their own money, "if they were entitled to it at all," to vote for Government candidates. The timing of the announcement by Mr. Brouillette was also criticized by Premier J. G. Gardiner of Saskatchewan, who said Mr. Brouillette "could very well have avoided any political reference being made by leaving the public announcement until next week" (i.e., until after the election).

The general effect of this disclosure upon the public just before the electors were going to the polls was to lead them to suspect the propriety of any payment being made to the Pools. This attitude was strengthened by the fact that it was known that the current level of wheat prices was not sufficiently high, if the account were closed out, to cover the costs incurred on the wheat and futures held by Mr. McFarland in the central selling agency during his period of operations.[9]

8*Ibid.*, Oct. 14, 1935.   9*Ibid.*, Oct. 10, 1935; April 2, 1936.

The defeat of Mr. Bennett's administration on October 14, 1935 led to considerable speculation, in view of the circumstances under which the agreement had been negotiated, about whether the incoming Government would recognize its validity. This arose in part from the prevailing belief that the Wheat Board would ultimately be forced to dispose of the big surplus at a heavy loss to the country, and in part from doubts about whether the Order-in-Council had been properly passed. Although four ministers of the Crown had signed the order, the number required to validate such a document, it was alleged that no Cabinet meeting had been held in Ottawa between October 3 and the date of the election, only one cabinet minister being in the city.[10] Mr. Bennett's notation on the order requiring an auditor's certificate was also said to be irregular. It was understood that a careful survey of the position would be made by Mr. King's administration, and that after this survey the Cabinet would make a decision.

It is to be noted that the Liberal party was pledged to a more vigorous attempt to sell wheat; one of the reasons given for the compulsory retirement of Mr. McFarland from the chairmanship of the Canadian Wheat Board was that his methods had induced sales resistance abroad and that he would have difficulty in making such a policy effective. Just how a policy of aggressive salesmanship would be implemented remained a problem. To the suggestion that the Board would be forced to "dump" grain on the market to achieve its ends the Minister of Trade and Commerce responded that there would be no "fire sale" of Canadian wheat. World changes in demand for wheat, however, came to the aid of the Government and relieved its anxiety on this score.

For some time there had been indications that a change was taking place in the world wheat situation. Crop disasters were reported in Australia and in Argentina. In the United States the wheat crop was estimated to be over 250,000,000 bushels below the average yield of the 1928-32 period. Shortly after the new Wheat Board was appointed the action of the Argentine Government on December 13 in authorizing a national grain board to purchase wheat from farmers at a price equivalent to about 90 cents a bushel in Canadian funds, or a price nearly double that authorized by them in the previous year, caused wild excitement in the wheat markets of the world. Frenzied buying occurred. It was estimated that on the

[10]*Ibid.*, Oct. 16, 17, 1935; Feb. 5, March 26, 27, April 2, 1936.

Winnipeg Grain Exchange on December 14 about 10,000,000 bushels
were sold on export account during the trading session. In ten seconds
at the opening of the market wheat prices reached the 3-cent limit
of advance permitted under the regulations of the Exchange. Although
no important additional advances were registered until nearly a year
later,[11] the export market continued active.   During the month of
December alone the Canadian Wheat Board sold 28,151,146 bushels
of the 1935 crop and 22,099,862 bushels of the old wheat it had taken
over on December 2 from the central selling agency.[12]   Large sales
continued to be made in the early part of 1936.

The effect of this dramatic change in the situation was to relieve
somewhat the tension at Ottawa and to hold out hopes that the surplus
would be liquidated without the colossal losses previously expected.
The possibility began to be considered that advancing prices might
enable the Board to dispose of the surplus at price levels that would
recoup the Government for the expenses it had incurred in meeting
its guarantee, as well as allow for a payment to the central selling
agency for the holdings which it had surrendered; in brief, that
"Canada's speculation in wheat" might turn out to be successful. As
is well known, this finally proved to be true.

Another event which apparently played a part in the ultimate disposal of the issue was the federal by-election in the constituency of
Assiniboia in southern Saskatchewan on January 6, 1936. In forming
his Cabinet Mr. King selected Hon. J. G. Gardiner, Premier of
Saskatchewan, for the position of Minister of Agriculture, and a seat
in the House of Commons was opened for him by the resignation of
the sitting member for Assiniboia. Under ordinary circumstances a
newly appointed minister after a federal election would not be
opposed, but in this instance the C.C.F. placed a candidate in the field
against him. The latter made the Government's wheat policy the sole
issue before the electorate. In the stress of the hot campaign which
followed Mr. Gardiner announced that the question of adjusting payments to the farmers for the 1930-31 crop would be settled as quickly
as possible. He said auditors had been put to work and that as soon
as they verified the claim the money would be paid. In the event that
the auditors did not approve the payment, "we will sit down with the
Wheat Pool to get a proper agreement under which a proper amount

[11]*Report of the Grain Trade of Canada for the Crop Year Ending July 31,
1936* (Ottawa, 1937), p. 173.
[12]Canadian Wheat Board, *Report*, 1935-36, pp. 4, 10.

can be paid."[13] This was the first direct intimation that the new Government contemplated making a payment to the Pools. Up until this time there had been persistent rumours emanating from Ottawa that no payment would be made.   Mr. Gardiner's statement was commonly taken to pledge the Government to a settlement based on the auditors' report, irrespective of any loss that the Dominion Government might incur in disposing of the surplus stocks.

With the auditors' report before it the Government, in the ensuing session of Parliament, took authority by legislation to make a payment to the Canadian Wheat Board of a sum not to exceed $6,600,000 for the primary producers in Manitoba, Saskatchewan, and Alberta who had delivered wheat, other than Durum wheat, through the respective Pool organizations in each province, with an initial payment of less than 60 cents per bushel basis No. 1 Northern delivered at Fort William.[14] For Durum wheat the basis was 66.27 cents per bushel for No. 1 Amber Durum delivered at Fort William. The Government chose to provide for the settlement by legislation, since it appeared that there were certain doubts with respect to the validity of the Order-in-Council and, in any event, the payment was a "most extraordinary" one which should be approved by Parliament.[15]

The settlement authorized differed from that set out in the Order-in-Council, which had provided for a sum sufficient to make an additional payment amounting to $890,658 to producers of coarse grains who had delivered to the Pools but who had received less than the initial payment originally established, and also for a payment of $862,487 to cover the 1930 operating cost of the Pools. The settlement decided upon was in accordance with the auditors' certificate in these respects. The Order-in-Council which authorized the Canadian Wheat Board to purchase outright the wheat holdings of the central selling agency was based on section 7 of the Canadian Wheat Board Act of 1935, and no authority was contained in this section to deal with coarse grains or to pay the Pools for their operating costs in 1930. The Government had guaranteed the banks against loss in financing the coarse grain pools but had made no stipulations with respect to profits. In the view of the existing Government the coarse grains were not used as part of Mr. McFarland's general stabilization policy. The settlement, however, made provision that any net credit surplus

[13]*Winnipeg Free Press*, Dec. 31, 1935.
[14]Statutes of Canada, 1936, c. 12.
[15]*Winnipeg Free Press*, Feb. 19, 20, March 26, 1936.

arising out of the operations in coarse grains should be returned to the Pools for the benefit of the primary producers concerned. The barley pool showed a profit of $15,720; the flax pool, $210,926, and the rye pool, $124,276. In the case of the oat pool there was a loss of $200,000 which the Government absorbed. To the demands of producers who were not members of the Pools that they should also receive an adjustment, the Government turned a deaf ear.

From the time that it became known that a payment to the Pools was contemplated until the issue was decided in Parliament, the propriety of making such a payment was a subject of acute public controversy. The political angles to the question and the intense competition that existed between the Pools and private grain companies aggravated the discussion. The basic reason maintained by the Pools for demanding a payment was that the use of their surplus was essential to Mr. McFarland's stabilization policy. The validity of this contention may be conceded to this extent: the use of the surplus reduced the amount of credit that the Government had to place at Mr. McFarland's disposal when he began stabilization operations. With additional government credit Mr. McFarland could have purchased the holdings of the Pools outright at current prices at any time during his tenure of office. But it must not be forgotten that Mr. McFarland entered upon his task with two purposes in view. One was to rescue the Pools from their predicament, and the other to protect the federal Government from losses under the guarantee it had given to the banks. When a formal accounting did finally occur in December of 1935 the Dominion Government accepted an apparent loss, estimated on then current wheat values, of $15,856,645.31 arising out of the Government's guarantee to the banks.[16]

The "providential disasters" of short crops in 1936 and 1937, however, leading to an increase in the price of wheat from around 85 cents a bushel in December of 1935 to as high as $1.50 in July of 1937 enabled the Government to come out on a basis of profit. The Wheat Board in its report for 1937-38 reported a surplus in its operations on "old wheat" account of $25,485,526.66, which worked out, after paying advances from the Dominion Government, to a net profit of $9,268,881.31. The Board reported that it had retained 6,954,000 bushels, represented by futures, to meet the needs, particularly of Saskatchewan, for seed grain. These futures were sold to the Saskatchewan Government on the basis of the average future prices

[16]*Report of the Royal Grain Inquiry Commission, 1938,* p. 37.

ruling between August 1, 1937 and February 28, 1938. Since the price range during this period was somewhat lower than in the preceding months, the final statement on the transactions completing the marketing of Mr. McFarland's surplus showed a net profit of $8,953,343.07.[17] Deducting from this sum the amount paid to the Pools under the settlement agreement, the final outcome for the Dominion Government was a profit of approximately $2,500,000. Mr. McFarland's holding policy had, in fact, proved successful.

Had the Government in dealing with the claims of the Pools for wheat made the settlement on the same basis as that for the coarse grains pools and waited until the surplus was finally realized before making an accounting to them, this balance would have properly accrued to them. But at the time the settlement was made to them neither the Government nor the Pools could foresee that wheat in a very short period would almost double in price.

It was claimed that the reason the Government made a settlement with the Pools was the belief that the Order-in-Council of October 10 had created a responsibility that it could not evade. Prime Minister King said that in view of the policies followed under the previous Government in handling the 1930 Wheat Pool surplus, producers of wheat who had accepted an initial payment of less than 60 cents per bushel, basis No. 1 Northern at Fort William, were justified in expecting these payments to be augmented to bring the total price received up to that level. Hon. Mr. Gardiner, instead of taking this ground, in a press statement said that "the conclusion that payment should be made is based upon the fact that this wheat was used for stabilization purposes."

A farm group with some reason to feel aggrieved at the Government's policy were the non-Pool wheat producers. In 1930 these growers had been forced to sell their wheat on a basis of less than 60 cents per bushel for No. 1 Northern delivered at Fort William. They felt that if the Dominion Government was making a payment to the Pools to enable the latter to adjust prices to this level for their members, they were entitled equally to receive relief. Government intervention was making it possible for Pool members to receive a stabilization payment while the losses of non-members for that year were not recognized as entitling them to relief. They felt their case was made stronger by the fact that the general principle of stabilization was, in effect, being continued by the fixing of initial delivery

[17]Canadian Wheat Board, *Report*, 1936-37; 1937-38.

prices for wheat as part of the operations of the Canadian Wheat Board.

Within a very short time after the Pools had received settlement from the Dominion Government they again found themselves the focus of public discussion; this time before the Royal Grain Inquiry Commission appointed in June of 1936. Under the terms of the order, Mr. Justice Turgeon, among other subjects, was specifically charged with investigating "co-operative or pool marketing" and its effects upon markets.[18]

In the prolonged inquiry that followed Pool affairs received a great deal of attention. The Pools, while strongly defending before the Commissioner the policies they had followed, took occasion to give a detailed review of their operations from the inception of the three provincial organizations and the central selling agency. They submitted to the Commissioner a statement setting out their views on the course grain marketing in Canada should follow. The Pool organizations recommended as the first step in the development of an adequate marketing programme that:

(1) A national marketing board should be given complete control of the entire wheat crop of Western Canada, charged with the duty of marketing it at the best possible price.

(2) Such board should set a reasonable initial payment at the time of delivery and make further arrangements from time to time as the grain is disposed of.

(3) Such board should establish a sales office overseas and appoint agents in the principal importing countries for the purpose of pushing the sale of Canadian wheat and increasing consumer demand.

(4) The board should have the power to subsidize the farmer in periods of depression.

(5) The board should provide a uniform price for grain of like quality.

(6) In the creation of the board provision should be made so that growers should have a voice in its operation.

The Pools added to their submission that they believed that the way should be kept open for the possibility of co-operation between exporting and importing countries in dealing with the world wheat problem.[19]

It will be recalled that the Commissioner's report took an almost completely different view of what Canadian public policy should be. Mr. Justice Turgeon rejected the idea of a national wheat board in

[18]See above, p. 40.

[19]See the Directors' report, Canadian Co-operative Wheat Producers Limited, 1937, issued in conjunction with provincial Pool reports.

favour of open marketing, though recommending the organization of comparatively limited pools similar to those in Australia which hedged their purchases and operated overseas "with the trade and not against it." Commenting on the report the directors of the Central Selling Agency said, "The report was disappointing to our members, and we believe that the country at large was not greatly impressed by the conclusions arrived at and most of the recommendations submitted."[20]

While the Pools lost their round before the Royal Commission, there was a different story when the Government went to Parliament and endeavoured to dispense with the Wheat Board. The Wheat Board was retained, and under the conditions created by the war has become firmly established as a national marketing board with functions beyond the sale of wheat. With the closing of the futures market for wheat of the Winnipeg Grain Exchange in 1943, practically all the policies urged by the Pools before the Turgeon Commission became part of the system of marketing Canadian wheat.

The next issue to confront the Pools was that of the taxation of their income. With the outbreak of war the Dominion Minister of Finance began searching out every source of revenue to meet the obligations created by Canada's war effort. With the Pools reporting large annual surpluses, it was inevitable that their legal liability under the Income War Tax Act should be carefully examined by the law officers of the treasury. Beyond the main incentive of securing more revenue there was the additional fact that bitter complaints of discrimination were being made to the Government by the private grain companies who were in competition with the Pools. These companies found that the major portion of their profits was being drained away under the extremely high rates of the Income War Tax Act and the Excess Profits Tax of 1940 while the Pools escaped. The sharpness of their complaints was not mitigated by the policy of the Pools, which were, on the whole, aggressively carrying on competition with the private trade.

In the original Income War Tax Act of 1917 the income of mutual corporations not having share capital was exempt. It was not clear from the Act that either a producers' or a consumers' co-operative could be considered a mutual company. In practice, however, the income tax officials tended to ignore most co-operatives, the majority of which were comparatively small organizations. Where taxation of co-operatives was attempted the department ruled that patronage

[20]*Ibid.*, 1938.

dividends were to be considered as discount deductible before arriving at taxable income, a position subsequently to be reversed on a ruling from the Department of Justice. The income tax department also held that dividends paid to shareholders as interest on capital were profits and liable to assessment, a position successfully maintained before the courts in 1929 in a case affecting the Fraser Valley Milk Producers' Association.[21] This decision was followed by representations to the Government by various co-operatives, including the Pools, with the result that in 1930 the Income War Tax Act was amended by the insertion of paragraph (p) in section 4. The intention, as stated in Parliament, was to exempt all co-operatives of the marketing and consumer type. The terms of the paragraph later proved to be ambiguous; they applied clearly only to co-operatives operating on a contract basis. Quite obviously the amendment confirmed the *de facto* exemption already enjoyed by the Pools as they were then operating; but shortly afterwards they ceased to carry on as contract pools and it was later to become a matter of contention whether or not the paragraph applied to them under the changed circumstances.

In 1940 came a sharp increase in the rates of income tax and the imposition of a heavy tax on excess profits, and at this time the section relating to co-operatives in the Income War Tax Act was strictly interpreted, with the result that various forms of gain accruing to them were held to be exigible. The main point at issue with respect to the Pools was whether, after the abandonment of pooling in 1931, they actually were operating on the basis which was covered by the Act. It was argued that the legal obligation to turn over to the members profits from sales, less expenses and reserve, was no longer binding upon the Pools since the organizations had become ordinary purchasers of grain able to sell on their own behalf. With its overpowering need for revenue manifest the attitude of the Department of National Revenue was that all taxable concerns should be taxed. In line with this view the Pools were assessed for tax on surpluses earned after the change in methods that occurred in 1931. On their part, the Pools indignantly denied liability and gave notice of an appeal. The Minister of National Revenue said in the House of Commons that he imagined the question whether the Pools were or were not co-operatives would come before the courts for final decision.[22]

The situation did not clarify quickly, although the private elevator

[21][1929] S.C.R. 435.
[22]*Canada Year Book*, 1946, p. 618; *Winnipeg Free Press*, July 22, 1942.

companies and other interests adverse to co-operatives were active in urging the Government to take action. The Pools resumed the payment of patronage dividends with the crop year of 1940-41 but made no provision in their distribution of earnings for the payment of income or corporation taxes. Meantime, eight private elevator companies announced the payment of patronage dividends. These companies argued that if the Pool elevators were permitted to distribute funds as patronage dividends without paying income tax, they should possess the same right since considerable goodwill would accrue to firms that could share their profits with their customers. The issue thus raised had serious implications for the Dominion treasury, for income tax revenue would decrease if ordinary business firms were permitted to distribute patronage dividends and deduct the amount from their income and excess profits taxes. A ruling on the point was sought by the private companies from the income tax department. The Minister of National Revenue announced that the payments being made by both the Pools and the line elevators in the form of patronage dividends or equivalent bonuses had not been allowed as deductions under the Income War Tax and Excess Profits Acts. The legal position still remained to be defined. The question was recognized to be most important, since it was obvious that if the deductions were generally allowable the practice would spread widely throughout the business world.

The controversy widened out into the political arena. A spokesman for the C.C.F. stated in Parliament that it supported the position that the Pools should not be taxed and said that a vote would be demanded on the issue. The Government replied that it was felt desirable that the question of fact and the law pertaining to the liability of the Wheat Pools to taxation should be brought before the courts for investigation and final determination. The Department of Justice had advised that the most practical method of getting these matters before the courts was to assess the Pools so that they might appeal from the assessment in the usual way. The Government's decision to assess the Pools had been taken after an examination of their legal position by the Department of Justice and a ruling by it that they were liable under the law as it stood.[23]

While the legal preliminaries to litigation were in progress public controversy continued between the interested parties. The Co-operative Union of Canada had made representations against the taxation of

[23]*Ibid.*, Oct. 22, 23, 31, 1942; Feb. 26, March 23, 1943.

co-operatives over an extended period to the Minister of Finance, but nothing came of these discussions. Early in the crop-moving season on October 2, 1944, the three Wheat Pools announced a reduction in their handling charges on grain of 2 cents per bushel in the case of street grain and 1 cent per bushel on consigned grain, retroactive to August 1. This reduction followed reports that the Pools had decided they would avoid income taxation by cutting handling charges to a level that would eliminate surpluses. The reduction seemed likely to place the Government in an embarrassing situation. The privately owned companies were in the position of having to meet the cut in charges or to surrender a large part of their custom to the Pools; on the other hand, they claimed that such a reduction would entail heavy losses.[24]   Obviously a general reduction of this magnitude would markedly curtail the earnings of all the country elevator companies and thus mean a serious decline in revenue to the Dominion treasury at a time when the exigencies of the war meant that every source of revenue must be levied upon to the greatest degree possible.

The Government stood firm on the taxation issue and arrangements were completed to hear the appeal of the Alberta Wheat Pool against their assessment before the Exchequer Court in November of 1944. The Alberta case would be followed in due course by the hearing of the appeals of the Saskatchewan and Manitoba Pools. In view of the paramount importance of the issue both the Dominion Government and the Pools engaged eminent counsel to represent them. A long period of litigation was expected before the question was finally settled.

Before the appeal reached the court John Bracken, leader of the Progressive Conservatives, put his party on record as opposing the taxation of the western co-operatives.   Mr. Bracken declared that "savings effected by a co-operative on behalf of its members are not income and therefore not taxable."[25] The issue was thus fast ceasing to be a legal determination of whether or not the Pools were in fact exempt under the wording of the law as it stood and was becoming one of public policy.

This was the situation when the Minister of Finance announced that a Royal Commission would be appointed to consider the tax treatment of the co-operatives, and that in the meantime the test case to be taken to the courts by the western Wheat Pools would be

24Ibid., Oct. 3, 1944.
25Ibid., Oct. 24, 1944.

held in abeyance. In making the announcement, the Minister of Finance said it was found that there was a "reasonable doubt about the manner in which the courts would interpret the existing provisions of the Income War Tax Act in so far as they affect the co-operatives."[26] Pending the report of the commission and legislative clarification, the treatment of co-operatives generally was to remain as it was in the past.

The Royal Commission on Co-operatives was appointed November 16, 1944, and consisted of four members, representative in a broad way of the varied interests affected, with a judge of the Court of King's Bench as chairman. Lengthy hearings were held in all parts of Canada and a great mass of evidence was accumulated. Three members of the Commission visited the United Kingdom to pursue inquiries there. The report, dated September 25, 1945, was signed by all five members with certain reservations by three members which did not seriously disturb the main conclusions reached.

On the principal issue the Commission reported: "It is our unhesitating opinion that the association [i.e., co-operative associations] and its members, as a result of the trading venture which they undertake, do make a profit. The difficulty arises in determining to which of the two, the members or the association as such, this profit inures. In the hands of one or the other, it is assessable to tax. Thus, while originally 'mutuality' may have had great potency in support of an argument that in fact no profits were made from the venture, it has lost much of its former vigour in those aspects of co-operative business which now confronts us."[27] With respect to patronage dividends the Commission said: "Functionally, then, the so-called patronage dividends may partake of the nature of a return of profits to the members, or a return of excess charges, or a return of investments, or an expense of the association. These practices, be it noted, are not to be regarded as devices adopted by the co-operatives to avoid payment of taxes. Rather they are characteristic of the ordinary co-operative way of doing business." The Commission found it impossible to lay down definitely as a general rule how much of their surplus the associations were actually obligated to return to their members, or on what date, or on what terms. This, the Commission said, constituted the difficulty of "deciding what amounts may reasonably be considered, for income tax purposes, to be income received directly by the member and tax-

[26]*Ibid.*
[27]*Report of the Royal Commission on Co-operatives*, p. 33.

able only in his hands, and what amounts can reasonably be considered to be the distinct income of the association and taxable in its hands, even if later distributed to the member."

The Commission found no basis for the view that the freedom of co-operative associations from income taxes had, in the past, induced the associations to engage in unreasonable direct price competition. It considered debatable the contention that the ability of the associations to pay patronage dividends gave the associations a competitive price advantage, and concluded that the chief competitive advantage which the co-operative associations enjoyed as entities by reason of their tax-exempt position lay in their capacity to set aside larger reserves than they could if they were taxed on the same basis as were their competitors.

Examining the contention that co-operative associations were un-usually difficult to initiate, the Commission observed that associations built up on the basis of share capital with large unallocated reserves appeared to be quite stable organizations. It admitted that the position of the "agency-type" association, financed largely by means of allocated reserves, was less clear, but pointed out that in practice members in the past were not able to obtain repayment of allocated reserves except with the approval of the association. Both types, having reached maturity, were capable, in the opinion of the Commission, of bearing the burden of taxes. There followed the conclusion that there was "no justification for the complete exemption of either of these types of co-operative associations on the grounds that, as companies, they have no ability to pay taxes."[28]

As an outcome of these conclusions the Commission recommended that the Income War Tax Act and the Excess Profits Tax Act should be amended to provide for the taxation of co-operative associations on the same basis as other bodies or persons. It qualified this recommendation by the proviso that patronage dividends or bonuses should be deductible before income tax was paid provided that such amounts were distributed to the members within six months after the annual meeting of the relevant fiscal period. To maintain parity of treatment it recommended that the same privilege should be granted to joint-stock companies and other business concerns. In order to avail themselves of this privilege, however, co-operative associations and other concerns must hold forth the prospect to their customers that payments of this nature would be made to them in proportion to their

[28]*Ibid.*, pp. 34 ff.

patronage. One concession was made to the co-operative associations as such. In response to the plea that co-operative associations encountered serious difficulties in becoming soundly established, the Commission recommended exemption from income tax for co-operative associations meeting certain requirements for the first three taxation years after commencement of business.

The findings and conclusions of the Commission were disappointing for different reasons both to the Pools and to the private grain companies. The former had failed to establish their main contention that they were non-profit organizations and therefore not liable to income tax; the latter did not like the Commission's recommendation that patronage dividends should be deductible before income tax was paid, even though it was proposed to extend the privilege to all business concerns. The payment of patronage dividends as a competitive factor in securing business was recognized to be of considerable significance in the grain trade, but in the case of the Pools the distribution of these dividends would be largely to the shareholders of the organization, whereas with the private companies their payment would represent a deduction from the shareholders' profits.

In the 1946 session of Parliament the Government introduced legislation amending the Income War Tax Act to give effect to the recommendations of the Commission. During the course of the debate certain modifications to the original proposals were accepted. But the two basic principles were adopted: (1) that there should be no tax exemption for co-operatives except for a limited period for those newly formed; and (2) that patronage dividends should be exempt. With respect to the latter the proviso was made that if the payment of these dividends should reduce earnings to less than 3 per cent of the capital employed, income tax should be payable on the basis of 3 per cent earnings on capital. This provision was made equally applicable to private concerns, but the chief significance was that it established a minimum on which income tax would be payable on the earnings of the Pools. The latter could not disburse all their earnings as patronage dividends and thus avoid income tax. Concessions made to the co-operatives included permission to distinguish between payments made to members and non-members and they were given twelve months instead of six in which to declare and pay tax-free dividends.

The legislation enacted did not settle the question of whether the Pools were liable to pay income tax in the years 1944 and 1945.

When the Government announced its policy the Minister of Finance stated that the principle of "good faith" suggested by the Commission concerning retroactive payments would be given consideration. The income tax administration would not "be required to collect tax from any co-operative in respect to any year during which it had reason to believe it was exempt and in respect of which it was led to believe by the income tax branch that it was exempt." However, referring particularly to the Pools, the Minister said that exemption would not be allowed for the years 1944 and 1945 because well before 1944 the Pools were aware of the legal opinion of the Department of Justice that they were taxable. The Government believed this to be a reasonable compromise but if this were not acceptable to the organizations concerned "the courts must determine the issue."[29] The amount involved was large, variously estimated for the Pools at around $14,000,000, of which about $8,000,000 would be payable to the Government on patronage dividends and $6,000,000 on retained surpluses. After protracted negotiations the Government agreed to exempt the amount paid out as patronage dividends but insisted that the tax on retained surpluses must be paid. The Pools vigorously protested against payment of the latter amount but a compromise was finally agreed upon and a settlement reached on the basis of a payment of around $4,000,000. In agreeing to make this payment the Pools, it was stated, "decided it was preferable to accept the Government compromise offer rather than risk millions of dollars in a legal action."[30] On the basis of parity of treatment the concession to exempt earnings paid out as patronage dividends in 1944 and 1945 was also extended to private firms which had set aside funds for this purpose. Thus ended an involved and acrimonious dispute with the broad result that the Pools became subject to income tax on the earnings of their capital up to 3 per cent but above that amount could deduct payments made by way of patronage dividends to their members, this privilege being also extended to private organizations.

[29]*Winnipeg Free Press*, June 28, 1946.
[30]*Alberta Wheat Pool Budget*, Jan. 3, 1947.

6

The Canadian Wheat Board and the war

WHEN the Canadian Wheat Board Act was passed in 1935, the powers to be given to the Board were the subject of heated controversy both inside Parliament and out,[1] and before the measure became law the Government found it expedient to make concessions in view of the determined opposition of the private grain interests. As a result, the bill that was finally passed was a compromise measure which incorporated within it certain provisions designed to leave a field open to the private trade. Legislation of this sort, involving compromise between interests and breaking new ground as well, often requires very soon after enactment a series of amendments that experience demonstrates to be necessary to give the new organization reasonable flexibility in operation. But in this instance the necessity did not immediately develop; the changes made in the Act during the first ten years of its existence were remarkably few. In fact, it stood for the first four years without receiving any amendments whatever. In 1939, 1940, and 1942 some amendments were made, but, with one exception, in no case was a vital change made in the rules under which the Board was to conduct business. The closing of the wheat futures market of the Winnipeg Grain Exchange by an Order-in-Council in September of 1943 did involve important changes in the Board's method of operations, but these changes were a consequence of the major decision that was made at that time under the stress of war conditions to eliminate futures trading in wheat. The action was not taken primarily to initiate a new procedure in the methods employed by the Wheat Board.

[1]See pp. 34 ff.

The only really significant change, arising from a shift in Government policy, occurred in 1939 when it was determined that the minimum "price" received by the producer on the delivery of his wheat should be set by Parliament rather than by the Wheat Board.[2] The 1935 Act provided that the basic price should be such "fixed price" as might "be determined by the Board with the approval of the Governor-in-Council." This provision implied an administrative decision of a practical nature based on a business-like appraisal of the relevant facts of the general wheat situation. It might be deemed to be such a price as, with regard to the coming year, the general marketing conditions warranted. Clearly, to go beyond this basis and to fix a price higher than marketing conditions warranted would be in effect to invade the legislative powers of Parliament. The Board in the exercise of its function had set a price in 1935 of 87½ cents per bushel for No. 1 Northern wheat for the crop year of 1935-36. This price was continued for 1936-37, but with the proviso added for that year by the Governor-in-Council that it should become effective only if the market price for wheat dropped below 90 cents per bushel for No. 1 Northern in store Fort William. This basis was continued for the crop year of 1937-38. In the autumn of 1938 the Board found itself faced with world-wide surplus wheat conditions, and in view of this situation fixed the delivery price with the approval of the Governor-in-Council at the lower figure of 80 cents per bushel.

The large yields of wheat in producing countries at this time were leading to very keen competition for export sales, and both Argentina and the United States had resorted to subsidies in an endeavour to dispose of their surpluses. The growth of the surplus building up in the world's carryover and the continuation of favourable growing conditions in 1939 in most wheat areas portended a further decline in wheat prices. It was foreseen that this would mean that the Canadian Wheat Board would be forced again to reduce the farmer's delivery price. In view of the marketing outlook there was fear that the reduction would be drastic. Indeed, a minimum price of 60 cents per bushel began to be mentioned as the figure that would probably be determined upon. The western grain growers fought bitterly against the possibility of a 25 per cent reduction in price which, they held, would once again seriously affect their standard of living. Their position in this respect was strongly championed in Parliament. The pressure exerted upon the Government by its supporters from the

[2]Statutes of Canada, 1939, c. 39.

West caused it to amend the Act by writing directly into the statute a delivery payment of 70 cents per bushel for No. 1 Northern wheat, basis in store at Fort William–Port Arthur or Vancouver, depending on the point from which it was shipped. The original procedure was retained for settling the payments for the other grades of wheat to bring them into proper relationship with the basic price established for No. 1 Northern. By this decision the wheat producers obtained a statutory floor price for their wheat that was not determined solely by marketing considerations, but involved regard for the maintenance of their standard of living and, it may be inferred, took into account the political effects of the decision. The effect of the change in method was that it made the determination from time to time of the basic price that the farmer was to receive a political question rather than an administrative problem. As it turned out, the deficit from the operations of the Wheat Board on the 1939 crop account amounted to approximately $8,250,000.[3]

That the minimum as fixed would include an element of subsidy was tacitly acknowledged by the limitation that was put upon deliveries to the Board at this price. A further amendment to the Act made at the same time provided that wheat growers could not sell to the Board an amount in excess of 5,000 bushels in any crop year. Thus, any subsidy that the price fixed upon might contain for the wheat growers was contemplated as giving assistance only to growers on small and moderately sized farms, and not to the larger operators beyond the above limit. At the same time the provisions of the Act were extended to include wheat produced in Eastern Canada so that the wheat producers of Ontario would share equally in such benefits as might accrue under the statute.

The amendments to the Wheat Board Act in 1940 were more comprehensive. They included additions that reflected an attempt to solve the mounting difficulties involved in handling and storing very large crops and carryovers, and others that sought to satisfy the demands of the producers for greater returns per bushel for their wheat without the Government's being forced to resort to a higher basic price.

The pressing need for additional storage space to hold wheat over an uncertain period, and the tremendous strain placed upon railway and lake transportation facilities by the prodigious demands for their services arising out of the war, made control measures clearly neces-

[3]Canadian Wheat Board, *Report*, 1943-44, Exhibit VI.

sary. This was recognized by the grain growers upon whom the
incidence of this situation ultimately fell. To deal with the problem of
excess supplies the Board was given the power to regulate deliveries
at country and terminal points, and to fix the maximum amount of
any kind of grain that a producer might deliver in any period of
time. By this amendment to the Act the Board became the administrative instrument through which the Dominion Government not
only worked out its policy of control over wheat acreage, but also
dealt with the necessity of making maximum use of the limited transportation and elevator facilities available in Canada under war conditions. To put teeth into the control measures, more severe penalties
for any failure to observe the Board's regulations were now included
in the Act.[4] At the same time the Government introduced certain
other amendments, among them one conceding the producers' demand
that they should be paid storage dues for wheat stored upon their
own farms when they were delayed in delivering their crop to market.
Payments of this nature were to be made for such periods as the
Wheat Board in its sole discretion might fix, the amount payable
not to exceed the tariff rates for storage in country elevators filed
with the Board of Grain Commissioners. By virtue of this amendment,
farm storage commenced on October 8, 1940, and was paid on all
grades of wheat delivered to the Board between November 1, 1940 and
July 31, 1941. The total amount disbursed to producers under this
clause of the Act during this period was $6,147,524.03. In the follow-
ing crop year payments were made on the same basis but amounted
to only $648,647.98. The smaller crop and the relatively heavy market-
ing possible previous to November 1, 1941 greatly reduced payments
to the producers for 1941-42.[5]

A surprising and short-sighted innovation included in the
amendments of 1940 was undoubtedly a direct concession to the
demands of the producers for greater returns from their marketings.
This was the establishment, by an amendment effective July 24, 1940,
of a processing tax or levy of 15 cents per bushel payable by the
manufacturers and importers of flour or other products manufactured
from wheat intended for human consumption in Canada. The western
farm organizations had conducted a lengthy agitation for the imposition of this tax. They argued that such a levy would not affect noticeably the price paid by the consumers of bread, since so many other

[4]Statutes of Canada, 1940, c. 25.
[5]Canadian Wheat Board, *Report*, 1941-42, p. 6.

factors entered into the cost, and would be absorbed by the processors. This argument was accepted by the Government. It was provided that the yield of this tax should not become part of the ordinary revenue of Canada, but should be paid over to the Canadian Wheat Board as an addition to its income, the purpose being to increase thereby the amount of any surplus that might arise from the Board's transactions. Since the Act provided for the issue of producers' certificates entitling the holder to a share in any surpluses that might accrue from the operations of the Board in any year, the intention was in this way to lay a burden either on processors or on domestic consumers of wheat for the benefit of the wheat producers.

The formal defence for this bit of legislation, put forward by the Minister of Trade and Commerce, was that circumstances compelled Canadian wheat to be sold for export at a low price, but that these circumstances should not govern the prices paid for wheat supplying the domestic market. The Minister said he considered that the rate of levy should not require any change in the retail price of bread.[6] The levy was criticized by supporters of the tax on the ground that the rate imposed was not sufficiently severe. John H. Wesson, President of the Saskatchewan Pool, said it was "merely a gesture, although a step in the right direction."[7] Subsequently, a submission by the Canadian Federation of Agriculture suggested that the levy should be raised to 50 cents per bushel.

Although the tax was obviously part of the Government's policy of political appeasement of the farmers for its failure to raise the basic price of wheat, it could hardly be contended that the imposition at this time of a processing levy was well thought out. Its abrupt repeal after being in force for only a little over one year was evidence of this fact and was not surprising to those familiar with the situation. As a device to bring substantially increased returns to the wheat producers, it rested upon a faulty analysis of the circumstances governing the marketing of Canadian wheat. Unlike the United States, Canada has a small domestic consumers' market relative to the amount of wheat produced in the country. A much larger portion of her supply is marketed abroad. This meant that a levy would fall upon only a small proportion of the total amount of wheat brought to market. Hence, unless the processing tax was imposed at a very high rate the return to the producer on his total marketings would not be

[6]*Winnipeg Free Press*, July 25, 1940.
[7]*Ibid.*, July 27, 1940.

of great significance. When the Government's policy was announced, it was estimated in the public press that a yield above $20,000,000 might be expected from the tax.[8] This figure was based on an assumed annual disappearance of wheat in Canada of around 150,000,000 bushels. The deduction made therefrom was obviously erroneous, since this figure included the use of wheat in Canada for any purpose. The relevant figure was the much smaller amount actually entering into human consumption in Canada. This soon became manifest, for during the course of the year and seven days the levy was collected, the total revenue accruing therefrom amounted to $5,966,791.63. This indicated that wheat used for human consumption in Canada during this period amounted to about 40,000,000 bushels. After deducting the expenses of administration, the sum available for distribution among the wheat producers was $5,867,129.40, which was allocated to a handling in round figures of 397,000,000 bushels of wheat for the crop of 1940. The additional returns from this measure to the producer were thus slightly under 1½ cents per bushel.[9]

Implicit in the prediction of the Minister of Trade and Commerce that the tax would be absorbed by the processors was the assumption that the processors were in the enjoyment of such a high rate of profit that it would be reasonable for them to carry on without a change in the price of their product under what was equivalent to an increase to them in the price of wheat of 15 cents per bushel. That the war was causing a general increase in costs and that prices of raw materials were an important factor in the situation seems to have been ignored entirely by those instrumental in pushing through the processing levy, although the difficulty of preventing a drastic rise in the cost of living was becoming more apparent daily. The assumption that the processors could absorb the levy without raising the price of their product was hardly realistic as experience was soon to demonstrate. A few weeks after the levy became operative the Government found it necessary to remit the tax in the case of wheat flour sold for future delivery by contracts made prior to May 15, 1940, on the ground that "it would hinder the Government in its efforts to prevent a rise in the price of bread." When it became clear that the effect of the tax was to accelerate a tendency to increase bread prices in various parts of Canada, the Wartime Prices and Trade Board issued a standstill order freezing bread and flour prices as of July 23, 1940. After

[8]*Ibid.*, July 25, 1940.
[9]Canadian Wheat Board, *Report*, 1940-41, Exhibit D.

an investigation, however, this order was rescinded in September of 1940. Later in the crop year, by another Order-in-Council, the levy was remitted with respect to wheat grown in Quebec and the Maritime Provinces and locally gristed for home consumption.[10] When the cost of living continued to rise in the summer of 1941, and inflationary tendencies became alarming, the wheat processing levy was precipitately dropped by an Order-in-Council under the War Measures Act effective July 31, 1941. The reason given for the repeal was that the lapsing of the tax would prevent a threatened increase in the price of bread.[11] Later in 1941, to combat inflation, an over-all price ceiling on all goods and certain designated services was established.

Finally, another innovation, contained in the amendments of 1939, disappeared after one year's experience. The limitation to 5,000 bushels on deliveries to the Board by any one grower was repealed in 1940. This discrimination against the large grower had been bitterly resented. During the course of the year in which it was in effect, large producers at times had found it difficult to find a market for their surpluses on account of the limited demand prevailing on the open market. Moreover, for part of the year the Wheat Board delivery price was higher than that obtainable on the open market, and during this period large producers who had to sell were forced to dispose of their stocks in excess of 5,000 bushels at prices below that currently available to farmers with stocks not over that amount. The elimination of this restriction removed a grievance harboured by a very influential group of wheat producers, and on the whole was well received by the public. Moreover, the Wheat Board had found the limitation very difficult to apply in practice on account of the diverse types of ownership prevailing, and the division of property and income between various members of a family. The Wheat Board in its annual report referred to the "virtual impossibility of settling questions as to what actually constituted a farm or a farm unit."[12]

The only amendment made in 1942, in addition to one which made good a minor omission in the Act, was to increase the delivery price for wheat from 70 cents to 90 cents per bushel.[13] No other amendments to the Wheat Board Act were made by Parliament until after the end of the war. The explanation is that the Dominion

[10]P.C. 1/4181, 134/813, 1941.
[11]*Winnipeg Free Press*, Aug. 1, 1941.
[12]Canadian Wheat Board, *Report*, 1939-40, p. 2.
[13]See p. 90.

Government legislated by taking advantage, as the occasion demanded, of Orders-in-Council passed under the authority of the War Measures Act. These orders were used both to overrule provisions of the Wheat Board Act and to give additional grants of authority to the Wheat Board to perform the additional functions with which it was charged. In fact, the Wheat Board in this respect enjoyed great flexibility in conducting business; if it found its powers of action curtailed in any direction it could, with the approval of the Governor-in-Council, secure what was in effect additional legislation without public notice or without the delays incidental to going to Parliament. Many Orders-in-Council relating to the Wheat Board were passed to facilitate its operations. During the war period it is estimated that the number of orders reached approximately six hundred, although certain of these were renewals or replacements.

II

To obtain a clear picture of the methods by which the Wheat Board carried on its operations, and the growing scope of its activities, it is convenient to deal first with its marketing methods during the period between its establishment in 1935 and the suspension of trading in wheat on the futures market of the Winnipeg Grain Exchange on September 28, 1943. The latter date marked the setting of a new initial price of $1.25 per bushel, and the acquisition by the Wheat Board of all stocks of cash wheat at the closing prices of September 27. During these years the Board developed an established technique of marketing which underwent little change except in the export field after the outbreak of war.

The directive embodied in the Canadian Wheat Board Act of 1935, as a result of the compromise worked out at that time between the principles of state trading and private enterprise, specified that it should be the duty of the Board in selling and disposing of wheat "to utilize and employ without discrimination such marketing agencies, including commission merchants, brokers, elevator men, exporters and other persons engaged in or operating facilities for the selling and handling of wheat as the Board in its discretion may determine." Thus, while the Canadian Wheat Board was given general powers of selling the Canadian wheat delivered to it, it is clear from this directive that the general process of handling it as it moved forward from the producer to final markets was to remain within the framework of the organized trade. In brief, the Board, in accepting wheat from the producers, would use units of the organized grain trade as its agents to handle it and place it in the positions it desired for ultimate sale.

The technique devised involved, as a primary step, handling contracts between the individual country elevator companies on the one hand, and the Wheat Board on the other. These contracts were similar in content in each instance, and the negotiations leading up to agreement were carried on collectively. Country elevator companies bound themselves to perform, when wheat was delivered in carlot quantities (Class A wheat), all the services that they would ordinarily perform for a shipper until the wheat was in store in a terminal elevator and immediately available for direct sale or export. When the wheat was in this position in the terminal it was turned over to the Wheat Board, the elevator companies receiving for their services the usual tariff, fixed by the Board of Grain Commissioners, of handling and cleaning charges, plus freight and a 1-cent per bushel "service" charge. The latter was really paid in lieu of the 1-cent commission fee which the elevator company would, in the ordinary course of business, have received from the producer for selling his wheat on the market.

When wheat was delivered in quantities of less than a carlot (Class B wheat–"street wheat"), there came into effect a schedule of prices for each grade of wheat delivered in each freight rate area which was part of the agreement. The companies agreed to pay these prices to the producer on delivery, and at the same time to issue to the producer a producer's certificate in a form to be determined by the Board. This was the producer's claim to any additional payment that might be made with respect to the deliveries in any crop year where the operations of the Board resulted in a profit sufficient to make an additional payment to the farmer. The companies also agreed to "carry" the wheat until it was delivered to the Board at a terminal point. This meant that the elevator companies financed the operation until the wheat was in store at a terminal.

The prices in the schedule to cover Class B wheat were arrived at after deducting from the basic price the Fort William or the Vancouver freight charges, whichever rate was the more advantageous to the producer, and after deducting a sum of 4½ cents per bushel. The latter deduction represented the amount paid to the elevator companies for handling this street wheat at country points, paying the producers for the wheat when delivered, forwarding it to the terminals, and absorbing freight on dockage and fees for weighing and inspection. The original deduction was 4½ cents but it varied in subsequent years as the result of negotiations and was as low as 3 cents.[14] When street wheat was not shipped immediately to the terminals, the Board paid to the companies a daily carrying charge covering storage and interest. This charge was calculated from the date the wheat was reported to the Wheat Board by the company to be in store at the country point until the wheat was unloaded at the terminals or at any other destination directed by the Board. The carrying charge was limited by the proviso that it should not be paid for more than thirteen days after the wheat was shipped from the country point.

The agreement provided that where the Board diverted wheat from the country elevator to an interior terminal for storage, the Board would pay a diversion charge of 1 cent per bushel. When this wheat was reshipped to a terminal point, the company originally making the shipment was entitled to control the destination of a proportional amount of the wheat so shipped. In the event of shipments to interior mills, the diversion payment was 1½ cents per bushel. These provisions were designed to protect the elevator companies against loss of revenue suffered when wheat that was received in their country elevators was diverted by the Board to interior mills or to government interior terminal elevators instead of being forwarded to the companies' own terminals.

These were the main features of the agreements negotiated from year to year with the grain companies. Other provisions covered such matters as the requirement to keep the wheat insured, the date of payment of accrued storage charges, and the methods of dealing with a variety of minor problems bound to arise in connection with the handling of a business as large and complicated as purchasing and moving the Canadian wheat crop, or a substantial portion of it, from the points of production to the terminals.

As wheat reached the terminals at Fort William and Port Arthur or Vancouver, and the elevator companies under their agreement turned over the unload documents and warehouse receipts to the Wheat Board, the Board accumulated stocks of wheat and was in a position to offer wheat for sale in either the domestic or the export market. Since wheat tends to move into consumption at a regular rate throughout the year, large deliveries made to the Board in the autumn months cannot all be sold immediately but accumulate in

---

[14]This deduction was voluntarily reduced to less than one-half for a time by the Pool organizations and subsequently by the private companies.

the terminals, where such stocks may remain for a considerable period as part of a carryover. The Board, when faced with holding surplus stores of wheat until sales could be accomplished, had the option while the futures market was operating of carrying these stocks either as cash wheat or in the form of futures. If carried as cash wheat, the Board simply retained the warehouse receipts delivered to it by the elevator companies and turned these over to purchasers of wheat when sales were negotiated either with Canadian mills or with exporting agencies. By the other method, the Board would sell the cash wheat to intending exporters or back to the elevator companies and purchase futures contracts for similar amounts. This was the policy initiated by Mr. McFarland when he became Chief Commissioner of the Wheat Board, and continued by his successors until the futures market was closed.

The Board's cash wheat was purchased very largely by the terminal elevator companies, which in this way acquired title to a variety of grades of wheat. The purchase meant they were more certain of earning storage revenue by keeping their elevators full, and were in a position to make any profits that might arise from mixing the lower grades with a view to enhancing the value of this wheat for ultimate disposal. There were also advantages from the standpoint of the Wheat Board. As wheat futures were "spread" forward into future months, the Board at times was able, by negotiating prices with the terminal elevator companies, to carry the wheat at a slightly lower cost than if it were paying the tariff charges filed by the elevators for the storage of cash wheat. Moreover, the method adopted introduced the least disturbance into the ordinary practices of trading followed before the Wheat Board came into existence. It was the method best calculated to "utilize" existing marketing agencies as directed by the Act. Until the war broke out, the Canadian Wheat Board disposed of its stocks at the Lakehead or Vancouver through ordinary trade channels.

The war led to a change in this procedure. Prior to the outbreak of hostilities, the open market price of Canadian wheat was well below the Board's delivery figure of 70 cents per bushel,[15] and did not show any marked advance until after war was declared. On September 2 the holdings of the Board amounted to 89,500,000 bushels, most of which was 1938 crop, with 30,000,000 bushels delivered at country

[15]On August 21, 1939, the open market price for No. 1 Northern wheat was 56⅝ cents per bushel.

points on Board account, against which sales of over 9,000,000 bushels had been made. After September 3, 1939 the open market price advanced rapidly on the Exchange. By September 6 the price of No. 1 Northern wheat had risen to 79½ cents per bushel. In the meantime, the British Government, while it had made some comparatively small purchases previously, was establishing administrative machinery to handle purchases on a much larger scale and arranging credits to finance the transactions under the changed conditions brought about by the war. In this period it was not buying wheat in Canada, nor did it for some months. Other sales, of course, were being made by the Board to Northwest Europe and the Mediterranean, which had not yet come under the power of Germany.

In October of 1939 a Canadian delegation headed by Hon. Thomas Crerar, which included the Chief Commissioner of the Wheat Board, visited England. After lengthy discussions, a clearer understanding was arrived at with the Cereals Import Committee, the body now charged by the British Government with the responsibility of importing wheat supplies. A plan of operations was devised to meet the changed conditions brought about by the war. The method adopted was for the Cereals Import Committee to purchase futures from the Canadian Wheat Board, these futures being held by the Wheat Board for use as needed when shipments went forward. The Cereals Import Committee quite early appointed a representative in Montreal who acted as the co-ordinating and liaison officer in supervising wheat shipments. This official was in touch with shipping conditions, was informed of sailing dates, and was furnished with information showing the position of stocks of wheat in Canada or the United States available for export. The Cereals Import Committee accepted offers from the Canadian exporters for wheat delivered at seaboard points designated by its representative. With the sale of the cash wheat the futures were cancelled out.

The first large sale reported under this arrangement was in January of 1940 when the Cereals Import Committee entered the market and Board sales were made to it of nearly 25,000,000 bushels. Much larger sales were negotiated subsequently. In August of 1940 the Board sold wheat futures for 100,000,000 bushels to the United Kingdom. In May of 1941 a further sale of 120,000,000 bushels was arranged. Throughout the war the United Kingdom continued to obtain the largest part of its wheat requirements from Canada. By buying futures in large blocks, the United Kingdom Ministry of Food assured itself that a sufficient amount of wheat would be available for shipment to Britain as needed. At the same time it established the over-all price that it would have to pay for these supplies.[16] The method left to the Canadian exporting agencies the business of forwarding wheat from the Lakehead to the eastern seaboard. For obvious reasons, most of the shipments went from Atlantic points. The shortage of shipping reduced the number of cargoes from Vancouver to a trickle. The urgent need for storage space to warehouse the large accumulation of grain that developed in Canada during the war years, however, led to an arrangement between the Wheat Board and the Pacific terminals by which they were kept filled, though at a reduced tariff for storage. From time to time, as freight vessels were completed and put into service on the west coast, some wheat would be taken from the Pacific terminals as part of the initial cargo carried.

The Order-in-Council passed to implement the Government's decision to end trading in wheat on the Winnipeg Grain Exchange[17] after September 27, 1943 empowered the Canadian Wheat Board to purchase for government account all unsold wheat stocks in commercial positions in Canada, including wheat held in the Board's 1940-41, 1941-42, and 1942-43 crop accqunts, at the closing prices as registered for each grade on September 27, 1943; to accept delivery of wheat produced by the 1943-44 crop at an initial price of $1.25 per bushel basis No. 1 Northern in store Fort William–Port Arthur or Vancouver for the remainder of the crop year; to distribute final payments to producers on outstanding participating certificates of the 1940, 1941, and 1942 crop accounts; to appropriate on government account all commercial stocks of western wheat for which there was no outstanding sales contract as of September 28, 1943 and to pay for wheat stocks so acquired on the basis of closing prices for the preceding day; finally, to sell wheat stocks held on behalf of the Government to fill domestic and mutual aid requirements.

This comprehensive order threw a vast amount of internal administrative work upon the staff of the Wheat Board. The closing of the earlier crop accounts on the basis determined resulted in the distribution of a combined surplus of $61,080,046 to western wheat growers. Of this sum there was payable to holders of certificates for the crop

[16]For the technique used in such arrangements see D. A. MacGibbon, *The Canadian Grain Trade* (Toronto, 1932), p. 293.
[17]P.C. 7942, Oct. 12, 1943.

of 1940, $26,081,800; for the crop of 1941, $15,305,476, and for the crop of 1942, $19,692,770.[18] The increase in the initial price from a basis of 90 cents to $1.25 also made it necessary for the Wheat Board to provide the elevator companies with price lists for the purchase of all grades of wheat at each country point. In the interim, while this schedule was being compiled, the elevator companies made advances to those producers who delivered wheat. In other respects the methods employed in handling producers' wheat at country points and moving it forward to the terminals remained practically unchanged.

The closing of the futures market made unavoidable the final clearing of all outstanding futures contracts. This operation was completed on October 16.[19] Estimates of the amount affected by the closing out of wheat futures contracts ranged between 200,000,000 and 300,000,000 bushels. The clearing of these contracts was an intricate operation, necessary for determining the values at which the Wheat Board assumed ownership of all Canadian wheat in commercial positions. The purchase of the wheat stocks held by the various elevator companies, as well as the Pools, resulted in very substantial profits to them. These profits accrued from the fact that the technique adopted in closing out the futures enabled them to buy in their October hedges on a basis that did not reflect the full advance that had taken place in the price of cash wheat. A large part of these profits was subsequently distributed as patronage dividends.

Ownership of cash wheat by the Board made necessary a change in the methods employed by the exporting agencies in their relations with the representative of the Cereals Import Committee at Montreal. The practice of offering wheat for export at seaboard points to the British agency was discontinued. Instead, the Wheat Board and the exporters worked out together a cost schedule covering the moving of wheat from the terminals at Fort William and Port Arthur to the various ports of shipment on the eastern seaboard. This schedule included a payment to the exporters for their services in making the necessary arrangements incidental to conducting a movement. Practically all the other cost items involved, such as elevator charges, weighing and inspection fees, lake and railway rates, were under the control of regulatory bodies and, of course, subject under certain circumstances to the approval of the Wartime Prices and Trade Board.

[18]Canadian Wheat Board, Report, 1943-44, Exhibit VIII.
[19]Winnipeg Free Press, Oct. 16, 1943.

The Wheat Board supplied the wheat to the exporters, and it was moved forward on the instructions of the agent of the Cereal Import Committee. Under these circumstances competition between the different exporting agencies was practically reduced to one in quality of service, and the business largely came to them on this basis. Shipments intended for export to the United Kingdom, which composed the bulk of the business, thus became purely a directed movement controlled and guided by the representative of the Cereal Imports Committee at Montreal.

III

The preceding section has set forth the different methods employed by the Board since its establishment in the performance of its main function of accepting the delivery of wheat from producers in Western Canada and selling it abroad. The Wheat Board also sold wheat to the Canadian mills. Under wartime conditions, when the price of wheat was advanced from 70 to 90 cents per bushel, the Wheat Board, acting on behalf of the Wartime Prices and Trade Board, undertook responsibility for the payment of drawback claims from the flour millers and other processors of wheat for human consumption in Canada. These drawbacks were in furtherance of the Government's policy of keeping down living costs by avoiding a rise in the price of bread.

When the Board was empowered to accept wheat from producers in Eastern Canada in 1939, it appointed a representative in Ontario with headquarters in Toronto. The delivery price fixed for the highest grade of wheat marketed in Ontario was the same as that for the West, namely, 70 cents per bushel, on the basis of delivery at Montreal export rail freight rates. In 1939 the Board received 4,254,935 bushels of eastern wheat. In 1940 deliveries fell to 1,354,315 bushels. In 1941, owing to a small crop in Ontario, the price for Ontario wheat rose much above the Board's initial price and only a very small amount of wheat was delivered to it by one producer. As a result, the Government by an Order-in-Council released the Wheat Board from accepting Ontario wheat at country points except in the event of the market price for the basic grade falling below 80 cents per bushel, basis export rail freights to Montreal. The Order-in-Council also authorized the Board to return to the producer the small amount that had been delivered that season. As part of the price control policy of the Government, on December 2, 1941 a ceiling price of $1.26 per bushel was established on Ontario wheat. Since the market price remained above the floor price of 80 cents per bushel, no further deliveries were made to the Board. In 1943 the basic price was increased to 90 cents per bushel to keep it in line with the western price. When the basic price was raised to $1.25 per bushel in the West, the basic price of Ontario wheat also became on September 27, 1943, $1.25 per bushel. Wheat, however, was not deliverable to the Wheat Board unless the price fell below 95 cents per bushel basis Montreal. As the market price remained in excess of this figure through the 1943-44 crop year, no deliveries were made to the Board.

The nature of the Ontario wheat trade led to a change in policy for the crop year of 1944-45. The Board's obligation was confined to supporting a floor price of $1.25 per bushel for the top grades delivered at Montreal. The wheat was handled by private traders and, since the price continued above the floor price, no action by the Board became necessary. The Dominion Government recognized, however, that producers were entitled to share in export prices obtainable for flour made from Ontario wheat when this flour was sold abroad at a price in excess of the domestic ceiling price plus forwarding costs. The Ontario Wheat Flour Equalization Fund was established, and equalization fees were collected from the private traders. Returns to the producers from this source on the 1944 crop amounted to $198,317. The Equalization Fund was continued for the crop year of 1945 and fees were collected on flour exports and a small quantity of export Ontario wheat, the distribution to the producers amounting to $262,114. In 1946-47 the Board was directed to administer a treasury payment of 9 cents per bushel, over and above the maximum price, for deliveries and to pay to the producer a fixed and final equalization payment of 5 cents per bushel. These payments were made through the dealers, who later were reimbursed by the Board. Since the maximum price for Ontario wheat on a Montreal basis, established in 1941, had been continued at $1.25 per bushel, this brought the maximum price obtainable by the Ontario producers to $1.39 a bushel. The disbursement to them from this arrangement amounted to $580,543, with a net cost to the treasury of $309,025. In June of 1948 the Government announced that the ceiling price of Ontario wheat was being removed and the treasury bonus eliminated. As a result, the price of Ontario wheat jumped immediately and within a short time had advanced by 39 cents per bushel.[20] The maintenance of

[20]*Ibid.*, June 19, 26, 1948. See also Canadian Wheat Board, *Report*, 1944-45, 1945-46, 1946-47.

returns to the Ontario wheat producer raised administrative difficulties, but, compared with western operations, it was a very minor part of the Board's activities.

IV

Apart from the direct marketing of wheat a tremendous expansion of the activities of the Wheat Board occurred between 1939 and 1946. This was scarcely realized except by those whose business kept them closely in touch with the Canadian grain trade. Part of this expansion was due to the Board's dominant position with respect to wheat marketing, which soon involved it in various measures designed to alleviate the situation created under war conditions by large crops, mounting surpluses, and reduced export outlets. It was confronted with difficult problems arising out of the control of deliveries at local shipping points, the shortage of storage space resulting from large carryovers, and the urgency of securing maximum utilization of the limited transportation facilities actually available for moving wheat forward from the local points to the terminals.

When the 1940 crop of over 500,000,000 bushels began to move forward in August, the Board, under the powers granted to it by the amendments of that year, instituted a system of quota deliveries effective at local shipping points with a view to enabling all producers to deliver at least a portion of their wheat and coarse grains when harvested. The necessity of this measure was obvious, since it was estimated that on account of the heavy carryover from 1939 the net storage capacity available for the new crop would not be more than 160,000,000 bushels. Without a quota, those producers whose grain ripened first would be able to deliver all their crop, while those whose crop ripened later would be out of luck. The Board's regulations provided that no wheat, oats, or barley could be delivered without a permit from the Board.[21] The permits had to be obtained from an elevator agent and the producer was limited to one delivery point except when he operated widely separated farms. Each delivery was recorded by the elevator agent in the permit book and aggregate deliveries were not to exceed the established quota. The quota was computed on the basis of the number of seeded acres of wheat, oats, and barley, and these grains were not interchangeable. Initial deliveries were fixed at 5 bushels per acre; as the season progressed and grain moved forward from the terminals the amount deliverable

[21] *Ibid.*, 1940-41, Appendix A.

per acre was increased. In the case of barley, when it became apparent early in September of 1940 that the bulk of the crop would be retained on the farm for feed, the quota restrictions were removed. For the same reason restrictions on the delivery of oats were dropped a week later.

The handling of the wheat crop itself presented the real problem in 1940. The relaxation of quota restriction began at individual shipping points where circumstances, such as sufficient storage space in the local elevators for local needs, made it feasible to permit more generous deliveries. A general increase in the quota to 8 bushels per acre was announced for September 14, and in November the quota was raised to 10 bushels per acre. By mid-December deliveries up to 12 bushels per acre were authorized. Delivery restrictions were removed altogether on April 21, 1941. This did not mean that the great crop of 1940 had been practically all delivered. Much remained in the farmers' hands. The usual practice of farmers is to hold a certain quantity of their wheat until they see how the new crop is likely to turn out. In this instance, the producers had an additional incentive to retain wheat on the farm in that they were able to collect a payment from the Government for its storage.[22]

The methods developed in 1940 by the Wheat Board to regulate deliveries in order to give all producers an equal chance in making use of restricted facilities of storage and transport were applicable to marketings for the crop year of 1941-42.[23] In 1941-42 the Dominion Government limited marketings to approximately 230,000,000 bushels for all of the West. An "authorized acreage" for delivery purposes was established by the Board for each producer on the basis of 65 per cent of his declared wheat acreage in 1940, the rule in certain instances being modified to correct inequities arising from the use of a single base year. When, however, it became apparent early in December that on account of the small crop in 1941 the total of prospective marketings was not likely to exceed 230,000,000 bushels, restrictions on deliveries were dropped. Restrictions were again applied in 1942 when a record production of all grains occurred; because of the congested condition of country elevators, deliveries of wheat for the crop year were limited to 280,000,000 bushels.

The general condition of strain on facilities, while acute in the country, extended throughout the whole structure for handling the western crop and conveying it to market. Transportation facilities

[22]See p. 94.   [23]See p. 56.

within Canada were being stretched to the extreme limit to cope with war demands; hence, there were fewer cars available for the carriage of grain. To maintain equity these cars had to be apportioned between the different shipping points and between the elevators located at each point. Since the amount of grain that a country elevator could receive was determined by the rate of shipment out, the distribution of cars between country elevators became a problem into which trade competition entered very sharply. The realization of this situation developed suddenly. To cope with it, early in August of 1940, under the chairmanship of a member of the Board of Grain Commissioners, a car control committee was established on which all interests were represented. Car distribution at country points between elevator companies was based on the amount of licensed permanent storage possessed by each company. This was admittedly a rough and ready method of allotting cars, adopted in the face of the urgent situation that had arisen. The system did not satisfy the Pool organizations, which claimed with some justification that it tended to reduce their proportion of total handlings for the year because at many points they handled more grain through their elevators for a given amount of space than their competitors. The duties of the car control committee were later taken over by the Wheat Board, and in 1943, to meet the protests of the Pool organizations, an attempt was made by the Board to base car distribution on the volume of grain handled by each company at each local shipping point during the crop years of 1938-39 and 1939-40. A good many difficulties were encountered in endeavouring to apply this principle, and the system was never put completely into operation. Easier transportation conditions developed by the spring of 1944, and the distribution of cars was regulated once more by the rules laid down under the Canada Grain Act.

Meanwhile, all grain-handling organizations were feverishly increasing their storage capacity at country points by the construction of temporary annexes. In the crop year of 1940-41 temporary storage to the extent of 72,485,477 bushels, was provided, the high point being reached in 1943-44 with 112,657,126 bushels. The Dominion Government encouraged the building of country annexes by a concession with respect to the rate at which depreciation could be written off. At Fort William and Port Arthur the urgent necessity of providing for additional storage space before the 1941 crop would be ready for delivery led to an agreement early in that year between the Dominion

Government and the terminal elevator companies for the construction in those cities of temporary storage annexes with a total capacity of 50,000,000 bushels. The main points of the agreement, embodied in an Order-in-Council,[24] were (1) that all tariff charges prevailing for the storage of grain should be continued without any reduction until July 31, 1943, in effect, a two-year guarantee of earnings; (2) that the Minister of National Revenue should allow each company constructing a temporary storage annex to write off as depreciation 50 per cent of the actual cost of the annex in each of the two successive years of 1942 and 1943. (An agreement between the various participating elevator companies provided for scrapping the constructions as soon as the emergency had passed.) After two years, if the Wheat Board continued to store grain in these annexes, it was agreed that a new arrangement would be negotiated in regard to the tariff for storage, based on the operating experiences gained up to the end of July 1943.

The provisions of the Order-in-Council became effective when the terminal elevator companies filed agreements with the Wheat Board contracting to make the storage available. The construction of the temporary storage space at the terminals was pushed with great energy by the companies during the summer of 1941, and most of it was available for use by the time the crop of that year was ready to move forward. The construction of these annexes increased storage capacity at Fort William and Port Arthur from 92,567,210 bushels to 146,730,210, and the additional space was invaluable in giving relief for some years to the congested situation in the country. After serving their purpose the annexes were scrapped in 1946. By the terms of the Order-in-Council, temporary storage annexes could be constructed under similar terms in Eastern Canada, and advantage was taken of this privilege by one elevator company to build two annexes with a capacity of approximately 3,000,000 bushels each, one at Sarnia and the other at Three Rivers.

V

While the large carryovers of wheat were creating handling difficulties, problems were arising with respect to the coarse grains. With the increased emphasis on the production of meat, bacon, and dairy products to supply British needs, greater supplies of the feed grains were required to make the fulfilment of Canadian commitments pos-

[24]P.C. 1225, 1941.

sible. When the Government met the wheat producers' demands for an increased price of wheat by raising the initial price from 70 cents to 90 cents a bushel, it was clear that if increased supplies of barley and oats were to be forthcoming, similar price guarantees for these products would have to be made. Merely to point out to the farmer that it was his "patriotic duty" to curtail wheat production and to grow more oats and barley would not be sufficient to achieve the ends desired.

In March of 1942 the Government announced its programme. The Canadian Wheat Board was empowered to buy barley at a price that would assure barley growers 60 cents per bushel for the top grades, with lower grades at an appropriate discount. In the case of oats, with the same powers given to the Board, the price established for No. 2 Canada Western oats was 45 cents per bushel, the price of other grades being scaled to this minimum. (In determining the actual level at which minimum prices for grains should be fixed, an important consideration was the influence exerted by the general policy of the Wartime Prices and Trade Board of keeping prices as low as possible with a view to preventing inflation[25] and an increase in the cost of living.) The establishment of these minimum prices brought the coarse grains within the scope of the Wheat Board should a marked decline from their current prices occur. In 1942 there was an increase estimated at 35.8 per cent in the acreage sown to barley and, in the case of oats, an increase estimated at 18.6 per cent. Increased sowings and favourable growing conditions combined to produce greatly increased yields. The increases in acreages were no doubt in part due to the establishment of minimum prices, but it is probable that other factors entered into the situation as well. Actually, when the Government's programme of minimum prices was announced, barley was selling on the open market at 64¾ cents per bushel and oats at 49½ cents, so that the chief inducement offered in the minimums fixed was a guarantee against a fall in prices. Another cause of the increase in acreages was the fact that the Canadian farmers in response to the exigencies of war, particularly to British requirements, were greatly expanding their production of cattle, hogs, and dairy products, and this expansion involved greater supplies of feed grains for use on their own farms. Also important was the limitation placed on the marketing of wheat which tended to drive the producers into coarse grains or, as an alternative, into summer-fallowing.

[25]Chairman of the Wartime Prices and Trade Board, Winnipeg, April 14, 1942.

In 1943 the ceilings were 51½ cents per bushel for oats and 64¾ cents per bushel for barley, while the level of prices for these grains was very much higher in the United States. In order to establish a method whereby the difference between domestic prices and the higher prices obtainable on export could be shared generally by western producers, the Board was empowered to assess equalization fees when licences were obtained to export western-grown oats and barley and their products. The proceeds of these levies were placed in two funds, the Oats and the Barley Equalization Funds, which were distributed, less administrative costs, to the producers on the basis of their commercial marketings.

The Board entered the market to support prices on two occasions only. In the crop year 1942-43 the Board purchased 32,601,645 bushels of oats and oat futures, and 22,970,429 bushels of barley and barley futures. These purchases were subsequently sold at a profit of $336,346.35 which was remitted to the Dominion Government. Again in the crop year of 1944-45 the Board purchased and sold 896,000 bushels of oat futures. A small profit on this transaction was turned over to the 1944 Oat Equalization Fund.[26] Profits arose from the fact that part of the stocks purchased were exported to the United States, where higher prices prevailed.

Government policy was amended in the fall of 1943. The supply of oats and barley was insufficient to support the large export movement possible and to provide enough feed for Canadian livestock producers in Eastern Canada. To protect the latter, sales were made to them, but the Canadian Government guaranteed equalization payments to the producers on their commercial deliveries and on authorized farm-to-farm transactions. Under these conditions advance equalization payments made to the producers of oats exceeded fees collected for the crop years 1944-45 and 1945-46 by $1,664,999. In the case of barley, the discrepancy between equalization fees collected and amounts disbursed to the growers for 1943-44, 1945-46, and 1946-47 amounted to $23,150,011. These deficits were absorbed by the Dominion Government. Essentially they represented a subsidy to eastern feeders incurred in recouping the western grain growers for some part of the higher prices they might have obtained for their oats and barley had exports been freely permitted. Total advance equalization payments made between the crop years 1942-43 and 1946-47

[26]Canadian Wheat Board, *Report*, 1946-47, p. 16.

inclusive amounted to $47,755,333 for oats and to $53,726,433 for barley.

The spring of 1947 brought a major change in Government policy with respect to coarse grains. On March 17 the Minister of Agriculture announced the discontinuance of advance equalization payments, which had been in effect since the fall of 1943. At the same time the maximum price for oats was increased from 51¼ cents per bushel to 65 cents per bushel, and for barley from 64¾ cents per bushel to 93 cents per bushel. An adjustment payment of 10 cents per bushel was provided for barley producers who had sold their barley before the new order became effective. With the advance equalization payment that they had received it was considered that this adjustment would place them on a substantial equality with barley producers who had held their barley and would be able to take advantage of the new maximum price. In the case of oats no adjustment payment was provided, as the advance equalization already received was deemed sufficient to give the oat producers approximately the same return as they would have received under the new maximum. For the coming crop year of 1948-49 the Board was empowered to buy No. 1 Feed barley at 90 cents per bushel and No. 1 Feed oats at 61¼ cents per bushel, and given authority to fix appropriate prices for the other grades. These changes were in line with the Government's policy with regard to the Canadian Wheat Board as contained in the amendments to the Canadian Wheat Board Act introduced into Parliament earlier in the session.[27]

Along with these changes the Minister of Agriculture announced that the Canadian Wheat Board would become the sole exporter of oats and barley. (In practice the Board did not actually export, but licensed dealers to do so.) To give effect to this policy all stocks of oats and barley in commercial positions were vested in the Board.[28] Under the provisions of the Order-in-Council the Board acquired 29,853,967 bushels of oats and 20,992,099 bushels of barley at the previous maximum price; that is, at 51¼ cents per bushel for oats and 64¾ cents per bushel for barley. Subsequently these stocks were disposed of by the Board at a net profit of $6,596,589, and this sum was credited to the Dominion Government, becoming part of the general revenues of the country. What really happened was that the grain was sold back to the former owners at the new price level.[29]

[27]See below, pp. 162-4.   [28]P.C. 1292, 1947.

[29]Canadian Wheat Board, *Report*, 1946-47; *Winnipeg Free Press*, April 23, 30, 1948.

The new policy represented a further encroachment of the Dominion Government into the domain of private trading, and the legality of the expropriation of these large stocks of oats and barley by the Board did not go unchallenged. The Order-in-Council was passed under the powers conferred upon the Government by the National Emergency Transitional Powers Act of 1945, and the preamble of the Order recited "the continued existence of the national emergency arising out of the war against Germany and Japan" as the reason for the decree. The necessity for such a step was disputed, and the issue was carried to the courts by the refusal of a Winnipeg firm of grain dealers, Hallet & Carey Limited, to deliver to the Board 40,000 bushels of barley held in storage for a Chicago grain merchant, who threatened them with court proceedings if they made delivery. The Canadian Wheat Board entered action against Hallet & Carey Limited and the terminal elevator companies who were acting as warehousemen for the grain, but were unsuccessful. The case was heard by the Chief Justice of the Court of the King's Bench for Manitoba, who said he was satisfied from the evidence presented that no emergency existed in Canada with respect to oats and barley. However, his decision rested upon what was held to be a deliberate omission from the transitional act of clear, distinct, and unequivocal powers of appropriation. Briefly, this meant that the Dominion Government in passing the Order-in-Council had exceeded its powers. The final effect of this decision will not be known until its validity is tested by the Privy Council. The Government lost the second round when the Manitoba Court of Appeal unanimously upheld the judgment given in the Court of King's Bench.[30] Subsequently, when the case was carried to the Supreme Court of Canada, the decision of that body was against the Canadian Wheat Board. One of the last appeals from Canada to the Judicial Committee of the Privy Council will be the one entered by the Government of Canada against the Supreme Court decision. Politically, the Government's action with respect to oats and barley represented a further departure from traditional Liberal policy, a departure which was more definitely indicated in the amendments to the Canadian Wheat Board Act which were being considered by Parliament at the time the Order-in-Council was passed.

[30]*Western Weekly Reports*, 1948, vol. I, p. 945; *Winnipeg Free Press*, March 12, 1949.

VI

The circumstances under which the Wheat Board took over control in 1942 of the marketing of flaxseed, and later of soybeans, sunflower seed, and rapeseed, were somewhat different than those under which control of the coarse grains were given to the Board. Canada has never produced enough oil seeds to meet domestic vegetable oil requirements, but has drawn important supplies from the Far East and from Argentina. Japanese conquests in the Pacific cut off supplies of coconut and palm oil from the former region, while transportation difficulties virtually eliminated the import of flaxseed from Argentina. These conditions put vegetable oils in short supply. The situation was serious. To meet this emergency an intensive campaign was begun by officials of the Dominion Department of Agriculture, in co-operation with provincial governments, to increase the acreage devoted to oil seeds, particularly to flax. Flax has not been a popular crop with western farmers, and it was realized that if the acreage was to be increased, price inducements were necessary. While there was at this time practically an unlimited demand for flaxseed, the objective was set of securing a crop of 20,000,000 bushels as compared with a production of 3,049,000 bushels in 1941.

Under the authority conferred on it by a series of Orders-in-Council[31] the Wheat Board took over all flaxseed in store in Canada on March 19, 1942, and at the same time became the sole purchasing agency to which flaxseed producers could make deliveries. Under this authority the Wheat Board acquired 1,986,427 bushels of flaxseed prior to the end of the crop year, July 31. This flaxseed was purchased at $1.64 per bushel for No. 1 C.W. flaxseed in store, the prevailing maximum price when the stocks of flaxseed in Canada were "frozen" on March 6. For the new crop year of 1942-43 the price of No. 1. C.W. flaxseed in store was set at $2.25 per bushel, a price considered sufficiently remunerative to encourage increased acreage. This proved to be an effective incentive; 1,492,200 acres were sown to flax in 1942 as compared with 996,500 acres in 1941. Production amounted to the greatly increased total of 14,922,000 bushels, though this was approximately 5,000,000 bushels under the objective set. In 1943 acreage increased to 2,947,800 and production to 17,911,000 bushels, the fixed price having been increased to $2.50 per bushel.

This was the high point reached in production. Although two

[31]P.C. 1636,1800, 2166, March, 1942.

further increases in price were made in the next three years, bringing it up to $3.25 per bushel for the crop year 1946-47, acreage declined to 840,900. In view of the hazards involved in growing flax the farmers did not consider these increases sufficiently attractive for them to devote large acreages to its cultivation. Moreover, the prices set for other grains were giving producers comfortable returns. For the crop year of 1947-48 the price was again raised, this time to $5.00 per bushel, and the acreage seeded increased to 1,571,000. The yield rose from a low of 6,208,000 bushels in 1946 to 12,240,000 bushels. On March 23, 1948, the Minister of Trade and Commerce announced that for the crop year 1948-49 the ceiling price of $5.00 per bushel would be removed and a floor support price of $4.00 per bushel would be initiated which would only be paid if the market dropped to that level. The removal of the ceiling would enable the buyer and the seller to trade freely at prices above the support level. Export controls were continued, but it was stated that the Wheat Board would be able to make available a larger supply of flaxseed for export. The Minister said that there were definite signs of improvement in the world situation with respect to oil seeds, and that there was a distinct possibility that the serious shortage that had prevailed for some years would no longer have to be faced.[32]

Up to July 31, 1946, the Wheat Board, while paying producers on the basis of the maximum prices established, was supplying the domestic market at a maximum price of $1.64 per bushel. Beginning with August 1, 1946, it was instructed to increase the price to processors to $2.75, and later on in the crop year, on February 1, 1947, the price was further increased to $3.25 per bushel. Thus the Board had been selling flaxseed for consumption in Canada at substantially lower prices than were being paid by it to the producer. This was in accord with instructions from the Government. As a result, the Board incurred substantial deficits in its operations in those years when domestic requirements reduced export sales to a minimum. These deficits were absorbed by the federal treasury. During the period extending from March 5, 1942 to July 31, 1947, the Canadian Wheat Board acquired a total of 44,683,840 bushels of flaxseed. Over half of this quantity was sold to domestic consumers; the balance, except for small stocks on hand on July 31, 1947, was exported. In the crop year 1946-47, 4,877,596 bushels were acquired and only 11,820 bushels were exported. The over-all result of the Government's policy of subsidizing

[32]*Winnipeg Free Press*, March 25, 1948.

domestic consumers was a net deficit of approximately $5,728,000.[33] Subsidizing the domestic consumer, of course, was part and parcel of the Government's general policy pursued during the war of controlling prices. The Canadian Wheat Board merely acted as its agent in implementing its policy in this field.

While steps were taken to encourage the production of soybeans, rapeseed, and sunflower seed, these proved to be comparatively small crops, though they helped to a small extent to relieve the critical vegetable oil situation. Beginning with the crop year 1943-44 and continuing up to the end of the crop year 1946-47 the Board handled 18,427,883 pounds of rapeseed and 23,250,902 pounds of sunflower seed. The Board also handled 92,537 bushels of Eastern Canadian soybeans. As part of the endeavour to keep down prices, by an arrangement with the Vegetable Oils Controller, Board purchases were resold at purchase price.

VII

The widening scope of the Wheat Board's control powers during the war years presents some technical aspects of interest. When the Canadian Wheat Board, in addition to marketing wheat, was empowered to control grain deliveries at local points, to determine the nature of the flow of shipments from local points to the terminals and to the mills, and from the terminals to the seaboard, this represented an expansion of its activities in depth; in brief, almost complete control of the movements of grain. The Dominion Government's selection of the Board to be its agency for carrying out government policy with respect to the marketing of coarse grains and oil seeds entailed expansion of a horizontal nature, or expansion in width. These additions to the Board's normal functions undoubtedly fell to it on account of the situation created by the war, but the effect was to reduce the field of private enterprise and to strengthen the trend towards state socialism in the grain trade.

The importance of wheat supplies to the Allies, especially the United Kingdom, during the war made it necessary that the Wheat Board should be in intimate touch with London and Washington with respect to wheat and the shipping situation. In 1936 the Board had appointed a European representative with headquarters in London whose principal duty was to promote the use of Canadian wheat over-

[33]Canadian Wheat Board, *Report*, 1946-47, p. 19.

seas. With the onset of war this official's services were centred on liaison work between the Board in Canada and the Cereals Import Branch of the Ministry of Food in the United Kingdom. He also conducted the Board's transactions with the Treasury department of the United Kingdom. In 1943 large sales of wheat to the United States and the concentration of wartime activities in connection with grain in Washington made it advisable for the Board to have a representative there. The problem of transporting wheat and flour to Great Britain, and later to the Continent, required the closest collaboration with the officials of the United States and of the United Kingdom. In this connection, the Board's representative at Washington served on the Cereals Committee of the Combined Food Board and represented Canada.

Broader contacts came to the Wheat Board through the numerous conferences, constantly occurring, of an international nature with reference to the future control of wheat production, food programmes in the post-war years, and the distribution of supplies to destitute countries following the collapse of the enemy powers. On occasions of this nature, the Board, by reason of its position, represented Canada either on a technical or on a higher level.

Within the Dominion the Board's position in the marketing structure of the grain trade brought it into close touch with various control organizations utilized by the Dominion Government, such as the Wartime Prices and Trade Board and the Transport Controller. A member of the Wheat Board headed a committee established by the Lumber Controller to allocate supplies of lumber for the construction of additional grain storage space. In brief, the Canadian Wheat Board became an integral part of the system of controlled economy built up in Canada by the Dominion Government, chiefly by means of Orders-in-Council, under the powers granted to it by the War Measures Act.

The magnitude of its operations stands out when one examines the record of producers' marketings through the Board and the latter's sales for export and domestic consumption. The volume, of course, varies from year to year, depending on a variety of circumstances, the limiting factor in producer deliveries being the size of the crop. From 1939 to 1944 inclusive, annual wheat production in Canada fluctuated between a high of 529,000,000 bushels in 1942 and 267,000,000 bushels in 1943. The total production for the six-year period amounted to approximately 2,550,000,000 bushels. The largest amount marketed with the Board in any one of these crop years was from the crop of 1940 when western producers delivered 395,357,243 bushels with initial payment of $268,265,988. Initial returns to producers from the 1944 crop were greater, although marketings were down by roughly 40,000,000 bushels. Delivery payments on this crop amounted to $427,916,283. This was largely because of the advance in the basic price of wheat to $1.25 a bushel. These figures present one side of the picture, the relationship of the Board to the producer. The other side appears in the records of the Board's sales. As Canada had large surpluses of wheat throughout the war years, fluctuations in sales did not arise from the volume of producer marketings but were due to such factors as the loss of European markets by the advance of the enemy, the requirements for wheat in the United Kingdom, the availability of shipping facilities, and a feed shortage in the United States. Within the period covered by the crop years 1939-40 to 1944-45 the Board sold around 1,726,000,000 bushels of wheat, of which 1,654,000,000 bushels was received direct from the producers; the balance consisted of purchases of terminal and country elevator overages, inter-crop transfers, deliveries through the clearing house, etc. This cash wheat sold for a total of $1,859,000,000, or on the average, approximately $1.07½ per bushel. In general terms, during these years the Wheat Board was conducting an annual business that varied in magnitude from $300,000,000 to $600,000,000. For the size of the enterprise administrative costs were kept remarkably low. For the crop year 1946-47 they amounted to $1,777,062, of which $1,307,539 was chargeable to marketing the producers' wheat and distributing the final payments.

During the strenuous years of the war the Canadian Wheat Board carried out the various duties delegated to it without arousing serious criticism. An isolated challenge to its methods of dealing with surpluses accruing from sales above the minimum price was an attempt by a producer named Oatway, acting on behalf of himself and other producers, to obtain through a court action an accounting from the Wheat Board covering its operations for the five years from 1938 to 1943. The complainant claimed that he was entitled to a share in the Board's surplus for each year. The Wheat Board maintained that it was an agent of the Crown, entitled to all the Crown's prerogatives and accountable only to the Crown for its public actions. This view was sustained in the Appeal Court of Manitoba.[34] Subsequently, an appeal

[34]*Winnipeg Free Press,* Oct. 5, 1944.

was carried to the Supreme Court of Canada where it was held that
the Orders-in-Council giving the Wheat Board power to take over all
wheat sales and to distribute surplus moneys wiped out the previous
action brought by Oatway.[35]

By the end of the war the Canadian Wheat Board was established
in a position that had every appearance of stability. The producers
appeared to be satisfied that they were being fairly dealt with by
the Board.   Even the difficult task the Board faced in determining
the "authorized acres" which were the basis of the producer's deliverable quantity, when limitations were placed upon marketings, was
accomplished with practically no complaints of unfair discrimination.
Moreover, this was not because of laxity in administration, for the
Board was prompt to prosecute attempts at evasion of the limitations
imposed. Various farm organizations passed resolutions to the effect
that the Wheat Board should be continued as the sole agency to
market Canadian wheat.   The Pool organizations were particularly
active in whipping up support for this point of view. Resolutions
of a similar tenor were also passed with varying degrees of support
by the western legislatures.

With the private grain trade the Board had ironed out most
differences and reduced procedure in dealing with it largely to routine.
But while the operations of the Wheat Board had been gradually
adjusted to the use of the facilities of the private elevator companies,
to the functions of the exporters, and to other factors in the trade,
it would be difficult to prove that it had reduced the over-all cost of
marketing Canadian wheat. Substantially, the Canadian Wheat Board
had been superimposed on and meshed into the existing organization.
Except in the elimination of a small number of futures grain brokers,
no significant reduction in grain trade personnel was discernible.

[35]*Ibid.,* Feb. 27, 1945.

7

The British Wheat Agreement

In the past twenty years nothing in the eventful history of the Canadian grain trade has evoked sharper controversy than the British Wheat Agreement negotiated in 1946. The end of the war laid upon the federal Government the necessity of deciding upon its future wheat policy. The impending disappearance of price controls found western wheat producers highly critical of the relatively low prices at which Canadian wheat under government directives was being sold to the United Kingdom and other countries abroad as well as to Canadian consumers. The growers were also anxious for some degree of stability in the price of their product. In Winnipeg private traders were urging that the futures market for wheat on the Winnipeg Grain Exchange, suspended in 1943, should be allowed to resume operations. These matters required consideration and they were closely related to the crucial question of the future status of the Canadian Wheat Board. With regard to this latter problem the Liberal administration had, on the whole, seemed to favour the continuance of an open market.

The first indications of government policy appeared in the autumn of 1945. On September 19, 1945, the Minister of Trade and Commerce announced in Parliament that the Government would put a "floor" under wheat prices by guaranteeing a minimum price of $1.00 a bushel for the next five years, from August 1, 1945 to July 31, 1950. The Minister said that this was in return for the sale by the Canadian Wheat Board of wheat for export at $1.55 per bushel. He admitted that Canadian wheat might be sold at higher prices for a limited period but he said that it was in the interest of Canada and of the grain growers themselves that the importing countries should be able to continue to obtain Canadian wheat at prices not in excess of those prevailing at the end of hostilities. It was also announced that, for

119

the balance of the 1945-46 crop year at least, the Canadian Wheat Board's advance to growers would continue at $1.25 per bushel, the figure at which it had been set two years previously.

During the following months there was some criticism of the five-year guarantee established by the Government, mainly on the ground that the minimum payment had been fixed too low.[1] Canadian wheat growers, despite the measure of protection afforded, were becoming increasingly alarmed about the future stability of world prices. Abroad the international wheat situation continued to be very confused. The exporting countries were unable to agree upon export prices and the lack of credit resources in the importing countries was making the international price structure decidedly artificial.

In May of 1946 an international conference of thirty-one countries concerned with agricultural prices met in London. At this conference representatives of Western Canadian farm interests were present. Mr. J. H. Wesson, of the Saskatchewan Pool, proposed an international wheat agreement. The idea was discussed by the grower and government representatives present but apparently remained merely in the discussion stage.[2] Of more importance was the fact that in the fall of 1945 and in January 1946 Mr. MacKinnon, Minister of Trade and Commerce, and Mr. Gardiner, Minister of Agriculture, were in Britain and are known to have discussed a long-term wheat agreement with the British Government. Mr. Wesson during his visit to London in May was also in touch with the British Minister of Food and officials of his department, and it appears most probable that a bilateral agreement came under consideration as an alternative, if there was no immediate prospect of launching a world wheat agreement. In June Mr. Wesson, in a statement in the *Western Producer*, referred to negotiations in progress between Canada and Britain for a wheat marketing agreement. Until an international agreement could be achieved, he stated, he believed it to be in the interests of the western wheat growers that such an agreement with Great Britain should be reached.[3]

On June 18 the British Minister of Food, Mr. Strachey, arrived in Ottawa on what was termed a one-day "courtesy" call while en route to Washington. At the same time despatches from London reported that he hoped to secure a long-term wheat contract from the Canadian Government. From this date events began to move more rapidly. The

[1]*Winnipeg Free Press*, March 16, 27, June 14, 1946.
[2]*Ibid.*, May 21, 23, 1946.
[3]*Ibid.*, July 13, 1950.

negotiations were quietly carried on at Ottawa and were concluded by the signing of the agreement on July 24, 1946.

Under the terms of the agreement Canada undertook to supply to the United Kingdom 600,000,000 bushels of wheat during the course of the next four crop years. She would make available 160,000,000 bushels during the crop years of 1946-47 and of 1947-48 and 140,000,000 bushels during the crop years of 1948-49 and of 1949-50. The agreement further provided that if the United Kingdom required more wheat from Canada than the amount set out in the agreement any additional quantity that Canada was prepared to make available would be subject to the same terms as those specified.

The agreement set out that for the crop years 1946-47 and 1947-48 the basic price should be $1.55 per bushel for No. 1 Manitoba Northern wheat in store at Fort William or Port Arthur or at Vancouver or Churchill. In respect to wheat sold in the crop year of 1948-49 the stipulation was that the minimum basic price should not be less than $1.25 per bushel and for 1949-50 not less than $1.00 per bushel. The actual prices to be paid in these two years were to be negotiated annually not later than December 31, 1947 for 1948-49 and not later than December 31, 1948 for 1949-50.

Clause 2 (*b*) of the agreement included a proviso that in determining the prices for 1948-49 and for 1949-50 the United Kingdom would "have regard to any difference between prices paid under this agreement in the 1946-47 and 1947-48 crop years and the world price for wheat" during these two crop years. The "have regard to" proviso did not cover the last two years of the agreement except in so far as it was to be one of the factors entering into the negotiations determining the prices to be paid in 1948-49 and 1949-50.

When the agreement was signed the world price of wheat was around $2.00 per bushel. Hence, the immediate reaction to it was one of distinct surprise that the Canadian Government should enter into a long-term wheat contract with the United Kingdom on the basis of a price that was so much below current world wheat values. The Government countered with the statement that the price agreed upon would enable it to increase the minimum floor price to producers, which it had announced in September of 1945, effective until July 31, 1950. Six days after signing the agreement the Minister of Trade and Commerce announced that the initial delivery price to the producer for the period between August 1, 1945 and July 31, 1950 would be raised from $1.00 per bushel to $1.35. On the 1945-46 deliveries, which had been based on a delivery payment of $1.25 per bushel, an additional 10 cents per bushel would be paid on all grades to bring the price up to the new basis of $1.35. The balance of the surplus from the sale of the 1945 crop was to be placed in a five-year pool, together with any surpluses that might accumulate from the disposal of the crops of 1946, 1947, 1948, and 1949. Payments on the participation certificates for this five-year pool would only be made after July 31, 1950.

At the same time the Minister announced a change in policy with respect to export sales of Canadian wheat, which were being made at the pegged price of $1.55 per bushel. While the price to the United Kingdom by virtue of the agreement would continue at $1.55 per bushel, a serious effort would be made to sell whatever additional supplies of wheat Canada had available for export at prices roughly corresponding to those obtained by the United States.[4] In the Canadian trade circles such wheat was known as Class II wheat while wheat sold to the United Kingdom was known as Class I wheat. The Canadian Wheat Board, in accordance with the new directive, raised the price of wheat for export to countries other than the United Kingdom from $1.55 per bushel for No. 1 Northern wheat in store at Fort William or Port Arthur to $2.05 per bushel. The additional sum accumulated from such sales was to become part of the surplus available for distribution at the end of the five-year pooling period.

The significance of these measures was that while the Government continued its marketing monopoly, it had placed the western wheat producers in a somewhat more favourable position than they had occupied. The guaranteed floor price had been substantially increased while the retroactive feature of providing a 10-cent per bushel additional payment on the wheat delivered during the crop year of 1945-46 would add forthwith approximately $23,000,000 to the income the growers had received for that year. Finally the sale of Class II wheat on the basis of world value would increase the amount accumulating in the five-year pool.

These developments lessened the amount of criticism to which the wheat agreement, if considered by itself, might have been subjected. They shifted attention to the immediate benefits deriving from the Government's programme. The reaction, in fact, to the Government's policy was varied, depending to a very large degree upon the interests affected. The producers were pleased with the prospect

[4]*Ibid.*, July 31, 1946.

of receiving at once an additional $23,000,000 on the 1945 crop, as well as the increase in initial and floor prices. Pool officials, while guarded in their comments, emphasized strongly the stabilizing value of a floor price of $1.35 per bushel and their satisfaction at the continuance of the Wheat Board as the sole marketing agency. The private traders, on the other hand, were bitterly disappointed at this check to free trading and strongly criticized the agreement for failing to secure to the Canadian producer prices equivalent to the current world values for Canadian wheat.

In Parliament the leader of the Progressive Conservative party described the agreement with the United Kingdom as a bad bargain, but nullified his criticism by saying that even this agreement was better than no agreement.[5] The C.C.F. and Social Credit parties supported the "principle" of the agreement. On the whole the debates in Parliament illustrated one weakness of government trading. The discussions were coloured by political considerations and the question whether the agreement in the light of prospective demands for wheat was a good contract or a bad contract was not subjected to searching scrutiny. This observation is almost equally true with respect to comments appearing in the columns of the Canadian press. Only in the *Winnipeg Free Press* and in some publications sympathetic to the private grain trade were the terms of the agreement condemned as bad business. Adverse criticisms from these quarters, however, were combined with such strong advocacy of free marketing that they were discounted as not being purely objective analyses of the merits of the agreement from a commercial standpoint.

In view of the sharp fluctuations in yield per acre that occur in Canada from time to time the magnitude of the quantities that were to be delivered annually to the United Kingdom raised the question whether, in the event of a short crop during the period under commitment, Canada would be able to fulfil the terms of the agreement. Canada had just come through a period of bountiful yields. The average annual production for the five-year period 1941-46 was approximately 378,000,000 bushels compared with 248,000,000 bushels in 1933-37. There could be no certainty that unfavourable conditions might not again reduce production. Even if sufficient wheat were produced to cover the contract with the United Kingdom comparatively slight reductions in yield per acre or in total acreage might make it impossible for Canada also to supply wheat to her ordinary customers

[5]*Ibid.*, Aug. 15, 1946.

in Europe. This risk was, of course, implicit in the agreement.

The United Kingdom was given the right to sell any surplus of Canadian wheat she did not require for her own consumption. This feature of the agreement came in for criticism on the ground that the average use of Canadian wheat in Britain was less than the supplies she would receive from Canada. It was argued that with world prices higher than the cost of her Canadian purchases the United Kingdom would have a surplus for resale in competition with Canada. But while conceivably odd sales of this nature might occur the probabilities were all against the development of a substantial trade on this basis. The argument failed to take into consideration the United Kingdom's total wheat requirements. Over and above what she received from Canada the United Kingdom would still find it necessary to purchase a certain amount of wheat from other exporting countries. It was estimated that her post-war requirements would run around 210,000,000 to 215,000,000 bushels annually.[6] Hence, if she resold Canadian wheat for export she would have to go into the market to buy equivalent quantities from other exporting countries at higher prices. The more probable course appeared to be that the United Kingdom, particularly in view of the low price settled upon in the Canadian agreement and of her credit position, would tend to increase her consumption of Canadian wheat.

If the general reaction in Canada to the agreement was confused and hesitant it was not so in the United Kingdom. The announcement of the terms of the contract in the British House of Commons by the British Minister of Food, John Strachey, drew cheers from the members, and the news received a favourable reception in the London press. Later, the Minister in a public address triumphantly declared that the Canadian farmers were selling their 1946 wheat to the United Kingdom "at nearly a dollar [a bushel] cheaper than the price they could get in the open market."[7] Subsequently, Mr. Strachey, reaffirming in the House of Commons the historic British policy of buying cheap, argued that bulk purchases were the best method of obtaining supplies at low prices.[8] The Economist referred to the "size and comparative cheapness" of the transaction and pointed out that the price for the first two years was some 30 per cent below the current price in the

---

[6]Ibid., June 25, 1946.

[7]Ibid., Aug. 20, 1946; an address given in Dundee, Scotland.

[8]British House of Commons, Dec. 11, 1946; Hansard, column 1156. See Winnipeg Free Press, Feb. 27, 1947.

United States.[9] The British grain trade publication, the *Corn Trade News*, while critical of the contract on the ground that it would perpetuate controls for another four years, revealed its amazement at the terms of the agreement in the suggestion, promptly denied at Ottawa, that Canada had yielded to "British pressure" in entering into the arrangement.[10] Quite obviously the oldest and shrewdest traders in the world instinctively recognized that the United Kingdom, from its point of view, had obtained a stupendous bargain and wondered how it had come about.

The correctness of their judgment about the agreement was steadily confirmed by the continuing upward trend of world wheat values. This trend was clearly shown by the record of prices quoted for Canadian Class II wheat, the price of which was fixed to correspond as nearly as possible to prices ruling in the free markets of the United States. The price established in August 1946 for Class II wheat was $2.05 per bushel or 50 cents per bushel higher than the price at which the United Kingdom was to obtain wheat of a similar grade under the agreement. Thereafter, during the course of the crop year the price of Class II wheat steadily rose until it reached a high point of $3.10 per bushel early in 1947. At this time Canada was supplying wheat to the United Kingdom at about one-half of its value in other export markets. The price of No. 1 Northern Class II wheat declined later on to a low of $2.05 but by the end of the crop year had risen again and stood at $2.56 per bushel on July 31, 1947. For the crop year of 1947-48 the level of prices for this wheat was generally above this figure; for some months it exceeded $3.00 per bushel. On account of the relatively small crop of 1947 the bulk of the Canadian exportable surplus went to the United Kingdom on the basis of $1.55 per bushel to satisfy the contract. Thus for the first two years under the terms of the agreement negotiated by the Dominion Government the bulk of Canadian wheat for export was being sold at a price well below the international level of wheat prices.[11]

Meanwhile various estimates were being made in Canada of what the agreement had cost the producers. Some of these estimates undoubtedly were excessive but on July 17, 1947 the Minister of Trade and Commerce placed the loss on the deliveries made under the agreement for the crop year at 77 cents per bushel. For the total deliveries

[9]*Economist*, Aug. 3, 1946, p. 169.
[10]*Winnipeg Free Press*, Aug. 9, 1946.
[11]*Ibid.*, July 25, 26, 28, 1947.

this was computed by officials of his Department to amount to $123,000,000.[12] The term "loss" refers to the amount of money it was estimated the wheat producers of western Canada were deprived of obtaining by reason of the difference between the price fixed under the agreement and current export values of Canadian wheat as measured by the prices set by the Canadian Wheat Board for wheat sold by it to other countries. At the end of the second crop year of the agreement, the loss was computed at $206,000,000, making a total loss for the first two years of the agreement of approximately $330,000,000. The importance of the figure at this time rested upon the fact that it was this sum, or whatever sum negotiations between the two countries might settle on as the most accurate computation of the loss, that was to be taken into consideration in setting the prices for the remaining two years of the contract.

In view of the obvious losses incurred by the producers under the contract during the first two years the question of how well the "have regard to" proviso included in the document would stand up under the conditions of actual negotiations became of crucial importance to them. When the agreement was signed the generality and vagueness of the British undertaking had not escaped notice altogether. The *Corn Trade News* observed that this proviso was "dangerously open to differences of interpretation"[13]–an observation that was abundantly confirmed by subsequent events. In Canada the interpretation gained currency that the United Kingdom would recoup the Canadian producer during the last two years of the agreement for losses incurred under its terms during the first two years. For this interpretation responsibility chiefly attaches to Mr. Gardiner, Canada's Minister of Agriculture, but also to some degree to Mr. Strachey, the British Minister of Food.[14] Mr. Gardiner, in an address at MacGregor, Manitoba, on July 23, 1947, declared: ". . . as soon as the size of the new crop is known negotiations will be opened with Great Britain to establish a price for the farmer for his 1948 crop and also 1949 crop. This price will be established under the terms of the contract which takes under consideration any losses which may have resulted during the first two years by accepting $1.55." Two days later at Dauphin he expressed the opinion that Canadian wheat growers would receive returns higher "than even the world price" on the latter period

[12]*Ibid.*, July 24, 1947; July 28, 1948.
[13]*Ibid.*, Aug. 9, 1946.
[14]*Ibid.*, Feb. 27, 1947.

of the contract.[15] These assurances, though received with some scepticism, heightened interest in the outcome of the pending negotiations.

According to the agreement the price to prevail for the third year was to be negotiated not later than December 31, 1947. Although the negotiations which had led to the agreement technically fell within the scope of the Department of Trade and Commerce, actually, except in the preliminary stages, they had been conducted by the Minister of Agriculture. This fact the Minister of Trade and Commerce was careful to make clear when questioned in the House of Commons, although the instrument was signed by him on behalf of Canada.[16] Discussions were begun in England by Mr. Gardiner and completed by negotiations continued in Canada by cable after Mr. Gardiner's return. On October 1, 1947 the Prime Minister, Mr. Mackenzie King, announced that $2.00 per bushel had been agreed upon as the price for Canadian wheat to be sold under the contract to the United Kingdom for the crop year of 1948-49. The new price of $2.00 per bushel became effective on August 1, 1948.

The text of the Prime Minister's announcement included the statement that in determining the price both parties recognized the obligation contained in the contract to give regard to the difference in the first two years between world prices and the price paid to Canada under the Agreement.[17] While the official statement issued by the Ministry of Food at London contained no reference to the "have regard to" proviso it said: "The United Kingdom Government has recognized that in the present world conditions a price somewhat higher than the price of $1.55 per bushel fixed under the contract for the present year would be equitable."[18] To this may be added a further paragraph from Mr. King's statement: "The Government is satisfied that the considerations which have prompted the United Kingdom Government to offer and the Canadian Government to accept a price of $2 per bushel for 1948-49 will apply fully and in the same spirit in the negotiations for the settlement of the prices to be paid in 1949."[19]

However, at the time that the price was settled upon for the 1948-49 crop year the current price for exports of Class II Canadian wheat was around $3.15 per bushel. When the agreement was signed in 1946 for

[15]*Ibid.*, July 25, 26, 1947.   [16]*Ibid.*, July 28, 1947.
[17]*Ibid.*, Oct. 2, 1947.   [18]*Ibid.*
[19]*Ibid.*

the first two years the discrepancy between current world prices and the agreement price was approximately 50 cents per bushel. Under the new agreement covering 1948-49 the discrepancy at the time the price was fixed was approximately $1.15 per bushel. While improving conditions in Europe were not unlikely to result in some decline in world wheat values in the ten-month interval between the signing of the agreement and the date it would become effective, Class II Canadian wheat for export would have to fall over $1.00 per bushel before the United Kingdom would be paying for Class I wheat on the basis of the going free market price. Under the circumstances it is difficult to see in what manner regard had been had to recouping the western wheat producers for losses incurred during the first two years of the agreement. But even if, as was stated, the principle was recognized, the outcome did not offer much comfort to them. A moderate decline did occur in world values, but the Board's selling price for Class II wheat during the crop year 1948-49 varied from a high of $2.48 per bushel to a low of $1.91; the average selling price was $2.23. On the same basis of calculation as employed for the first two years, the loss on the third year of the contract was $27,000,000.[20]

In March 1948, by an amendment to the Canadian Wheat Board Act, the Government took power, hitherto held by Parliament, to make periodic advances in the initial wheat payments.[21] Under this legislation it subsequently increased the initial payment from $1.35 to $1.55 per bushel retroactive to 1945. The amount meant a distribution to the growers of approximately $155,000,000. Decision to increase the payment was based partly on the higher price of $2.00 for the crop year 1948-49 settled upon under the contract and partly on account of the funds accumulating with the Wheat Board as a result of its sales of Class II wheat on the world's markets.[22] Withholding returns over the minimum price for the entire five-year pool period had never been popular with the producers and making the change retroactive from 1945 would give them in effect a substantial interim payment and a higher delivery payment thereafter.

With respect to the basis of the $2.00 price determined upon, regard must be paid to a curious statement made by the Minister of Agriculture at Lethbridge, Alberta, on January 15, 1948. Mr. Gardiner is reported to have said that the price of $2.00 per bushel

[20]*Ibid.*, July 10, 1950; Canadian Wheat Board, *Report*, 1949-50, p. 10.
[21]Statutes of Canada, 1948, c. 4.
[22]*Winnipeg Free Press*, March 26, May 6, 1948.

was agreed to in order to establish parity between prices for British home-grown wheat and the cost of Canadian wheat laid down in Britain; the British farmer received $2.50 per bushel for his domestic production and the cost of shipping Canadian wheat from Fort William to Britain varied between 40 and 50 cents per bushel.[23] If this explanation for the price settled upon is correct it must be pointed out that there is nothing in the contract to indicate or require such a basis. Nor, as far as Canada was concerned, was its relevancy apparent.

If a strong buyers' market had appeared to be impending a price of $2.00 per bushel might represent some concession by the United Kingdom to Canadian claims. But this was not the situation at the time negotiations occurred. The world was being warned by experts that exportable surpluses of food grains were still in very short supply. On July 28, 1947, W. C. McNamara, Assistant Chief Commissioner of the Canadian Wheat Board, estimated a potential deficit of "close to 400,000,000 bushels" of wheat and coarse grains suitable for human consumption. In his view, the situation would be as serious as, if not more serious than, it was in the preceding year or had been since the end of the war.[24] On August 18, 1947, Dr. Dennis A. Fitzgerald, Secretary-General of the International Food Council, said that the bumper crop harvested by the United States would not offset the great declines in Canadian and European crops. The world food situation would continue to be very difficult. On August 26, 1947, the Department of Agriculture of the United States Government estimated that the world's wheat carryover was the smallest in eight years and there was a possibility that deficit nations would have to scrape along with even less wheat than they had expected from exporting countries.[25] The broad result of the 1947 negotiations was that the United Kingdom was apparently able to increase the margin of protection that she had obtained in the original agreement against the possibility of a decline in world wheat values.

Conditions were not as favourable to the Canadian negotiators when the time came in the fall of 1948 to settle upon the price at which wheat deliveries to the United Kingdom would be made for the crop year 1949-50, the final year of the contract. Large and in some instances bumper crops had been garnered by practically all the large wheat producing countries and the sellers' market of the previous years was showing signs of becoming a buyers' market. In the United States,

[23]*Ibid.*, Jan. 17, 1948.   [24]*Ibid.*, July 30, 1947.   [25]*Ibid.*, Aug. 19, 27, 1947.

particularly, an immense reserve of wheat was accumulating and under the European Recovery Programme that country was assisting the dollar-famished importing country to make purchases. The re-election of President Truman had led to a revival of interest in a world wheat agreement and steps were going forward in Washington to convene another world wheat conference. In the United Kingdom domestic controversies over food and finance slowed down British initiative.[26]

In 1947 the agreement between Canada and the United Kingdom covering 1948-49 had been reached by October 1 but in 1948 after preliminary unsatisfactory financial explorations negotiations lapsed for some weeks and it was not until early in December that Mr. Gardiner went to England to conclude a settlement. Canadian wheat producers were fully aware of the importance of the decision to be reached. The stage of the contract had now arrived when it appeared that final consideration would have to be given to the "have regard to" proviso with respect to the losses incurred in the first two years of the contract. Negotiations continued through December into January of 1949. It was reported that the the Canadian Government had asked for a basic price of $2.00 per bushel plus an adjustment to cover part of the loss sustained by the producers during the first two years of the contract. The British were said to have offered to continue the price of $2.00 for the first six months of 1949-50, after which a new price would be negotiated, which would take into consideration any offset to the losses sustained during the first two years that might have occurred during the first six months through a decline in world prices. Late in December Mr. Gardiner, the Canadian Minister of Agriculture, indicated that an extension of the agreement was under consideration, which, however, did not eventuate.

On January 20, 1949 Prime Minister St. Laurent announced that without attempting to reach a final settlement on the obligations of the United Kingdom under clause 2 (b) of the agreement the two governments had settled upon a price of $2.00 per bushel. The discrepancy between the agreed price and the current price at which Canadian wheat was offered for sale in the free market was now 31 cents per bushel. The official statement also said that the two governments had agreed that their representatives would meet not later than July 31, 1950 to settle any obligations of the United Kingdom which might then be outstanding under clause 2 (b) of the agreement. The statement added that "the extent to which any such obligation

[26]*Ibid.*, Nov. 18, Dec. 2, 9, 28, 1948.

will remain will depend largely upon the actual prices ruling for wheat during 1949-50." The problem of compensation under the agreement thus was shelved until the contract was running out of its term.[27]

Mr. Gardiner, who had represented the Dominion Government in the negotiations at London, said this was "just exactly what I asked for when I went to London." He said the establishment of a current price was "the natural thing since no one can tell what's going to happen 18 months ahead."[28] Deferring the question of compensation for losses sustained on the first two years of the contract until its termination was not an unreasonable decision since the two parties would then have practically complete data for the whole period covered by the agreement. In view of the improved conditions of production in Europe, the large surplus piling up in the United States, and the price levels being discussed in connection with a new international wheat agreement, it appeared possible that before the end of the contract wheat would become available to importing countries at a price below $2.00 per bushel. This possibility appears to have been taken into consideration when agreement was reached. However, during the crop year 1949-50 Class II wheat sold as high as $2.41 per bushel and as low as $2.04 with an average price of $2.16. In none of the four years covered by the agreement did the average annual price of Class II wheat fall below the agreed price.

During the last year of the agreement there were elements in the situation that make it difficult to calculate the results of differences in price between wheat sold to the United Kingdom and wheat sold to other countries. In March 1949 Canada signed the International Wheat Agreement. Under this agreement the minimum and maximum prices for the crop year 1949-50 were $1.50 and $1.80 per bushel. In September 1949, when the Canadian Government devalued the Canadian dollar, the maximum price of No. 1 Northern wheat in store Fort William for purposes of the international agreement was adjusted to $1.98 per bushel. The International Wheat Agreement made provision for the recognition of prior sales agreements between signatory countries. Hence, most of the wheat which Canada supplied to the United Kingdom under the prior agreement, while recorded by the International Wheat Council, was subject to the prices agreed upon by Canada and the United Kingdom in January 1949.[29]

[27]*Ibid.*, Jan. 21, 1949.
[28]*Ibid.*
[29]Canadian Wheat Board, *Report*, 1949-50, p. 2.

Had it not been for her commitment, the United Kingdom would have been able to buy wheat from Canada or elsewhere in 1949-50 under the International Wheat Agreement at prices below those settled upon for the last year of the British Wheat Agreement. Gains accruing to Canada as a result of this situation may be roughly equated against the loss sustained during the crop year 1948-49. The net gain or loss on sales made under the contract during these two years is only significant in so far as it represents a deduction from or an addition to the loss sustained during the years 1946-47 and 1947-48.

The deferment of a final settlement until near the end of the contract period stimulated discussion over the amount of compensation that might be received. Some idea of what the growers would have considered a fair settlement at this time may be gleaned from a statement made by the Chairman of the Alberta Pool in December of 1948 when negotiations over the price for 1949-50 were in progress. He said that the farmers knew that wheat sold on world markets by other countries had brought high prices in recent years. Western producers had not been so greedy and he did think they were entitled to some consideration. He declared that Western Canadian grain growers should get a minimum of $2.00 per bushel basis No. 1 Northern Fort William, for all wheat delivered from the 1945 to 1949 crops inclusive.[30]

No doubt to allay the rising feeling in the West, on February 24, 1949 the Government announced an increase of the initial basic price to the producers from $1.55 per bushel to $1.75. This price would apply on all wheat delivered to the five-year pool from August 1, 1945 to July 31, 1950. It was estimated that the producers would benefit to the extent of about $214,000,000. In making his announcement, Mr. C. D. Howe, who was now Minister of Trade and Commerce, referred to the substantial operating surplus held by the Canadian Wheat Board. Various factors had contributed to this surplus: the increase to $2.00 in the selling price to the United Kingdom for the last two years of the contract; substantial export sales made to countries other than the United Kingdom at prices in excess of $2.00, and also the recent increase in the price of wheat for domestic purposes to $2.00 per bushel. For these reasons, he said, the Government had been able to raise the initial price to the Canadian producer.[31]

[30]*Winnipeg Free Press*, Dec. 24, 1948.
[31]*Ibid.*, Feb. 25, 1949.

In May of 1950 Mr. Howe entered upon wheat talks in London
with the British Government. On his return he announced that the
bilateral agreement with the United Kingdom would terminate at
the end of the four-year agreement on July 31, 1950.[32] This news was
not unexpected since the International Wheat Agreement, to which
both countries were signatories, was now functioning. What was not
expected was his further statement a week later, in reply to a question
in the House of Commons, that there would be no further settlement
from the British Government under clause 2 (*b*) of the current contract.   Mr. Howe said that "the United Kingdom took the strong
position that it had fulfilled all its obligations under that clause."[33]
From figures submitted to the House of Commons' committee on
agriculture by officers of the Wheat Board it appeared that western
wheat growers could expect a final payment of something like 5 or 6
cents a bushel when the five-year pool was closed out in the autumn.
This would bring the total payment per bushel to $1.80, or slightly
over, on the 1,427,588,090 bushels of wheat delivered to the Canadian
Wheat Board between August 1, 1945 and July 31, 1950.[34]

Proponents of the Wheat Agreement had pinned their faith to
the "have regard to" proviso as protection against losses arising out
of the contract. When it became known that the United Kingdom was
not prepared to make any further payment there was a heavy ground
swell of disappointment in the western wheat-growing area. It was
not long before a delegation of western wheat growers appeared in
Ottawa and appealed to the Government to make the final payment
25 cents a bushel. It was known that Liberal members of Parliament
were active in suggesting that the final payment should be brought
up to 12 or 15 cents. Private traders, who favoured the maintenance
of the Winnipeg Grain Exchange and who had always been opposed
to the agreement, stressed the losses that had been incurred under a
bulk marketing agreement. Estimates of the loss went all the way up
to $600,000,000. Western newspapers devoted columns to the contro-
versy. In Parliament itself discussion of the pact led to sharp debates.
Although there had been no really forthright opposition, except from
a few individual members, when the agreement came originally before
the House of Commons, the Opposition parties emphasized the responsibility of the Government for its outcome. To Opposition charges that
the wheat producers had lost $600,000,000 Mr. Howe replied that the
Government would give consideration to the "alleged" loss when the

[32]*Ibid.*, May 29, 30, 1950.   [33]*Ibid.*, June 6, 1950.   [34]*Ibid.*, June 9, 1950.

pool was settled towards the end of the year.[35] There the matter rested officially, but in the country controversy continued with attempts being made to assess the responsibility for the agreement as between the Government and the farm organizations themselves.

As the time approached when a final payment from the Canadian Wheat Board might be expected a new development occurred. In an address at Regina to the Saskatchewan Wheat Pool delegates on November 17, 1950, Mr. Gardiner, Minister of Agriculture, said a further payment by Britain under the four-year agreement was still under discussion. "All I am going to say," Mr. Gardiner is quoted as declaring, "is that I don't think the gap has been completely closed and we will go on with discussions and see if there can be some conclusion arrived at which will be satisfactory not only to the farmers of the west and the Government of Canada but the Government of Great Britain as well."[36] Nevertheless, discontent was increasing in the West. Late in December the western Wheat Pools, which had been strong supporters of the agreement, made known that they had asked the Dominion Government for a final payment of 15 cents per bushel.[37]

In February the Dominion Government sent Mr. Gardiner to London in another attempt to obtain reimbursement for the loss under the four-year agreement. Mr. Gardiner was unsuccessful. The British Government made it clear that it was firm in its decision that it was not under any obligation to make any further payment.[38] On March 2, 1951, Prime Minister St. Laurent announced his Government's decision. He said it had decided to pay a federal subsidy of $65,000,000 to the western wheat farmers to compensate them for losses under the agreement. This amount plus the balance in the Canadian Wheat Board's account for five years' sales would make possible a final payment of 8.3 cents per bushel.[39] The net result of this decision was that the wheat producers in the five years from 1945-46 to 1949-50 inclusive would receive on their deliveries an average basic price of $1.833 per bushel. This would bring the total final payment to approximately $120,000,000.

The Government's decision satisfied no one. Western Liberal members were keenly disappointed that the amount provided was not larger. A number of private members on both sides of the House were opposed to a payment of $65,000,000 to the western wheat producers

[35]*Ibid.*, June 27, 1950.   [36]*Ibid.*, Nov. 17, 1950.
[37]*Ibid.*, Dec. 30, 1950.   [38]*Ibid.*, Feb. 19, 23, 24, 1951.
[39]*Ibid*, March 3, 1951.

merely because they had not realized as much as they believed they were entitled to under the contract. The Social Credit and C.C.F. parties contended that the final payment should be 25 cents a bushel. The Progressive Conservatives, while not taking the position that no subsidy should be paid, charged the Government with colossal blunders in conducting its bulk-marketing operations. With the other Opposition parties they castigated any suggestion that the United Kingdom was partly at fault and enlarged upon differences in the statements made in respect to the final negotiations by the Minister of Agriculture, Mr. Gardiner, and the Minister of Trade and Commerce, Mr. Howe.[40]

The most effective defence of the agreement on behalf of the Government was made by Mr. Howe. He described the five-year pool and the British Wheat Agreement as "an experiment in stability." Everyone recognized there were risks on both sides in such an agreement but the results of the Government's policy had been that Canadian wheat producers were paid on the basis of $1.833 per bushel for five successive crop years. The agreement had been of importance in influencing the United States Government to permit the use of Marshall Aid funds by the United Kingdom to buy Canadian wheat. Personally, he thought it was a mistake that there should have been included in the agreement such a loosely worded "have regard to" clause. Nevertheless, an agreement that was not subject to legal interpretation must inevitably be interpreted by the party doing the paying. He could not conscientiously say that the United Kingdom was in default under the agreement and he deplored the suggestion that the United Kingdom had not played fair with the Canadian people.[41] With its large majority in the House the Government easily defeated a motion censuring it for mishandling the sale of wheat since the negotiation of the agreement.

In Western Canada provincial political leaders "sounded off" on the inadequacy of the final settlement. The three Wheat Pools, meeting at Regina, issued a statement which said that the wheat farmers of Western Canada should not be made to suffer through the failure of the British Government to fulfil the terms of the agreement as it was interpreted to them by cabinet ministers of both the United

[40]A protracted debate in the House ended on March 16; see *Winnipeg Free Press*, March 17, 1951.

[41]*Canada, House of Commons Debates*, March 12, 1951, p. 1168.

Kingdom and Canada.[42] Although Prime Minister St. Laurent told a delegation from the three prairie farm unions that a further payment from the federal treasury was out of the question[43] demands for an increased payment continued to be pressed and these demands are shaping up as a first-class political issue in the Prairie Provinces.

Very wide discrepancies exist between the estimates that have been made of the total monetary loss incurred. It has been argued that some allowance should be made for the possibility that if no agreement had been entered upon Canada might not have sold her export surpluses at the prices she was able to obtain for Class II wheat, that without the contract the United Kingdom might have reduced her bread quota, leaving Canada and other exporting countries with larger stocks to sell elsewhere, and that this might have reduced the level of world prices. But in view of the fact that the United Kingdom was down practically to bed-rock in food requirements with an acute world shortage of wheat and urgent demands for it in all deficit countries, it does not appear likely that the British Wheat Agreement had any significant effect on the prices of wheat outside its scope.

On the basis of the calculations made by the officials of the Department of Trade and Commerce the loss incurred during the first two years of the contract was about $330,000,000.[44] This figure has been widely accepted. Against this amount Mr. Gardiner said in the House: "I had taken the position all through the negotiations in 1947 and 1948 for further payments as a result of any losses that might have been taken in the first two years that we did not agree that there had been a loss of $330,000,000 on any basis that you like to take it. . . . On the most favourable terms to Great Britain we figured the actual loss to be $166,000,000." Mr. Gardiner said that this loss had been computed by taking the actual figures that the United States farmers got for their wheat during the period and comparing them with the actual figures the Canadian farmers got for their wheat.[45] It is possible that the wide discrepancy between these two estimates might be accounted for partly by one estimate being based on "the most favourable terms to Great Britain" and the other on the terms most favourable to the western wheat producers. Beyond doubt there

[42]*Winnipeg Free Press*, March 8, 1951.
[43]*Ibid.*, April 9, 1951.
[44]See p. 126.
[45]*Canada, House of Commons Debates*, March 9, 1951, p. 1122.

are pitfalls in mathematical calculations in a complicated problem of this nature. Intangibles enter into the situation and implicit assumptions creep in. It is unlikely that common agreement on the amount of the loss sustained ever can be reached. The best that can be said is that we have a very rough indication of the order of its magnitude.

The much higher estimates of loss ranging from $500,000,000 to $700,000,000 that have been made cover wider ground than the losses incurred under the contract during the first two years of its operations. Mr. Ross, Progressive Conservative member for Souris, Manitoba, said that "on the entire contract the loss is estimated at close to $500,000,000." He held the Wheat Agreement responsible for losses suffered by the wheat producers in the domestic market because after September 1946, when other producers and wage earners were being freed from price controls, wheat continued to be sold to Canadians at less than world prices.[46] The western Wheat Pools allege that this policy resulted in an additional loss to western wheat growers of $48,000,000. Mr. Stanley Jones, President of the Winnipeg Grain Exchange, said that a computation based on the Wheat Board's Class II wheat prices for the period of the five-year pool indicated that "the western farmers lost more than $700,000,000 by not being able to sell on the free world market."[47]

Whether the monetary loss was $330,000,000, or greater or less, the sum does not take into consideration the sense of security and stability (even if not fully warranted) which a guaranteed floor price gave to the wheat producers—an item which escapes monetary valuation. The advantages of a stabilized price to the producer were strongly emphasized by officials of the Wheat Pools and by the president of the Canadian Federation of Agriculture. When the Canadian Government, underwriting the risk it had assumed when it guaranteed a five-year floor price of $1.00 a bushel on wheat, concluded the agreement with the United Kingdom it was able to increase the delivery price to the producer from $1.25 to $1.35 per bushel. It will be noted that the minimum prices agreed upon for the total quantity of 600,000,000 bushels to be sold to the United Kingdom averaged out to just over $1.35 per bushel.

The United Kingdom in becoming the chief risk-bearer in the transaction could reasonably claim that, if losses accrued to Canada,

[46]*Ibid.*, March 8, 1951, p. 1054.
[47]*Winnipeg Free Press*, March 10, 1951.

a deduction should be made in reaching a final settlement for the value of this service. But with such a contract there is no actuarial basis upon which the risk could be measured and valued. In the final analysis the prices agreed to in the contract represented a speculation about future supplies of wheat and the prices at which they would sell. On estimates of this sort it is obvious that different people would hold different opinions. The vagueness of the "have regard to" proviso reflects this situation and lies at the base of any ill feeling that has been engendered through disappointment over the United Kingdom's final settlement with Canada.

However, the importance to the wheat producer of an agreement fixing wheat prices for an extended period into the future has been greatly overrated. When an attempt is made to stabilize his net income, cost factors must be taken into consideration. As it turned out in this instance the value of a guaranteed minimum price for wheat for five years was greatly lessened by the fact that the Canadian wheat producers' costs were rising steadily as part of an inflationary spiral. The index number measuring the cost of farm operations in Western Canada, basis 1935-39, 100, reported as of August 1946, was 160.3 and as of August 1950, 213.7. Meanwhile the index for farm living costs for the same period advanced from 130.3 to 183.1.[48] Furthermore, because of the substantial quantities of wheat over and above the amount sold to the United Kingdom which the Wheat Board was able to dispose of at higher prices, much larger distributions were made to the growers than would have been possible if all the wheat exported during the period had been sold at the prices set under the agreement.

All of the reasons why the Canadian Government, in an era of scarcity and high world wheat prices, should have approached the British Government with the offer of a wheat agreement cannot be established with certainty. Admittedly, one consideration was the desire of the Government to increase the five-year guarantee of a floor price of $1.00 per bushel given in September of 1945 to a higher level without incurring the risk of a drain upon the federal treasury. Conditions existing in the Canadian political situation appear to have been influential also in leading the Government to come to the decision. It was well known that the pool organizations were con-

[48]Dominion Bureau of Statistics, Prices Section, *Prices and Price Indexes, 1944-1947* (Ottawa, 1948), p. 53; Dominion Bureau of Statistics, Labour and Prices Division, *Price Index Numbers of Commodities and Services Used by Farmers*, Aug. 1950, p. 2.

ducting a strong agitation for the continuance of the Canadian Wheat Board as the sole agency for marketing Canadian wheat and were exerting continuous pressure upon the federal Minister of Agriculture in that direction. The policy of government marketing was also being advocated strongly by the C.C.F. The C.C.F. had been making heavy inroads into Liberal representation in the House of Commons from Saskatchewan, a province from which the Liberal party had drawn a large part of its western strength. Undoubtedly it desired to regain its position there. Moreover, for many years the Pools had been active in promoting international conferences with a view to obtaining a world agreement regulating exportable surpluses and export prices. Failing the achievement of a world wheat agreement, an arrangement with the United Kingdom, Canada's leading customer, covering a period of time would go a considerable distance towards meeting their wishes. Hence, an advantageous wheat contract with the United Kingdom might be counted upon to satisfy substantially the large body of opinion represented by the Saskatchewan Wheat Pool and work to the advantage of the Liberal party in Saskatchewan, the Minister of Agriculture's home province.

Probably also some weight should be attributed to the view that if Canadian wheat prices rose sharply to the level of world values the effect would be to accelerate the inflationary trend in the Canadian level of prices which the Government was endeavouring to hold in check. A rise would occur directly through an increase in the price of bread to the Canadian consumer as price controls were relaxed. Indirectly, also, forces would be set in motion that would tend to increase the price of other foods. Additional purchasing power would be placed in the pockets of the wheat producers. Moreover, a sharp increase in wheat prices would almost certainly lead to the diversion of western farm acreage into wheat and away from the production of coarse grains. This would mean a reduced supply of these grains with a corresponding rise in their value which necessarily would affect the cost of dairy and meat products to Canadian consumers and would also, incidentally, reduce the quantities of animal food stuffs and cheese available for export. Wheat prices were a key factor in the general structure of Canadian prices which determined the cost of living in Canada.

When the contract was negotiated, and later when the price for the 1948 crop was determined, British newspapers particularly, commenting upon the advantages of the terms of the agreement from a

British standpoint, suggested that Canada was coming to the relief of the United Kingdom. It is conceivable that in view of the United Kingdom's difficult dollar problem there may have been a disposition by the Canadian Government to extend to Britain some aid in this way, but there is little evidence to support this view. The agreement was commended by its supporters on other grounds. But if considerations of this nature were a factor in Canada's agreeing to sell Canadian wheat cheap to the United Kingdom they were hardly fair to Canadian wheat producers since upon them was placed the burden of Canadian generosity instead of upon the Canadian people as a whole.

Another advantage of the agreement was that it enabled the Government to postpone making a final decision about whether the Canadian Wheat Board was to become the sole agency henceforth in marketing Canadian wheat. The decision it was faced with was whether to allow the Wheat Board to revert to its previous status of a stand-by emergency organization ready, by being willing to receive wheat from the producer at a given fixed initial payment, to guarantee a basic minimum price, or, alternatively, to endeavour to continue the Wheat Board as a compulsory marketing board through which all Canadian wheat would be marketed and sold. The first alternative meant a return to the open market; the second meant the continuance of a government monopoly.

The assumption of emergency powers under the War Measures Act of 1914 by the Canadian Government on the outbreak of war in 1939 had had the effect of overcoming for the time being constitutional obstacles to an expansion of the functions of the Canadian Wheat Board. Hence, the Government was able to utilize the Board as an important part of the system of controlled economy that prevailed in Canada during the course of the struggle. But as much of the authority the Board exercised was conferred upon it by Orders-in-Council which derived their validity from the War Measures Act it was obvious that the disappearance of emergency powers with the coming of peace would immediately raise the question of the Board's future status. It was widely recognized that this would necessitate one of the most important decisions on future policy that would confront the Government at the close of the war.

Traditional Liberal policy favoured the maintenance of free competition in the marketing of Canada's greatest cereal crop, and with that a continuance of the futures market. When the Bennett Government in 1935 introduced the original bill to establish the Canadian Grain Board, providing for a government monopoly in grain marketing which would make it impossible for the futures market to function, the measure was fought strenuously by the Liberal Opposition in Parliament. The Liberals favoured a temporary board to take over the McFarland holdings and to liquidate them as fast as possible. Hon. J. L. Ralston, chief spokesman for the Opposition on this issue, indeed urged the Government to insert a clause in the bill to indicate that it was an emergency measure and to provide that it would automatically lapse at the end of a year unless renewed by Parliament. As a result of the storm of criticism raised in both the House of Commons and in the country, the Government provided for the compulsory clauses to be held in abeyance; thus in effect it withdrew from its original position. The amended bill, frankly described by Premier Bennett as "a fair compromise," confined the Board's operations to wheat and authorized it to "utilize and employ without discrimination" existing marketing agencies.[49] This was regarded by the Liberal party as a partial victory for its policy.

In 1939, after the Royal Grain Inquiry Commission of 1938, which had been appointed to inquire into the operations of the Government in marketing wheat and to recommend a permanent wheat marketing policy for Canada, reported against the establishment of a compulsory wheat board, the Liberal administration accepted its recommendations and in due course announced a new wheat marketing policy.[50] Mr. Gardiner, the Minister of Agriculture, outlined the new policy to the House of Commons and said that three years' experience with the Wheat Board Act of 1935 had shown that it was legislation which could only be helpful with a marketing emergency and could not form the basis of a permanent system of marketing. He announced that the Government intended to carry out as far as possible the recommendations contained in the Commission's report and quoted the Commissioner's conclusion "that the Government should remain out of the grain trade and that our wheat should be marketed by means of the futures market system." However, on account of the vigorous opposition of western members the Government did not find it possible to go as far as it had indicated it wished to go and retained the Board as a voluntary emergency organization.[51]

[49]*Winnipeg Free Press*, June 14, July 5, 1935.
[50]*Ibid.*, Feb. 17, 1939.
[51]See above, pp. 46-7.

During the period in which the controls instituted under war conditions were in effect, the Government made no definite declaration of general policy. In 1945 Parliament passed the National Emergency Transitional Powers Act which continued certain powers the Government had exercised under the War Measures Act up to or into 1947. This measure gave the Government an additional period to consider and decide upon the permanent policy it wished to adopt.

In May of 1946, speaking on a bill introduced by a private member which would indirectly abolish the Winnipeg Grain Exchange, the Minister of Trade and Commerce declared that until the policies of importing countries became more clearly defined it would be a mistake on Canada's part to destroy the private trade of Canada. He said he considered it a very bad policy for Canada to define its future policy with rigidity. Referring to the section in the Canadian Wheat Board Act which safeguarded the position of the Exchange, he pointed out that it was a section that had been retained without change since the Board was first established, and was, therefore, the policy of both the Liberal and the Conservative parties. That the Government did not feel necessarily bound by this section could be inferred, however, from his further statement that it might be a disservice to wheat producers to cling to some arbitrary and inflexible method which failed to take into account changing circumstances of the world markets.[52]

Not until the negotiation of the British Wheat Agreement were any marketing arrangements entered into by the Government that would prejudice an early re-establishment of an open market for Canadian wheat. But with the signing of the agreement a new situation was created which raised the question whether the Government was shifting away from its previous policy and was prepared to consolidate the position of the Wheat Board as a permanent monopoly. It was at once recognized that the contract with the United Kingdom implied the continued closing of the futures market of the Winnipeg Grain Exchange. When queried at a press conference the Minister of Trade and Commerce agreed, but held that this did not necessarily mean closure of the other functions of the Exchange.

Since the period of time which the agreement covered extended beyond that of any likely continuing national emergency arising out of the war, it was clear that constitutional grounds would have to be found by the Government to validate, under conditions of peace,

[52]*Winnipeg Free Press*, May 18, 1946.

this encroachment upon the powers of the Canadian provinces. A constitutional basis could be found in several decisions of the Privy Council which had held that in certain instances, in order to fulfil obligations assumed under agreements with other countries, the Parliament of Canada could extend its powers of control into the provincial field.[53] At the time the wheat agreement was signed, the Minister of Trade and Commerce merely stated in the House of Commons that when the National Emergency Transitional Powers Act expired the Government would direct its attention to the form and authority under which the Board's powers might be further continued. This statement, however, did not receive much consideration in the debate that followed. Attention was then concentrated upon the terms of the agreement with respect to what they offered to the Canadian wheat producers.

Thus the agreement had the advantage of promising to settle for the time being a number of troublesome problems for the Government. It enabled it to combat the dissatisfaction of producers with its price policy by increasing the floor price while giving the grower added protection against a much-feared post-war slump in wheat values. The retroactive payment of $23,000,000 on the 1945-46 deliveries in addition was bound to allay criticism. With the contract in hand the Government on its own part had protected itself against serious loss in making good its guarantee should wheat prices register a marked decline. The continuance of compulsory marketing strengthened the political position of the Liberal party in Saskatchewan. Moreover, the terms of the agreement reduced the possibility of disturbance to the Canadian price structure from a sharp increase in wheat prices and of disarrangement of the delicate balance between wheat production and the production of meat and dairy products. Finally it enabled the Government, while continuing compulsory marketing, to postpone coming to a decision in regard to the ultimate status of the Canadian Wheat Board.

It must be emphasized that since it was the Canadian Government that wished to enter into an agreement and approached the British Government the benefits from such an agreement accruing to the United Kingdom had to be clear and substantial before the British Minister of Food would be justified in signing it. Under the circumstances the representatives of the United Kingdom were able to take

[53]In re Regulation and Control of Aeronautics in Canada, [1932] A.C. 54; In re Regulation and Control of Radio Communication in Canada, [1932] A.C. 304.

full advantage of the situation. While nothing has transpired to show that the Canadian Wheat Board, as an expert body, recommended the agreement on the price terms established there is some evidence to suggest that the willingness of the Canadian Minister of Agriculture to agree upon such a low price basis rested upon a more optimistic opinion of Europe's ability to return quickly to full agricultural production than the technical facts available appeared to warrant. In an interview after the agreement was signed, he referred to the rapidity with which Europe was coming back and warned Canadian wheat growers not to be "lulled into a false sense of security" by the existing world wheat shortage.[54] As Mr. Howe observed: "The time when you must decide whether an agreement is good or bad is when you sign on the dotted line, and we signed on that dotted line in 1946."[55]

The Wheat Agreement came under criticism both in Canada and abroad on the ground that it represented a departure from the principles of multilateral trading. It was not difficult to prove that the agreement was inherently discriminatory in that it enabled the United Kingdom to obtain the bulk of Canadian wheat available for export at prices greatly below those quoted to the other countries which customarily purchased wheat from Canada. With Canada vitally interested in maintaining her export trade, the benefits of a return internationally to the principles of freer trade were generally recognized but bilateral agreements, such as the wheat agreement, were precisely one of the main obstacles in the path of those nations which were endeavouring to promote, under the United Nations, an international return to non-discriminatory trade policies. The inclusion of an "escape" clause, providing for the modification of the agreement, if necessary, to bring it into conformity with any international agreement entered into to which both governments were parties, was not sufficient to silence criticism on these grounds.

[54]*Winnipeg Free Press*, July 30, 1946.
[55]*Canada, House of Commons Debates*, March 12, 1951, p. 1169.

8

The International Wheat
Agreement of 1949

DURING the crop year of 1949-50 the Canadian Wheat Board, while completing deliveries under the British Wheat Agreement, was also operating under the International Wheat Agreement, which came into force on July 1, 1949. For many years western wheat growers had looked hopefully to the negotiation of an international wheat agreement that would establish conditions under which wheat prices could be stabilized. The first agreement, signed in 1933 to cover the crop years of 1933-34 and 1934-35, had proved a failure. The idea of a new agreement, however, was kept alive by the International Wheat Advisory Committee constituted at that time, and negotiations were again in progress when war intervened in 1939. In July of 1941 discussions were resumed by officials of Argentina, Australia, Canada, the United States, and the United Kingdom—the four principal exporting countries and the leading country of import. The purpose of this conference was "to consider what steps might be taken toward a solution of the international wheat problem."[1]

The immediate reasons for these discussions while the war was still in progress were the large surpluses of wheat that were accumulating in the four exporting countries, the likelihood that wheat would be needed for relief purposes immediately after the war in many countries, the desirability of stabilizing the post-war international trade in wheat, and the probable difficulty of holding an international wheat conference immediately after the end of hostilities. It was

[1]*Wheat: Memorandum of Agreement between the United States of America, Argentina, Australia, Canada and the United Kingdom, and Related Papers,* Executive Agreement Series 384 (Washington, 1944).

145

foreseen that urgent problems relating to wheat requiring international consideration would arise with the close of the war.

Discussions on the expert level between the five countries extended over a period of many months and ended in the initialling of a memorandum of agreement and of a draft convention by the representatives of the five countries participating on April 22, 1942. The memorandum of agreement was to become effective as soon as it was approved by the governments concerned. Approval having been received, both documents and the minutes of the final session were made public on July 1, 1942 at Washington.[2]

The convention contained a draft of a proposed new international wheat agreement for submission to all wheat-exporting and wheat-importing countries willing to participate in a conference to be called to negotiate such an agreement. To replace the former International Wheat Advisory Committee the convention provided for a new administrative body, the International Wheat Council, which was to be located in London unless it should otherwise determine. In the meantime, in order that there should be no delay, the five countries agreed, by the memorandum of agreement, to regard as in effect among themselves the arrangements set out in the draft convention relating to the anticipated immediate post-war situation. The memorandum of agreement also brought the council into existence; it was decided that the headquarters of the organization should be in Washington while the memorandum was in force.

The arrangements regarding post-war needs provided for the creation of a pool of wheat which would be available for intergovernmental relief in the war-stricken countries and other areas requiring aid. The pool would be administered through the council which would use where possible such relief organizations as might be set up. To this pool the governments of Canada, the United States, and the United Kingdom agreed to give 25,000,000, 50,000,000 and 25,000,000 bushels of wheat respectively or its equivalent in whole or in part in flour. It was agreed that with the assent of the council the United Kingdom might contribute transportation of relief wheat or flour in lieu of part or all of its contribution. No specific commitments were made by Australia or Argentina but in common with Canada and the United States they were to contribute additional quantities to be determined by them

[2]For a comprehensive study of the provisions see Joseph S. Davis, *New International Wheat Agreements*, Wheat Studies of the Wheat Research Institute, Stanford University (Stanford, Calif., Nov., 1942).

in consultation with the council if the quantities already supplied appeared likely to prove insufficient. Another feature of the immediate programme included an undertaking by the four exporting countries to "adopt or maintain positive measures to control production with the object of minimizing the accumulation of excessive stocks," pending the conclusions of the contemplated conference. Upon the United States was placed the obligation of convening an international conference of the nations having a substantial interest in international trade in wheat when it deemed the time propitious. The object of this conference would be to consider the draft convention.

In order to make the International Wheat Council more fully representative of both wheat-importing and wheat-exporting countries, ten additional governments and the Food and Agriculture Organization (F.A.O.) of the United Nations were invited to join it. The F.A.O. and eight of the ten governments joined the council, but the Union of Soviet Socialist Republics and Yugoslavia declined. The enlarged council at a meeting in Washington on July 15, 1946 appointed a preparatory committee to revise the draft convention of 1942 with a view to calling a general conference. Subsequently, the council recommended to the United States Government that it should arrange for an international wheat conference to be held in London in March of 1947. The United Kingdom issued invitations to all governments which were members of the United Nations and to the F.A.O. to attend this meeting.

The conference opened on March 18, 1947, with delegates from forty countries present. Despite the fact that months of intensive preparation had preceded the calling of the conference, it was soon evident that the sharp conflicts of interests between the participants had not been reconciled. After two weeks of discussions Argentina, which had been indecisive about taking part in the deliberations, withdrew from the conference with the announcement that it was not for the present possible for her to become a party to an agreement. Since Argentina was one of the principal wheat-exporting countries her withdrawal increased the difficulties of the conference and threatened to impair the value of any agreement it might reach.

The conference continued until April 24. While agreement was reached on practically all points, on the question of minimum prices for the crop years of 1949-50 and 1950-51 producer interests and consumer interests deadlocked. The representatives of the United States favoured a minimum price of $1.20 per bushel for 1949-50 and $1.10

per bushel for 1950-51. The United Kingdom was unwilling to agree to these prices but they were carried by the conference in the face of British opposition.[3] The United Kingdom refused to accept this situation and followed this decision by a statement that it was "unable to associate itself with this wheat agreement." Without the participation of the largest wheat importer the other countries were unwilling to commit themselves and the conference ended without an agreement.

The United Kingdom delegation made it clear that it felt the scheme proposed would tend to keep prices too high and, therefore, would not be a party to it. During the course of the conference *The Times*, the *Economist*, and other British papers had attacked the proposals made, chiefly on the ground that the scheme envisaged would restrict rather than increase production by setting up an artificial structure under which neither supply nor demand would effectively function, with the final effect that importing countries would pay higher prices.[4]

While the conference ended in a failure, the idea of negotiating an international wheat agreement was not finally shelved. The draft agreement was remitted to the International Wheat Council in Washington for further consideration. In June 1947 discussions were resumed in Washington by the council, but these were unsuccessful. The council again returned to the problem in December and appointed a committee to consider a new basis of agreement. This committee consisted of representatives of the United States, Canada, and Australia and of five major importing countries. A special session of the International Wheat Council to consider the committee's report met in Washington early in 1948. This meeting included all countries with a substantial interest in wheat exports or imports with the exception of Russia, Argentina, and the Danubian states. These important wheat-growing countries again remained on the outside.

Discussions continued over several weeks, but this time greater success attended the efforts of the negotiators than was the case at London. The conference concluded with the signing of a five-year international wheat agreement on March 5, 1948. Thirty-six countries signed the agreement, subject to formal acceptance by the signatory governments before July 1, 1948. This time it seemed certain that a comprehensive wheat agreement was on the way to being achieved.

[3]*Winnipeg Free Press*, March 19, 29, April 23, 25, 26, 1947.
[4]*Ibid.*, April 9, 1947.

Again the hopes of the negotiators were doomed to disappointment. When the agreement was introduced into the United States Senate it was held up in the Foreign Relations Committee and, in spite of an urgent request from the President that it be ratified, did not reach the floor of the Senate to be dealt with before the Senate adjourned in June of 1948. Ratification by the United States before the required date of July 1 thus became impossible. Despite this fact Canada, a few days later, ratified the agreement, although without assurance of whether the agreement was alive or dead. The United Kingdom, on the other hand, exercised its right under the terms of the agreement to withdraw from the pact on the ground that the guaranteed sales of exporting countries whose governments had formally ratified the international wheat agreement were insufficient to ensure its successful operation.[5] Australia and the Netherlands also gave notice of withdrawal.

As a result of these unexpected developments the International Wheat Council, established under the agreement, reviewed the situation at its first meeting in July. Twelve countries had ratified the agreement and sixteen others had indicated they would ratify it but sought an extension of the period for formal acceptance. The council decided that without the adherence of the United Kingdom the agreement would be unworkable. While the agreement might have been considered to be in force between the countries' which had deposited their instruments of acceptance before July 1, 1948, it was clear that for all practical purposes the agreement had collapsed.

The failure to secure ratification in the United States Senate occurred a few months before the presidential and congressional elections, and at a time when both Houses of Congress were under Republican control. The re-election of President Truman, and the majorities for the Democratic party in both Houses of Congress in November 1948 renewed hope that a new agreement might be achieved. On November 24 before a meeting of the F.A.O. the President expressed regret that the agreement had not been ratified, and promised that if a new agreement were negotiated he would send it to the new Congress for approval.[6] With this encouragement the principal wheat-producing countries decided to hold another conference in Washington in January of 1949 to negotiate an agreement.

[5]*Ibid.*, July 9, 1948.   [6]New York *Times*, Nov. 24, 1948.

Forty-six countries, including Argentina and Russia, were represented at the conference. In the interval between the negotiation of the 1948 agreement and the convening of the new conference the wheat supply situation had greatly improved. This strengthened the position of the importing countries in the discussions which centred around the amount of wheat the importing countries would be willing to guarantee to purchase and the maximum and minimum prices which they would be prepared to pay. Discussions were arduous and protracted, and negotiations were frequently stalled by sharp differences of opinion.   Not until negotiations had extended over a period of nearly two months was an accord finally reached. On March 23, 1949 an international wheat agreement to run for four years was initialled for forty-two countries.

Neither Argentina nor Russia became parties to it. The Russians had originally asked to be allowed to supply 100,000,000 bushels, but Canada, the United States, and Australia objected that Russia was asking more than she was entitled to and proposed that the Russian allotment should be 50,000,000 bushels. The Soviets replied officially that "while they were interested in participating in an agreement they were not prepared to do so on any less than 75,000,000 bushels." During the course of the negotiations Argentina withdrew on the ground that the maximum prices being conceded were too low and that in addition the Argentine Government must receive imports of industrial goods for the export of wheat and meat, its two main export commodities.[7]

It is obvious from the record that a vast amount of thought has been devoted to the problem of working out and drafting an international agreement on wheat that would be acceptable to at least three of the principal wheat-exporting countries and to a large number of those countries which ordinarily rely in greater or less degree upon imports for their supplies of wheat. The draft convention prepared in 1942 represented a thorough-going attempt to avoid the weaknesses disclosed in the agreement of 1933. The agreement contained in the draft convention was worked over again at the London conference of 1947.   The conference of 1948 in Washington led to further study of the terms of the agreement.   The chairman of the final meeting of the Washington conference said on that occasion that while the Washington wheat meeting of 1941-42 laid the foundation for a post-war international wheat agreement, the London con-

[7]*Winnipeg Free Press*, Feb. 19, March 17, 1949.

ference constructed the superstructure and the Washington conference of 1948 "put on the roof—or should I say the ceiling."[8]

In general form and principle the agreement of 1949 did not differ essentially from the one negotiated in 1948. There were changes in arrangement and terminology; but the really important changes were that its duration was shorter, the quantities guaranteed were less, and the maximum price agreed upon was lower.

The agreement of 1949 consisted of a preamble and five parts containing twenty-three articles and two annexes.[9] The preamble of the 1948 agreement had stated that the Government on whose behalf the agreement was signed recognized that there was a serious shortage of wheat. This assertion was not made in the 1949 agreement, which began with the statement that the parties to the agreement intended "to overcome the serious hardship caused to producers and consumers by burdensome surpluses and critical shortages of wheat." The objectives of the agreement as set forth were to "assure supplies of wheat to importing countries and markets for wheat to exporting countries at equitable and stable prices."

The essence of the agreement was that Australia, Canada, the United States, France, and Uruguay guaranteed to sell to the importing countries 456,283,389 bushels[10] of wheat annually for a period of four crop years, beginning August 1, 1949 and continuing until July 31, 1953, at prices within the limits of an established maximum and minimum range of prices. On their part the thirty-seven importing countries agreed to buy from the exporting countries this amount within the same price limits. The amount, if any, of wheat flour to be supplied and accepted against the guaranteed quantities was to be determined by agreement between the buyer and seller in each transaction, except where the council might be asked to intervene where difficulties arose in purchasing or selling the guaranteed quantities. The guaranteed quantities represented the maximum amount that the importing and exporting countries would be required to buy or sell within the terms of the agreements. Transactions outside the price range would be possible, but would not count towards the fulfilment of the obligations assumed under the agreement except where

[8]Final Plenary Meeting of the International Wheat Council, March 6, 1948.
[9]Canada, *International Wheat Agreement,* Treaty Series, 1949, no. 10 (Ottawa, 1949).
[10]The amounts set out in the annexes to the agreement are stated in thousands of metric tons with equivalent bushels.

an agreement of purchase and sale existed prior to the International Wheat Agreement coming into force.

The allocations of the total quantity agreed upon between the exporting countries were as follows: Australia, 80,000,000 bushels; Canada, 203,069,635; France, 3,306,934; the United States, 168,069,635, and Uruguay, 1,837,185. These quantities showed the Canadian quota to be nearly 30,000,000 bushels below the quota allocated by the proposed 1948 agreement. The Australian quota was reduced by 5,000,000 bushels and that for the United States by about 17,000,000 bushels. Significant of the change in the supply situation was the fact that France, which under the proposed 1948 agreement had appeared as an importing country, guaranteeing purchases of 35,824,000 bushels, now became an exporting country. Uruguay was not a signatory to the 1948 agreement. Compared with the older 1933 agreement Canada's position remained substantially the same; Australia suffered a reduction of 25,000,000 bushels, and the United States obtained an increase of approximately 121,000,000 bushels.

On the importing side the United Kingdom guaranteed purchases of 177,067,938 bushels. Since the United Kingdom ordinarily imports around 215,000,000 bushels annually, this would leave her with a free purchasing margin of approximately 35,000,000 bushels annually. Nine other countries agreed to buy over 10,000,000 bushels annually. Among these nine, Italy accepted a quota of approximately 40,000,000 bushels, India, 38,000,000 bushels, and the Netherlands and Belgium over 20,000,000 each. Seven countries guaranteed to purchase less than 1,000,000 bushels each. In this group, Liberia undertook to purchase 36,744 bushels. Thus the ten largest importers guaranteed to purchase approximately 360,000,000 bushels, while the remaining 96,000,000 bushels was divided in varying amounts among the other twenty-seven signatories to the agreement.

The agreement included escape clauses to cover the situation where an exporting country was unable to fulfil its obligation by a short crop or an importing country found it necessary to safeguard its balance of payments or monetary reserves.

On the size of the Canadian quota there was very little comment in Canada, though it was pointed out that several good crops might lead to large carryovers. Alternatively, there was the possibility that less-than-normal Canadian harvests might make it difficult for Canada to fulfil her obligations under the agreement and that she might have to seek relief by an application to the council. The large increase in the quota allotted to the United States in 1949 compared to her 1933 quota was due to her strong credit position, the enormous supplies of wheat she was currently accumulating, and the fact that Argentina, which in the 1933 agreement had had a quota of 110,000,000 bushels, abstained from being a party to the agreement. Since the quotas allotted to the exporting countries were balanced by the guaranteed purchases of the countries of import it is obvious that implicit in the agreement was a threat to Argentina's position as one of the major exporters of wheat. In effect the agreement resembles the international cartels of big business. It apparently contemplated that, in years when imports were low, the United States, Canada, and Australia would divide up the bulk of the export market among themselves at the expense of Argentina, Russia, and other countries which remained outside its scope. However, it was foreseen that the amount the importing countries guaranteed to purchase under the agreement might be less than they would actually require, and sales to them, plus sales to certain countries that were not signatories to the agreement, might enable Argentina to market her customary quantity of wheat.

Much of the negotiation at Washington centred around the price schedule. Since there were prospects of increasing supplies of wheat for export, the exporting countries found themselves forced to give ground if they were to be successful in securing an agreement. The maximum price agreed to was $1.80 per bushel, compared with $2.00 per bushel in the 1948 agreement. Minimum prices were stepped up 10 cents a bushel for each year, the minimum for 1949-50 being $1.50, the price set originally to apply to the year 1948-49 in the previous agreement. The schedule is as follows:

Crop year	Minimum	Maximum
1949-50	$1.50	$1.80
1950-51	1.40	1.80
1951-52	1.30	1.80
1952-53	1.20	1.80

The prices fixed were in terms of Canadian currency at the parity for the Canadian dollar determined for the purpose of the International Monetary Fund as at March 1, 1949, and applied to No. 1 Manitoba Northern wheat in store Fort William or Port Arthur. As a result of a change in the value of Canadian currency in September 1949, the maximum price became $1.98 and the minimum prices $1.65, $1.54, $1.43, and $1.32 respectively in Canadian currency.[11] It will be observed

[11]United Nations, *Review of International Commodity Problems, 1949* (Lake Success, N.Y., Feb., 1950), p. 47.

that, while the maximum price was to remain fixed for the four-year period, minimum prices were established on the basis of a descending ladder going down from $1.50 per bushel for the crop year 1949-50 to $1.20 for the crop year 1952-53. These declining minima reflected the opinion that, with the agricultural recovery of Europe and with large crops in prospect in the United States, world wheat values would fall to lower levels. The alternative possibility that before the end of the four-year period short crops might make the maximum price of $1.80 per bushel unduly low was not provided for.

On March 23, 1949, the date of the initialling of the agreement, the price for Class II No. 1 Manitoba Northern wheat was $2.18 per bushel in store at Fort William. The maximum price agreed upon was thus 38 cents below the then existing world price level but it is quite impossible to forecast whether over the whole period covered by the pact the maximum or minimum prices settled upon will prove to be the more significant. Up to the present world prices have remained above the maximum, a situation similar to that which has prevailed under the British Wheat Agreement.

The prices incorporated in the agreement raised no strong protests in Canada although the maximum set was lower than the price currently effective under the terms of the British Wheat Agreement. The situation was different in Australia where the Federation of Australian Wheat Growers sent an emphatic protest to the British delegates at Washington. A representative of the federation commented adversely on the attitude of the importing countries in forcing the price of wheat down.[12]

The 1948 agreement had contained elaborate provisions with respect to the stocks the exporting countries should maintain with a view to price stabilization. Under certain conditions importing countries could also be called upon to accumulate reserves if the free market price were below the lowest minimum price set out in the agreement. These requirements were dropped in the 1949 agreement. The agreement simply provided that importing and exporting countries should endeavour to maintain adequate stocks at the end and at the beginning of each crop year.

Complete liberty of action was reserved by the contracting governments in the determination and administration of their internal agricultural policies. The agreement states: "Exporting and importing

[12]*Winnipeg Free Press*, March 22, 1949.

countries shall be free to fulfil their guaranteed quantities through private trade channels or otherwise. Nothing in this agreement shall be construed to exempt any private trader from any laws or regulations to which he is otherwise subject." In the case of the United States, where free marketing prevails, as long as the open market prices range between the maximum and minimum prices established for a given year, and sufficient quantities are sold in private trading for export to the importing signatory countries, the obligations of the United States are discharged. In Canada, sales are negotiated through the Wheat Board.

To head up the organization and to administer the agreement, a new International Wheat Council was established. On the council each contracting government may be represented by one delegate, one alternate, and advisers. In addition, the Food and Agriculture Organization, the International Trade Organization, the Interim Co-ordinating Committee for International Commodity Arrangements, and such other intergovernmental organizations as the council may decide, are entitled to have one non-voting representative at meetings of the council. Any country which the council recognizes as an "irregular exporter or irregular importer of wheat" may become a non-voting member of the council. For convenience in operation the council is empowered to establish an executive committee to be responsible to it and to work under its general direction. The council is also to have the assistance of an advisory committee on price equivalents. This committee is designed to advise the council on appropriate price relationships between the varieties and qualities of wheat, where these are not set out in the agreement, and technical problems of a similar nature.

The method of voting devised provides for due weight to be given to the importance of the various importing and exporting countries which are parties to the agreement. One thousand votes are to be held by the exporting countries and one thousand by the importing countries, distributed in proportion to the quota of guaranteed sales or purchases assumed by each signatory, but each delegate is to have one vote. By this arrangement any two of the principal exporting countries command a majority of the votes held by the exporting countries. On the importing side the United Kingdom has by far the largest bloc of votes. Important decisions require a majority of the votes of the importing countries and of the exporting countries, and, in certain instances, two-thirds of each.

The council must keep a record of all transactions in wheat made under the agreement and keep the contracting countries informed of the amounts entered in its records against guaranteed quantities. When the guaranteed quantity of any exporting or importing country for any crop year has been fulfilled, all exporting and importing countries must be notified immediately. Upon the council also devolves the duty of handling such problems as adjustments in the case of the withdrawal or non-participation of countries in the agreement and adjustments arising out of short crops or balance of payment difficulties, as well as disputes and complaints concerning the interpretation or application of the agreement.

To come into force the agreement required acceptance by countries responsible for not less than 70 per cent of the guaranteed purchases and by countries responsible for not less than 80 per cent of the guaranteed sales by July 1, 1949. Any exporting country which considered its interests to be seriously prejudiced by the non-participation or withdrawal of any importing country responsible for more than 5 per cent of the guaranteed purchases might withdraw before September 1, 1949. Under parallel conditions an importing country had also the right to withdraw.

On July 5, 1949 the International Wheat Council, meeting in Washington, reported that twenty-two of the forty-two original negotiators had ratified the agreement by July 1. These countries had guaranteed sufficient quantities of purchases and sales to make the pact effective. With the agreement a reality the council established the administrative procedure to implement it. London, England, was chosen as the permanent site of the council's headquarters. That part of the agreement which related to actual transactions in wheat became effective on August 1, 1949.[13]

The time limit for acceptances of the agreement was subsequently extended to February 28, 1950. In March 1950 the International Wheat Council accepted Western Germany's application. Other less important countries have become signatories of the agreement. The number of importing countries guaranteeing purchases is now forty-one; Australia, Canada, France, and the United States continue as exporting countries.[14] These changes involved adjustments in the annual quotas: from 456,283,389 bushels to 525,000,000 for the crop

[13]*Ibid.*, July 7, 1949.
[14]United Nations, *Review of International Commodity Problems, 1949*, p. 6.

year 1949-50, and to 562,000,000 for the duration of the agreement.
The annual quotas after 1949-50 from the exporting countries became:
Australia, 88,700,000 bushels; Canada, 221,600,000 bushels; France,
4,100,000 bushels, and the United States, 248,100,000 bushels. Of the
importing countries, thirteen agree to buy over 10,000,000 bushels
annually and together guarantee to purchase 472,000,000 bushels.[15]

The completion of the first year of the agreement showed that,
while the exporting countries guaranteed sales under its terms of
525,000,000 bushels, only 432,000,000 bushels were purchased by the
importing countries. Australia and France sold their quotas, Canada
with a quota of 205,100,000 bushels sold 183,934,000 bushels, and the
United States with a quota of 235,858,000 bushels sold 161,507,000
bushels. It must be understood that if an exporting country wishes
formally to force sales under the agreement the wheat must be offered
at the minimum price for the year. In 1949-50 the minimum price was
$1.50 per bushel. Since world wheat prices were above the agree-
ment maximum, sales at the minimum would have meant an additional
loss of 30 cents per bushel, which could hardly be considered in the
national interest.   With world wheat prices above the agreement
maximum throughout the year conditions were most favourable for
importing countries; nevertheless less than one-half of these countries
fulfilled their obligations under the agreement.[16]   The discrepancy
between the amounts guaranteed for sale and the amounts purchased
is explained on several grounds. Countries late in coming under the
agreement stated their requirements in terms of a full year. This was
an important factor in reducing purchases in some instances. Other
reasons given were good domestic crops and intergovernmental trade
agreements in which the higher price of non-agreement wheat was
not the only consideration. Under trade agreements Argentina sold
heavily to Brazil and Italy, both signatories of the International Wheat
Agreement.

The terms of the agreement exhibit the painstaking efforts that have
been made to devise a scheme that would have sufficient flexibility
in operation and at the same time bring a measure of control into
the international marketing of wheat. Nevertheless, it remains uncertain whether this attempt to control the marketing and price of

[15]Dominion Bureau of Statistics, *The Wheat Review,* March, 1951, p. 2.
[16]Dominion Bureau of Statistics, *Monthly Review of the Wheat Situation,*
Aug., Oct., 1950, p. 2.

wheat on an international scale will prove a successful antidote to "burdensome surpluses and critical shortages of wheat." There are several basic difficulties. An essential element in the situation is the ability to limit the quantities available relative to the demand. The technical aspects of the wheat problem in this respect are much more difficult to cope with than those which affect the supply of most commodities under international cartels. With these a monopoly of supply is usually in the hands of one or a few producers. Wheat, however, is the most decentralized of all commodities that enter into international trade. It is grown all over the world by small independent producers and in many countries the acreage can be increased if price conditions are favourable. This is especially true of certain countries of Europe. Exclusive of Russia Europe before the war had an annual average yield in excess of 1,500,000,000 bushels. In view of the relatively small portion of the total amount of wheat grown that enters into international trade, a slight general increase in acreage with good crops would easily upset the balance between export surpluses and the requirements of deficit countries.

The agreement implies that the signatory countries will be able and willing to exercise effective control over domestic production in the interests of stability. But where wheat producers constitute an important part of the farm population, effective control is often difficult to accomplish. If prices are established at a level satisfactory to the producers there is a tendency for them to increase their acreage even though explicitly advised by their government not to do so. In the fall of 1948 producers of winter wheat in the United States, in the face of government warnings to the contrary, increased the area sown by more than 3,000,000 acres. Moreover, in importing countries where the production of substantial domestic supplies is related to national security, wheat growers often occupy a favoured position, which injects a political factor of resistance into the situation, making it difficult for the government to obtain effective reductions in acreage. At the present time there is a strong incentive for importing countries to maintain or increase domestic production in the lack of foreign exchange. Until a true balance in international trading is achieved the tendency is likely to be in the direction of limiting wheat imports to the irreducible minimum by expanding domestic production. Surplus supplies in either exporting or importing countries are a threat to the stability of any international agreement.

The situation will not be made easier by the failure of Argentina,

Russia, and the Danubian countries to adhere to the agreement. It is not to be expected that Argentina will allow herself to be forced out of the export market without making a fight to retain this important factor in her national economy. Up to the present she has found it more remunerative to sell wheat on a government-to-government basis.[17] Her carryover at the end of the latest crop year, December 1, 1950, was estimated at the exceptionally low figure of 7,000,000 bushels.[18] Russia is also an uncertainty. She has at times a considerable volume of wheat available for export and is not likely to sell it in a way that would facilitate transactions under the International Wheat Agreement. If supplies became redundant, and Argentina or Russia chose to undercut prices, importing countries would be tempted to sabotage the agreement to buy their supplies in the cheapest market.

An uncontrollable element is the wide fluctuation which occurs from year to year in the yield of wheat per acre. If one country alone were favoured in a given year with a bumper crop, adjustments made through the agency of the International Wheat Council might prove capable of coping with the marketing problem that increased supplies would create. But if a whole continent were affected by exceptionally favourable conditions of yield, the circumstance would inevitably introduce stresses and strains into the operation of the agreement which would be very difficult to resolve except at the expense of the main object of the agreement, namely, the stabilization of wheat prices. The same considerations apply in the case of a series of short crops spread over a large area, except that in this case the boot would be on the other foot.

The fixing of a price range for wheat over a period of years is also subject to the fundamental weakness that, unless other prices are stabilized, the wheat producer may find himself caught in a spiral of rising prices that affects his costs while his returns remain constant. Stabilizing the price of wheat does not necessarily stabilize the producers' real income. This was clearly evident with respect to the British Wheat Agreement. The reason given by Argentina for her abstention from the 1948 conference was that price arrangements on other products should be discussed concurrently with arrangements to stabilize the price of wheat.[19]

[17] *Ibid.*, Nov., 1949, p. 27.
[18] *The Wheat Review*, Jan., 1951.
[19] *Winnipeg Free Press*, Feb. 3, 1948.

Moreover, there is always the danger that such an agreement may prove rigid and restrictive in operation and thereby reduce the consumption of wheat without being sufficiently powerful to check overproduction. The best remedy for excessive supplies in export countries is a price low enough to increase consumption in the poorer deficit countries.   Conversely, when scarcity of supplies prevails prompt advances in prices to induce increased production are necessary. The agreement signed at Washington permits a certain degree of flexibility in price changes by the spread agreed upon between maximum and minimum prices. Beginning with a spread of 30 cents per bushel for the crop year of 1949-50, the spread widens to 60 cents per bushel for the crop year of 1952-53.

But the differences that exist between the standard of living of the wheat producers in exporting countries and that of the consumers in importing countries make it difficult to satisfy each group that the price agreed upon is an equitable one. While there may exist a broad community of interest among the signatory countries the situation does not remain static and as time goes on marked changes in the world value of wheat may occur. This may lead to the agreement operating to the disadvantage of one group or the other or to the disadvantage of particular countries within the exporting or the importing group. It is idle to expect that under these circumstances prompt amendments to the agreement will be easily made. Amendments require a two-thirds majority of the exporting countries and of the importing countries.   Moreover, if an amendment is ratified signatories who do not favour it may withdraw from the pact at the end of the current year.

The administration of a commodity agreement affecting a large number of countries with conflicting interests tends to increase rather than to reduce friction.   In negotiations on a governmental level questions of national prestige enter into the situation. Again, the weight of national power can be used by a powerful country with ample credit facilities to turn the scale against its weaker neighbours more easily than under a régime of free trading. For instance, the threat of stopping off-shore purchases under the Marshall Plan was used by the United States to get Britain and other importing countries to accept the exporters' "final terms" in concluding the 1949 wheat agreement, though subsequently off-shore purchases were restricted by the refusal of the Economic Co-operative Administration to grant further authorizations.[20]

[20]*Economist*, April 23, 1949, p. 760.

Within the channels of private trade negotiations can be conducted with despatch and without the publicity and public controversy that attend the discussions of policies of state. When a breach of contract is alleged under conditions of private trade the courts are available to determine the issue but when the charge is made that a government or a government agency has failed to fulfil its obligations national susceptibilities are apt to be touched leading to delays and difficulties in reaching an amicable settlement. The settlement itself may be attacked for political reasons and those who are disappointed by its terms will cherish a grievance. The sale of Canadian wheat to the United Kingdom through the medium of an intergovernmental agreement for four years has not added notably to the reserves of mutual goodwill in the two countries.

These considerations lead to the conclusion that there are serious obstacles to the success of an international wheat agreement. It is hardly likely that the present international agreement, involving the sale and purchase of large quantities of wheat and bringing within its scope many countries, will escape the difficulties inherent in the nature of such arrangements. The value of the International Wheat Agreement of 1949 as a stabilizing agent in the international wheat market still remains to be demonstrated.[21] If one may judge from the level of prices for Class II wheat, producers are paying a high price for whatever stability the agreement may afford. A disturbing element in the present situation, and one not likely to improve quickly, is the chronic shortage of dollars at the disposal of importing countries to finance imports of wheat from Canada and the United States. Beyond this looms the grim threat of over-production and excessive supplies.

[21]For a careful study of wheat planning, see Paul de Hevesy, *World Wheat Planning in General* (London, 1940).

9

Post-War developments in the grain trade

EARLY in the session of 1947 the Government brought down its bill to amend the Canadian Wheat Board Act.[1] The *prime facie* reason for the proposed legislation was to enable the Wheat Board to carry through the British Wheat Agreement. The preamble recited the fact of the agreement and declared that it was "necessary to make provision for the carrying out of the arrangement." In this way the Government was able indirectly to extend the compulsory powers of the Board until July 31, 1950. That the Government did not wish, however, to go beyond the judicial grounds furnished by decisions of the Privy Council for authority to invade provincial rights[2] was made apparent during the progress of the bill through the Senate. When the measure was under examination before the Banking and Commerce Committee of that body the Minister of Trade and Commerce and the Chairman of the Wheat Board told the committee that the legislation was not intended primarily to implement the agreement with the United Kingdom but chiefly to establish a compulsory pooling of wheat during the term of the Government's price commitment to the Canadian wheat growers. But when, in view of these statements, a member of the committee attempted to incorporate in the preamble an amendment stating that its objects included the establishment of a five-year pool, as well as assuring a fixed wheat supply for the United Kingdom, the solicitor of the Wheat Board objected that the inclusion of this statement might lay the Act open to attack on constitutional grounds as a price-fixing measure.[3]

[1]Statutes of Canada, 1947, c. 15.
[2]See above, pp. 142-3.
[3]*Winnipeg Free Press*, May 3, 8, 1947.

While increasing the Board's powers in some respects, in the main the Act gave statutory authority to the powers exercised by the Board under Orders-in-Council passed during the national emergency created by the war. These powers included complete control over interprovincial and export trade in wheat as well as over the quantities to be delivered to elevators and railway cars and methods of delivery. The Act provided that the establishment of wheat quotas was to be subject to the limitation that the final quota in any crop year should not be less than 14 bushels per authorized acre. One significant feature of the revision was the repeal of the clause in the original Act which laid upon the Board the obligation to utilize existing marketing agencies. The new Act empowered the Board to "establish, utilize and employ such marketing agencies or facilities" as it deemed necessary for the purpose of its operations.

Further, the Act disposed decisively of the original idea of the Canadian Wheat Board as a quasi-independent government body designed to act as an agent for the grain growers' protection in marketing their wheat. It contained the specific declaration: "The Board is, for all purposes, an agent of His Majesty in right of Canada, and its powers under this act may be exercised by it only as an agent of His Majesty in the said right." Moreover, the Board's powers were strictly controlled by the authority of the Governor-in-Council to make orders, not inconsistent with the Act, directing the Board "as to the manner in which any of its operations, powers and duties" should be "conducted, exercised or performed." "Subject to regulations" the Board was empowered to sell grain, for such prices as it considered reasonable, with the object of promoting the sale of grain produced in Canada in world markets.

The bill emerged from Parliament with few changes. In the Commons the Government refused to send it to a special committee where officials of the Wheat Board could be examined and it was considered by the House sitting as a committee of the whole. While it was hotly contested clause by clause, there was no direct formal challenge by the parliamentary Opposition, and it was passed after four days of debate by a vote of 172 to 7. In the Senate it encountered stiff opposition. There it was characterized as exemplifying "a complete totalitarian technique of grain marketing for the country" by which the marketing of wheat was placed in a "strait jacket" from which there was no relief.[4] The bill was referred to the Senate

[4] *Ibid.*, March 22, 1947, ff.

Banking and Commerce Committee where attempts were made to restrict the powers of the Wheat Board but without much success. The only change of importance was the inclusion of a clause specifically providing for the repeal on August 1, 1950 of Part II, which related to the control of deliveries of grain to elevators and railway cars. A much criticized section, which gave the Board the power, under certain circumstances, to suspend the right of the producer to deliver grain under any permit book for a period not exceeding one year, had been dropped earlier.

The passage of this Act continued the rigid monopoly over the marketing of Canadian wheat until August 1, 1950. The Government did not indicate whether as a general policy it favoured compulsory wheat marketing. The Minister of Trade and Commerce told the House of Commons that the Government anticipated the continuation of the Canadian Wheat Board "in some form" after the termination of the agreement with the United Kingdom but did not add to this information.[5] It is not unlikely that in 1947 the Government hoped to negotiate a further agreement with the United Kingdom in 1950 or was looking forward to an international agreement. There was also the possibility that, if the Government wished to continue compulsory marketing indefinitely, some other method might be devised by which constitutional difficulties would be surmounted.

The latter possibility came to the fore in 1948 when the Government introduced a bill which included provisions for the compulsory marketing of oats and barley. Since these cereals were largely sold for domestic consumption and were not subject to an international agreement obviously a constitutional basis would have to be found to make the legislation effective.

When the Government, as part of its general policy of abolishing restrictions arising out of the war, removed price ceilings on oats and barley in October, 1947, trading in these grains on the Winnipeg Grain Exchange was resumed, with sharp increases in prices. At the same time the Government announced the discontinuance of the stock feeding subsidies of 25 cents per bushel on barley and 10 cents per bushel on oats. The payment of these subsidies had been a cause of discontent to the coarse grain growers and feeders in Western Canada who maintained that it gave the eastern stock feeders an unfair advantage over them in livestock production. Decontrol and the discontinuance of subsidies resulted in a substantial

[5]*Ibid.*, Feb. 27, 1947.

increase in feeding costs for the livestock producers and dairy farmers in Eastern Canada. This undoubtedly led them to look favourably upon a state system of marketing for coarse grains as being more likely to give them cheap food supplies than purchases made on the open market. But if this view were correct it could only mean that the western growers of oats and barley would get less for what they sold under the Board than they would get on an open market.

Although western producers welcomed the removal of the price ceiling and the discontinuance of the feeding subsidies, the Saskatchewan Pool continued to declare its unswerving opposition to futures trading in grain. At its annual meeting in the autumn of 1947, it asked for complementary provincial legislation that would guarantee the authority of the Wheat Board to market all grains.[6] This policy the C.C.F. party had sponsored in an unsuccessful amendment to the bill amending the Canadian Wheat Board Act when it was before Parliament earlier in the year. With reference to this amendment the Minister of Justice had said that he was told that if the Wheat Board were placed in the position of handling all or most of the volume of coarse grains on a compulsory basis, its acts would likely be unconstitutional.[7] Subsequently, the Minister of Agriculture, Mr. Gardiner, assured western producers that he was sympathetic to the "idea of placing the control of oats and barley under the Wheat Board" but said there was no authority by which this might be accomplished.[8] The leader of the provincial Liberal party in Saskatchewan also went on record to the effect that the party favoured the compulsory marketing of all grains by the Canadian Wheat Board. Since he was at that time a member of the House of Commons he promised to press for the necessary legislation at the next session of Parliament.[9]

Nevertheless, farm opinion in Western Canada was by no means wholly in favour of the Wheat Board taking over control of coarse grains. Many western producers feared that under state marketing the prices determined upon by the federal Government would inure more to the advantage of the eastern livestock and dairy interests than it would to them. Moreover, it was recognized that state marketing of oats and barley would differ from state control of the marketing of wheat, since oats and barley were sold mainly for domestic consump-

[6]*Ibid.*, Nov. 15, 1947.
[7]Montreal *Gazette*, Feb. 19, 1948.
[8]*Winnipeg Free Press*, Oct. 23, 1947.
[9]*Winnipeg Tribune*, Oct. 29, 1947.

tion and the major portion of the wheat crop was sold for export. The compulsory marketing of oats and barley by the Wheat Board would place the Board in the difficult position of acting as arbiter between the coarse-grain producers of Western Canada and the livestock, dairy, and poultry interests of the eastern provinces. Moreover, it was believed that the Wheat Board itself did not desire to assume such a responsibility. While no official confirmation is available it was reported that, when the control of coarse grains by the Board was considered by the Wheat Board Advisory Committee, an almost unanimous resolution opposing compulsory marketing through the Board was passed. The only dissenter to the resolution was said to be the president of the Saskatchewan Pool.

This conflict over marketing policy, where domestic producer and consumer interests were directly at issue, came to a head at the annual meeting of the Canadian Federation of Agriculture early in 1948. At this meeting the livestock and dairy farmers of Eastern Canada strongly urged that the marketing of coarse grains should be placed under the Wheat Board. Western farm organizations were split on this proposition. The United Grain Growers Limited, with its large western farmer membership, was opposed to government control. The Alberta Pool objected to the control of coarse-grain marketing by the Wheat Board but advocated the creation of another marketing board to be composed solely of the producers of coarse grains, which would act purely with the interests of these producers in view. The Saskatchewan and Manitoba Pools, on the other hand, sided with the eastern interests in supporting Wheat Board control. They appeared to be chiefly interested in the extension of compulsory marketing. The upshot was that the Federation passed a resolution which recommended to the Government that the Wheat Board should be made the sole marketing agency for all other grains in addition to wheat; in deference to western opinion a clause was included in the resolution to the effect that "such legislation be based upon the principle that the Wheat Board shall be an agency operating, primarily, for the benefit and in the interests of grain producers."[10]

Broadly, the situation that had developed was that in Eastern Canada the livestock and dairy interests were behind a drive for the compulsory marketing of coarse grains, and in Western Canada the Saskatchewan and Manitoba Pools were actively urging the same course of action. The key to the situation was Saskatchewan.

[10]*Winnipeg Free Press*, Feb. 7, 9, 1948.

In that province the C.C.F. party was in power with a provincial election impending. The attitude the federal Government would adopt on the question of a complete government monopoly in grain trading promised to be an issue in the approaching campaign. The amendment of the Wheat Board Act to provide for the compulsory marketing of oats and barley would largely eliminate this issue. This was the course the Canadian Government followed. The decision to do so strongly suggested that it was made on the basis of a calculation of the political advantages that would accrue to the provincial Liberal party in Saskatchewan. At any rate, there appears to be no reason to doubt that political considerations were influential.

The amending Act of 1948, in addition to authorizing the compulsory marketing of oats and barley, also gave the Government power to increase the advances made to wheat producers delivering to the five-year pool, strengthened the Board's control over interprovincial movements of wheat by including control over the movement of wheat products, and authorized the Board to establish a pension fund for its members, officials, and employees. The contentious part of the bill was the extension of the compulsory powers of the Board to include the marketing of oats and barley.

The Government was bitterly assailed for including in one bill the legislation providing for an expected increase in the initial payment on wheat along with that for establishing state trading in oats and barley. The increase in the advances on wheat deliveries, forecast at 20 cents per bushel, met with general approval, but there was very strong disapproval from one section of the House of placing oats and barley under the control of the Board. To delay the passage of the bill while the principle of state marketing of oats and barley was debated at length would postpone the ability of the Board to disburse the additional funds to the wheat producers. Protests from opponents to the control features of the bill were so sharp that the Minister of Trade and Commerce, to expedite progress, promised to divide the bill in order to permit committee hearings on the controversial issue. When the time came to fulfil this promise the Minister moved to divide the bill but at the same time gave a broad hint to the Government supporters that his motion should be voted down. He said the objective of saving time in debate, which had prompted his concession, had not been achieved. As a result the motion was defeated although a number of Liberal members voted for the motion along with the Progressive Conservatives and the Social Credit members.[11] In the Senate there was strong opposition. The Senate Banking and Commerce Committee struck out the oats and barley control section by a vote of 16 to 8. Subsequently the section was reinstated by the chamber itself on a vote of 25 to 17.[12]

The circumstances surrounding the development of the Government's policy, indicated by its decision to bring the marketing of oats and barley under the control of the Wheat Board, afford another illustration of the way political considerations may enter into ministerial decisions regarding a great national industry, affecting thousands of voters.

At the time the Act was passed the view was commonly expressed that the sections of the Act relating to coarse grains would be set aside as not being within the constitutional powers of Parliament to enact and that they would never become effective. The method employed to meet the test of constitutionality was that of concurrent legislation. The amended Act empowered the Governor-in-Council by regulation to extend to oats and barley the powers given to the Wheat Board with respect to wheat. Subsequently the Government announced that this part of the Act would not be implemented unless the western provinces passed concurrent legislation placing the marketing of coarse grains under the Wheat Board.

Saskatchewan enacted such legislation but no immediate action was taken by Alberta or Manitoba. The Premier of Manitoba said that there would be no legislation in that province until the Canadian Government could demonstrate that such action was necessary to make the federal statute valid.[13] This declaration was made after a meeting in Regina of the western premiers and cabinet members and representatives of the Canadian Federation of Agriculture had been informed that the law officers of both the Alberta and Manitoba governments had given opinions to the effect that there was no greater need for complementary legislation with respect to the marketing of oats and barley than there was in the case of wheat; and that, therefore, there was no need for provincial legislation to complement the 1948 amendment to the Canadian Wheat Board Act.[14] There were further approaches to the Canadian Government but no mutually satisfactory decision was reached. The Government of Alberta made it clear that it would be prepared to pass the legislation asked for by the federal Government provided the Wheat Board was instructed to handle coarse grains "in the interests of the producer."

[11]Ibid., March 12, 22, 1948.   [12]Ibid., March 25, 1948.
[13]Ibid., June 19, 22, 23, 1948.   [14]Ibid., May 12, 1948.

The Minister of Trade and Commerce stated definitely that the Canadian Government would only put the Act into force if the Prairie Provinces passed the legislation demanded. He said it was obvious that the Government could not give any undertaking that it would become responsible for marketing coarse grains solely in the interests of the producers of those products.[15]

The deadlock was broken when Alberta and Manitoba passed the complementary legislation demanded at the 1949 sessions of the legislatures. This was followed by an announcement by the Minister of Trade and Commerce that oats and barley would come under the Wheat Board on August 1, 1949. The initial payments by the Wheat Board would be 61½ cents per bushel for oats and 90 cents per bushel for barley. The Board would sell coarse grain through private dealers and would post daily prices in line with demand and the world situation.[16]   Western insistence that these grains should be marketed purely in the interests of the producer implied that the Board should endeavour to secure the highest prices possible. With control over supply the Board could exact monopoly prices when making sales on the domestic market but since the Board is not specifically a producers' board it is not bound by any obligation of this sort and is left with the problem of how to satisfy in its sales policy western producers and eastern consumers.

Its policy has been to sell oats and barley either on the Winnipeg market, which continues to function, or outright at Fort William, Vancouver, or country points. Private dealers can make use of the facilities of the futures market to hedge their stocks while making sales. The market is not an open market in the full sense of the term since the Board is in control of the situation through its control of supply, but since the Board makes reasonable supplies available from day to day the prices established in the market provide a guide to current values.

The method developed has evoked little criticism except from the more ardent partisans of state marketing, but the merit of state marketing for oats and barley continues to be a very controversial subject. Grain merchants complain that their business is being injured by a black market. Bootlegging occurs when a producer sells oats and barley direct to a dealer below the market price. The dealer is then able to undersell legitimate operators. The black market is attractive

15*Ibid.*, March 15, 1949.
16*Ibid.*, July 21, 1949.

to a producer when he needs full cash payment for his grain or when the price he can obtain is higher than the average he can expect to obtain from the Wheat Board.[17] The existence of continued criticism in Manitoba was revealed in February 1951, when the Premier of Manitoba announced that a special plebiscite would be held in that province after the returns for the 1950-51 crop were in. Manitoba producers of oats and barley were given an opportunity to express, after two years' experience, their opinion about the Wheat Board's handling of coarse grains. The plebiscite was held on November 24, 1951. The results of the referendum showed that some dissatisfaction might exist but that the large majority of producers were in favour of continuing the present system. The voting gave 31,252 persons in favour of the present system and 3,853 against.[18]

With the expiry of the British Wheat Agreement in 1950 Canadian participation in the International Wheat Agreement became the basis of the Board's authority to maintain compulsory marketing of wheat. In order to be able to fulfil the terms of the pact the Wheat Board's monopoly powers were continued to August 1, 1953. At the same time the Government provided for an increase in the membership of the Board should this become desirable. The Act now reads that the Board "shall consist of not less than 3 and not more than 5 members appointed by the Governor in Council." The present Board consists of 3 members. In 1951 a short act, making certain corrections in the 1950 statute, added a new section providing for the transfer of wheat in the accounts of the Board from a preceding pool period to the current pool period. The purpose of this change is to permit the Board to proceed with an earlier disbursement, after the end of a pool period, of any surpluses payable to the producers.[19]

Meanwhile, the disposal of Canadian wheat for export is presenting serious problems. In reporting on the crop years of 1948-49 the Board indicated some difficulty in selling the surplus available. It reported that at no time in the crop year was the demand for wheat buoyant and over the greater part of the period the demand was light and intermittent. The limited demand for Canadian wheat was attributed to large crops harvested in Europe in 1949, the continued supplying of substantial quantities of wheat to Western Europe by the United States under financing by the Economic Co-operation

[17]*Ibid.*, April 16, 1951.
[18]*Ibid.*, Feb. 10, April 18, Dec. 4, 1951.
[19]Statutes of Canada, 1950, c. 31; 1951, c. 50.

Administration, and the steady demand for Australian wheat within the sterling area as a result of the dollar shortage. The Canadian crop of 1950 has presented unusual difficulties in handling. An unseasonable August frost reduced the expected yield from 544,000,000 bushels to 427,000,000 bushels. It is estimated that not more than one-third of the total will grade in the choice milling grades while approximately 200,000,000 bushels will grade below No. 4 Northern in quality. Much of this wheat will have to be sold for feeding purposes and much of it will require drying to prevent further deterioration.[20] These conditions have created grave handling and marketing problems for the Wheat Board.

After fifteen years of operation the final status of the Canadian Wheat Board has not been determined. Originally established to dispose of an export surplus of wheat on the best terms possible the Board developed under the impact of war into an important administrative instrument through which the Canadian Government exercised a monopolistic control over the delivery and sale of Canadian wheat and other grains. Concurrently with this change in its nature the Board appears to have become to a large degree administrative in function, acting as an agency under the control of the wheat committee of the Cabinet. This rather intangible change is reflected in its composition. The first and second chief commissioners of the Board were leading figures in the grain trade before accepting appointment and enjoyed a considerable degree of independence in discharging their responsibility. From time to time other men high in the grain trade became members of the Board but one by one these men resigned and returned to private business. The present Chief Commissioner and Assistant Chief Commissioner are both former employees of the Board, and the third member was Assistant General Manager of Saskatchewan Pool Elevators. But within its scope the competence of the Board has not been questioned; in fact there would appear to be general agreement that on the whole, and at times under difficult circumstances, the Board, as an administrative body, is doing a good job. In recognition of its contribution to the national effort during the war, in the distribution of honours which followed, the Chief Commissioner, Mr. George McIvor, was appointed to the Order of St. Michael and St. George.

The recent establishment of a pensions system for members of

[20]Canadian Wheat Board, *Report*, 1948-49, 1949-50; *Winnipeg Free Press*, Dec. 30, 1950.

the Board and its employees as well as the purchase of extensive premises in Winnipeg are indications that the Government considers that the Board has become a permanent body. But the real issue concerning the Board remains to be fought out and settled, that is, whether after 1953 it will continue to be monopolistic in its operations or will provide merely an alternative method of marketing to that afforded by the private trade. There is still much difference of opinion on this question among grain growers but there is practical unanimity with respect to the necessity of guaranteed floor prices. Much will depend upon whether the International Wheat Agreement proves to be a more successful "experiment in stability" than the British Wheat Agreement. Neither of the principal political parties appears to have a firm policy on this question. The Liberal administration has followed what might be termed a day-to-day policy, acting in the light of existing political situations. The Progressive Conservative party adopted a plank in its platform in 1948 that favoured "the restoration of the Canadian Wheat Board Act of 1935 to serve its original purpose." The Board would be allowed to handle coarse grains, as well as wheat, on a voluntary basis, while guaranteeing "to all producers the right to market wheat or other grains by any other means."[21] This declaration of policy, however, was qualified by party leaders during the electoral campaign in Western Canada in 1949 by the promise that if the Progressive Conservative party were returned to power the producers themselves would determine the type of marketing agency they wanted to handle their grain.[22]

[21]*Ibid.*, Oct. 7, 1948.

10

The Growth of the Pool organizations

THE difficulties encountered in 1929 and 1930 caused some changes to be made in the formal organization of the three provincial Pools. With the disappearance of the five-year contract membership in the Alberta and in the Saskatchewan Pools rested in the ownership of a share in the organization procurable by a grain grower at nominal cost. The Manitoba Pool, based essentially on the local units, was reorganized and the administration centralized by placing the management of the locals, including accounts of the local organizations and their producer members, under the elevator company.[1] Ceasing to handle sales through the Canadian Co-operative Wheat Producers Limited (the central selling agency), each Pool developed its own marketing department. Since 1943 the Pools, in common with other grain companies, have acted as agents for the Canadian Wheat Board in the purchase and delivery of wheat. The Saskatchewan Pool also conducts an export business, buying wheat from the Wheat Board and selling to foreign buyers. This, however, is not an important aspect of its activities.

The Saskatchewan Pool is the largest of the three provincial Pools. This is natural since Saskatchewan is the largest wheat-growing province in Canada. The Pool began in 1924 with 47,000 members who signed the five-year contract. Growth was rapid and it had on record in 1931 82,870 operative wheat contracts. Certain members, however, while retaining their membership, failed to sign the 1928-32 contract. Their right to vote was taken away, but, with the disappear-

[1] *Report of the Royal Commission on Co-operatives* (Ottawa, 1945), p. 146. See also the brochure, *Twenty Five Years Service*, issued by the Manitoba Pool Elevators, 1949.

ance of the contract in 1933, they again became eligible to vote for delegates, and other restrictions were removed. It was at this time that the new policy of enrolling members on the purchase of a share for $1.00 was initiated. The shares issued under this arrangement increased from 104,354 by 1934 to a total of 129,412 by 1945.[2] In respect to members' equities in the commercial and elevator reserves a form of revolving fund is used by the Pool by which the rights of deceased members or members who have retired from farming may be realized upon. The rights are purchased and transferred to the credit of patrons who otherwise would receive cash refunds. By this method the original elevator and commercial reserves are retained in the organization with new investments by active members replacing investments by retiring members.[3]

After seven years of rapid expansion the Saskatchewan Pool had largely succeeded in covering its natural territory for operations and had provided itself with terminals. In 1931 it had 1,066 country elevators, five terminals at the Head of the Lakes, including two leased terminals, and one transfer terminal at Buffalo, New York. This gave it a command of an over-all capacity in all positions of approximately 63,300,000 bushels.

Since 1931 there has been an increase in the number of country elevators to 1,162, which, along with the addition of a number of permanent and semi-permanent annexes, has resulted in an increase in terms of country storage for grain of 5,600,000 bushels. On the other hand there has been a reduction in its terminal space during that period. One leased elevator was relinquished in 1933, the other in 1948, and the transfer terminal at Buffalo was disposed of by sale in 1945. To offset partly its loss of terminal space the Saskatchewan Pool completed the construction of an additional storage annex to one of its existing terminals at the Lakehead in 1949. At that time the total storage capacity of its permanent facilities was approximately 59,000,000 bushels.

In addition to its permanent storage facilities the Pool constructed temporary storage space for over 26,000,000 bushels at country points and temporary terminal space for 10,000,000 bushels at Port Arthur, Ontario, to meet the urgent demands for more storage facilities during the war years when Canada had excessive carryovers. In accordance

[2]Saskatchewan Co-operative Wheat Producers Limited, *Annual Report*, 1931, 1933, 1945.

[3]*Report of the Royal Commission on Co-operatives*, p. 142.

with the agreement under which the temporary storage space at Port Arthur was constructed these additional bins have since been dismantled. Part of its temporary storage at country points has also been demolished but there still remains space for approximately 18,000,000 bushels.

Figures significant of the growing strength of the organization are those which relate to the reduction of the debt owed to the Saskatchewan Government and to the Pool members' increasing equity in the Pool's assets. In 1931, as a result of the overpayment on grain delivered to the Pool in 1929, it emerged with a funded debt to the provincial Government amounting to $13,752,000. Interest and principal payments were consistently maintained throughout the years in accordance with its agreement and the final payment on its liability was made in 1949, two years ahead of its due date. In 1933 the members' equity in the assets of the Pool amounted to $8,585,583, or 39 per cent of the total value. With the completion of the repayment to the Saskatchewan Government the members' equity now stands at 100 per cent valued at $22,801,662.

Since its organization the Saskatchewan Pool has paid or credited to its patron members a total of $22,343,673 in the form of patronage dividends, and, in addition, has paid to its members a total of $3,378,697 in the form of interest on their investment in the elevator company. In recent years the Pool has handled through its country elevator facilities in excess of 50 per cent of all grain marketed in the province of Saskatchewan. The membership in the Pool numbered 136,668 as at July, 1949.

It owns three subsidiaries, two of which link up with the main activities of the parent organization. The Modern Press Limited was incorporated in 1931 to absorb from the publishers the *Western Producer,* a farm weekly, to which the Pool had advanced considerable money in order to provide itself with a publicity outlet. The publication of this organ entailed quite heavy annual losses to the Saskatchewan Wheat Pool up to 1944 but since that date surpluses have been reported. The Saskatchewan Wheat Pool Terminal Construction Company Limited was organized in 1929 to facilitate the carrying-out of elevator construction.

In 1944 the Pool branched out into a new field when it amalgamated with the Saskatchewan Livestock Pool. To make this possible amendments to the acts of incorporation of both organizations were passed by the legislature of Saskatchewan. The technical name of the parent organization was changed from the Saskatchewan Co-operative Wheat Producers Limited to the Saskatchewan Co-operative Producers Limited. Under the terms of the agreement all shareholders of the latter automatically became members of the Saskatchewan Livestock Pool. The Livestock Pool continues to function as a legal entity with the status of a subsidiary of the Saskatchewan Co-operative Producers Limited and to employ the assets of the old organization in its business.[4] Recently the Saskatchewan Pool has extended the range of its activities to include the production of flour and the extraction of vegetable oils from flax and rape seed. Large plants for these purposes are operated at Saskatoon.

The Saskatchewan Pool has been particularly active in maintaining close touch with its membership throughout the province. At nearly all shipping points Pool committees are in existence which are energetic in promoting the business of the Pool. An extensive programme of co-operative education is carefully organized. As media of publicity the Pool employs the radio, advertising in the *Western Producer* and other Saskatchewan weeklies, Pool calendars, and folders and other literature given out at booths set up at the principal agricultural exhibitions in the province. The Pool is also developing a lending library service for the use of its members. As a result of these measures the Saskatchewan Pool up to the present has been markedly successful in avoiding the fate of many co-operatives—the loss of interest in its activities among its membership.

The Alberta Wheat Pool, while not as large as the Saskatchewan Pool, occupies substantially the same position in Alberta that the Saskatchewan Pool does in Saskatchewan. It began operations in October of 1923, a year earlier than the Pools in the neighbouring provinces. The general lines of its organization are similar to those of the Saskatchewan Pool.[5] As with the latter, certain changes were made in its organization to meet the situation created by the difficulties of 1930. Originally membership rested upon the signing of a marketing agreement and the purchase of one share in the enterprise. In 1929 share capital was abolished and moneys received for share capital were repaid to the members. When the second five-year contract expired in 1933 the Pool obtained an amendment to its act of incorporation whereby members who had signed this con-

[4]Saskatchewan Co-operative Wheat Producers Limited, *Annual Report*, 1944, p. 28.
[5]Alberta Wheat Pool, *Annual Report*, 1933, 1945.

tract would continue to be able to vote until a new sign-up was effected or the act of incorporation was again amended. No new sign-up of members was attempted and the act of incorporation was not amended until 1939. In the intervening period there was no method by which new members could be accepted into the organization. One result of this curious situation was that the voting strength of the Pool declined from year to year, because of deaths, removals, or other causes.

The amendments to the act in 1939 established a procedure for enrolling new members. Membership now became open to any grower, upon application, who had not signed a marketing agreement, if he had delivered 500 bushels of grain from 1935 to the date of application, and had acquired a certain interest in the elevator or commercial reserves. Voting privileges were also restored to those members who had signed the first contract but had failed to sign the second, thereby forfeiting voting rights. Provision was also made to enable the Pool to make use of the device of a revolving fund with a view to maintaining an active membership and of buying out old members. An amendment to the by-laws permitted the Pool to purchase reserve certificates and reissue them to new members. As a result of these changes there was a large increase in the Alberta Pool membership. When the second five-year contract expired in 1933 contract signers numbered 43,527. Under the procedure adopted in 1939, by November of 1946 13,492 new members had been enrolled.[6]

For a number of years the Alberta Wheat Pool differed in its practice from the other Pools with respect to the licensing of its line of country elevators. At the outset these elevators, as a general policy, were licensed as private country elevators, thus limiting their activities to the needs of the Pool membership. The changes in marketing methods caused by the difficulties of 1930-31 led the Alberta Pool henceforth to license these elevators as public country elevators and to carry on a general country elevator business.

From the beginning it pursued a vigorous policy of expanding elevator facilities throughout the province with the result that by 1931 it was operating country elevators at practically all the important shipping points in Alberta. In 1931-32 it had under licence 438 country elevators. In 1947 it added to its system 30 country elevators purchased from the Northern Grain Company Limited. Included in the purchase were 28 annexes and 16 dwellings. This purchase brought the total

6*Ibid.*, 1937-38, 1945-46.

number of country elevators owned by the Alberta Wheat Pool in 1949 up to 485 situated at 431 shipping points in Alberta, with two located in British Columbia. Total storage capacity including annexes amounted to 30,700,000 bushels.

Beginning with the leasing of terminal elevators at Vancouver and other points on the Pacific coast the Alberta Pool subsequently built a terminal of its own at Vancouver. This terminal, with a capacity of 5,150,000 bushels, went into operation in 1928. At the Head of the Lakes the central selling agency for a time managed a terminal owned in partnership by the three provincial Pools. This terminal later was sold to the Manitoba Pool. In 1939 the Alberta Pool purchased the Union Terminal at Port Arthur with a storage capacity of 2,000,000 bushels. This terminal is operated by the Manitoba Pool Elevators under a profit-sharing agreement with the Alberta Pool and provides an outlet for a substantial percentage of the latter's handlings which move into export via the eastern route.

The financial position of the Alberta Wheat Pool has greatly strengthened since the setback encountered in 1930. The overpayment of 1929 left it with a funded debt to the Government of the province of $5,649,00. In addition, the Pool owed $1,750,000 on the new terminal at Vancouver. By the terms of its agreement the provincial debt was to be repaid with interest in annual instalments of approximately $453,000. The first payment, which fell due on September 1, 1933, amounted to $170,000 on the principal. This sum, together with interest, was duly paid, and succeeding instalments on principal and interest were consistently paid. In 1947 the whole amount was paid off and the terminal debt had likewise been liquidated.

In addition to paying off this indebtedness the Alberta Pool substantially increased its financial resources. In 1931 the value of its properties and equipment was placed at $9,648,028. At the end of the business year in 1949 the investment in its elevator system was $14,142,520. Working capital had expanded from $2,672,303 to $4,168,086. As a result of turning back net earnings into the organization to clear its indebtedness the reserve holders' equity increased from 43 per cent of net elevator and commercial reserves to 105 per cent. This represents an increase of nearly $4,000,000. Through the purchase of commercial and elevator reserves to the extent of $4,834,000, approximately 57.1 per cent of the original deductions have been returned to the signers of the first and second five-year contracts. From the time of its organization up to 1949 the Alberta

Wheat Pool, over and above the sums paid for the grain marketed, has made cash payments to its members of $9,354,906, as patronage dividends, interest, and the purchase of reserves.[7] During the crop year 1948-49 the Alberta Pool handled 34.39 per cent of the total grain marketed in the province of Alberta.

Moderate in outlook, it did not take up enthusiastically the idea of a 100 per cent pool enforced by legislation, a policy advocated by the members of the Saskatchewan Pool. In 1931 the Alberta Pool conducted a referendum on this question. The total vote recorded was 7,429, with a majority of 1,047 against such a measure. Nor has it extended its collateral activities as widely as the Saskatchewan Pool, though like the latter it maintains an elaborate field service to keep its members actively interested in the organization. While it issues a weekly bulletin, the *Alberta Wheat Pool Budget*, it relies upon the radio as its principal method of publicity. In the promotion of agricultural education and research it has given aid to various organizations, particularly those engaged in working among young farm people. The Manager of the Alberta Wheat Pool, R. D. Purdy, has occupied that position since 1925, and the present Chairman of the Board of Directors, Ben S. Plumer, was one of the original directors elected in 1923.

The reverses of 1929 and 1930 created the severest difficulties for the Manitoba Pool, the smallest of the three provincial Pools. This was in part because of the form of organization which had been adopted by the wheat growers of Manitoba who united to form the Pool. The principal difference between the Manitoba organization and the Pools in the other two provinces was with regard to the position of the local organizations and their relationship to the central body and to the Manitoba Pool Elevators Limited, the subsidiary holding and operating elevator company created by the Pool in 1925. The local co-operative associations were conceded local autonomy and operated within the organization on the basis of a contract with the elevator company. Membership in the Manitoba Pool was obtained by signing a five-year contract to deliver grain to it for marketing. Contracts between the local association and the marketing agency authorized the latter to make commercial and elevator deductions from the farmers' returns on the grain sold, in return for which it issued participation certificates. The money accumulated by the Pool

[7]*Alberta Wheat Pool's Record of Progress*, pamphlet issued by the Pool, July 31, 1948. See also *Report of the Royal Commission on Co-operatives*, p. 144.

in this way was largely advanced to the elevator subsidiary which constructed or acquired elevators as rapidly as possible at each point where a local co-operative association was organized. The elevators were leased to the associations by Manitoba Pool Elevators Limited with an option to purchase. By the end of July, 1931, loans by the Manitoba Wheat Pool to the elevator company amounted to $2,503,690.

During the first six years of its development the Manitoba Pool, like the other two Pools, expanded rapidly and by 1931 was operating 153 country elevators as well as terminals. Throughout the period the elevator company had very limited capital resources. In 1931 it reported a paid-up capital of $10,000 and a contingency reserve of $48,462.35.[8] Working capital was largely borrowed from the banks on the basis of a guarantee from the Wheat Pool itself. Under these circumstances the Pool was in no position to cope with the situation created by the disastrous fall in grain prices in 1929-30. The Government of Manitoba was forced to come to its aid in 1930 by guaranteeing its bank loans and took a first lien on its property which included its subsidiary the elevator company.[9] The liability incurred by the Government from this guarantee was subsequently determined in November of 1931 at $3,374,940 while the realizable assets were estimated at $2,400,000, in the form of obligations payable to the elevator company by the local associations on leases and purchases of elevators.

Meanwhile, the Manitoba Pool had to face a royal commission of investigation appointed by the Government of Manitoba to probe certain charges made against it by James R. Murray in a letter to the Premier of Manitoba, dated March 10, 1931. These charges came as an aftermath to public exchanges of views in 1929 between Mr. Murray, who at that time was Assistant General Manager of the United Grain Growers Limited, the older farm co-operative, and the management of the Manitoba Pool. It was generally believed that they were provoked by the aggressive policy of the Manitoba Pool in 1928-29 in providing itself with its own line of country elevators. In the background was the fact that when the Pool was being formed in 1924 representatives of the United Grain Growers Limited had endeavoured to come to an agreement with supporters of the Pool whereby the duplication of elevator facilities by farmer companies

[8]Manitoba Pool Elevators Limited, *Financial Statement and Report for the Year Ended July 31, 1931.*
[9]Statutes of Manitoba, 1931, c. 57.

might be avoided.[10] These negotiations had broken down, however, on account of the hostility of the Pool members to farmers' grain being sold under the methods employed by open market. At the time that Mr. Murray wrote his letter to the Premier he had ceased to be an officer of the United Grain Growers or to have any connection with that organization.[11]

The substance of Mr. Murray's charges was: (1) that the Pool was building elevators at many points throughout the province where they should never have been built, and where there was no reasonable chance of their being anything but a burden on the members of the local association; (2) that, through the operation of the delivery contract, members at a number of points had been taxed through excessive overages and undergrading of their grain to meet the extravagantly high expense; (3) that the financial statements supplied to the local associations by the Manitoba Pool Elevators Limited had never shown clearly to the members just how much per bushel the expenses amounted to on their grain and what they had contributed through overages and undergrading; (4) that many of the elevators could not meet expenses and overhead charges if the farmers delivering their grain to them were given a deal equal to that which they could get at any competing elevator.

After a lengthy and detailed investigation the Commissioner, Mr. E. K. Williams, K.C., of Winnipeg, reported his findings on each charge: (1), substantially proved; (2), proved; (3), proved literally, but in so far as overages and grade gains were concerned the information was available to any person who sought it; (4), considering the vagueness of this charge and the absence of any proper standards of comparison, not proven.

The investigation clearly showed that the optimism of the directors and members of the Pool, combined with local pressures to have Pool elevators at given shipping points, had led the Pool into what, at the time, were unwise expenditures. The original decision of the Pool to build no elevators except at points where it had at least 10,000 acres signed up by Pool members, or where it would have at least 75 per cent of the tributary territory after two years, had been relaxed. Of the total number of elevators operated, 119 had been acquired (leased, bought, or built) with less than 10,000 acres signed

[10]See p. 191.
[11]Royal Commission on Manitoba Pool Elevators Limited, *Report* (Winnipeg, 1931).

up. Initial calculations had been based on an elevator cost of between
$12,000 and $13,000. While 30 elevators had been purchased at an
average cost of $12,611, 122 new elevators had been purchased at
an average cost of $21,783. More than $3,000,000 was invested in
elevators. This included all elevator deductions, the Pool's commercial
reserve, and a bank loan of $750,000.

While the Commissioner found that the Manitoba Pool Elevators
Limited was shortweighing and undergrading at certain shipping
points, he said he was of the opinion that the "entirely fallacious"
theory, widely held and consistently preached, that profits from overages and grade grains went back to the persons contributing, was
partly responsible for these practices developing. Another cause, he
was convinced, was the desire of the directors to avoid wherever
possible making assessments on the members of local associations
at the end of the year to cover deficiencies in income.

The Commissioner's report was followed by an announcement of
policy by the Premier of Manitoba which set forth how far the
Government was prepared to go in assisting the Pool and the terms
under which the assistance would be granted. His proposals were
submitted to the local associations of the Pool and after negotiations
an agreement was reached between the interested parties and signed
on August 1, 1931.[12] The agreement involved four parties, the local
associations, the elevator company, the Pool, and the Province of
Manitoba. The Pool, which by this time had suspended operations,
was included in the arrangement because of its previous pledge of
all the assets of the organization, which included the elevator company,
to the Manitoba Government in connection with the guarantee the
Government gave to the banks after the overpayment made by the
Pool to its members on the 1929 crop. By the terms of the agreement
the leases of the elevators by the elevator company to the local associations were cancelled, and the local associations were required to buy
them from the elevator company at an aggregate price of $2,100,000.
The purchase money was to be collected by the elevator company
from the locals and held in trust payable on demand to the Government. Payments to the Government were to be completed in twenty
years and the rate of interest agreed upon was 5 per cent. The Government, in agreeing to accept $2,100,000 with interest, as full payment
of its claims, thereby absorbed a loss ultimately of around $1,275,000

[12]Statutes of Manitoba, 1932, c. 52.

arising out of its 1929 guarantee to the banks. The Government also met the immediate financial problem of the elevator company by advancing $300,000 as a callable loan. This loan continued to be shown as a deferred liability, reduced to $258,089, at the year ending July 31, 1946 but has since been paid off. To safeguard its interests the Government insisted that it should have representation on the Board of Directors of the Manitoba Pool Elevators Limited, and two members subsequently were appointed. The Manitoba Pool Elevators Limited was reorganized, the Manitoba Wheat Pool having suspended operations. The reorganization resulted in the election of a new president of the Manitoba Pool Elevators Limited and the retirement of the official in charge of country operations.

The assistance that the Government of Manitoba gave to the Pool organization at this time of crisis in its affairs enabled it to continue to function but, despite this assistance, it had to go carefully on account of its financial weakness. Prior to 1931 the Manitoba Pool had operated two terminals at the Head of the Lakes, No. 1, which was purchased from the central selling agency in 1928, and No. 2, which was leased from the Gillespie Grain Company. In August, 1931 Manitoba Pool Elevators Limited assumed operation of Terminal No. 1 and during the year acquired title to it subject to a mortgage held by the Alberta and Saskatchewan Pools. At about the same time, on account of a particularly poor crop in Manitoba in 1931 the Manitoba Pool terminated its lease with the Gillespie Grain Company which still had two years to run. As a result of this action legal proceedings were instituted against the Manitoba Pool by the Gillespie Grain Company. Judgment in favour of the latter was given for $77,486.30. Following the failure of the Pool to pay off the judgment, execution was issued against the Pool's assets. The sheriff returned a report that the Pool had nothing upon which he could seize. Thereupon, on November 5, 1932, an order was obtained from the court putting the Pool into bankruptcy. This development, however, did not affect the Manitoba Pool Elevators Limited and it assumed the general functions of the Wheat Pool.

At the annual meeting of the Manitoba Pool Elevators Limited in 1932 its board brought to the attention of the delegates the desirability of changing its method of operations to bring it more into line with that used by the Pool organizations in Alberta and Saskatchewan. The change was accomplished by a supplementary agreement arranged between the local associations and the Manitoba Pool Elevators

Limited. This agreement provided, in effect, that the central organization should operate as a line of elevators to the extent of paying operating expenses and interest and principal on its indebtedness to the Province of Manitoba. The local units retained their corporate identity; when they had surpluses, after certain allocations were made, these were placed to their credit but were retained by the central organization as contributions to the working capital of Manitoba Pool Elevators Limited and carried as deferred liabilities to the respective associations.

In 1936 this agreement was modified to permit any association to pay out one-half of its surplus as a patronage dividend to its members. Where a local association had contributed to working capital 50 per cent or more of its capital cost it was given the right to distribute all of its surplus as a patronage dividend. It was felt that it was hardly fair or equitable to require the more successful local associations to contribute indefinitely whatever surpluses they might have to the general organization for working capital. The change made possible the payment of patronage dividends to their members by local associations in successful years. In making refunds to contributors to the working capital reserve the revolving fund principle is applied.[13]

Manitoba Pool Elevators Limited was originally incorporated with a capital stock of 5,000,000 shares of $1.00 par value. Subsequently 2,100,152 shares were issued and outstanding on which $10,000 was paid up. In 1940 this capital stock was cancelled by an act amending the act of incorporation. In keeping with the new act all elevator associations received authority to cancel their capital stock and they now operate on a $1 membership basis. In 1944 legislation was passed providing for the deletion of the word "Limited" from the title, "Manitoba Pool Elevators Limited" and from all the titles of elevator associations in which the word "Limited" appeared. While Manitoba Pool Elevators is now the correct name for the organization it is popularly known as the Manitoba Pool.[14]

Since 1932 the Pool has shown steady growth. In 1934 it again leased the Gillespie Grain Company's terminal, subsequently purchasing this elevator in 1936. In 1938 a third terminal was purchased from the Federal Grain Company. In 1938 it also entered into an agreement with the Alberta Pool to operate a terminal purchased

[13]Manitoba Pool Elevators Limited, *Annual Report*, 1933, 1936, 1937.
[14]Manitoba Pool Elevators, *Twenty Five Years Service.*

by the latter at Port Arthur. The four terminals are operated as a unit, and, under a handling agreement, profits are shared on a per bushel basis between the two Pools. In 1948 the Pool sold one of its small terminals and purchased a larger terminal from the Reliance Grain Company. In addition in 1948 it leased the Canadian National Railways' terminal No. 6 under a yearly arrangement which it renewed for the 1949-50 season. With these facilities the total terminal capacity operated by Manitoba Pool Elevators is 15,750,000 bushels.

Expansion has also taken place in its line of country elevators. In 1940 the Pool purchased 41 country elevators from Western Canada Flour Mills; in 1943, 14 from the Federal Grain Company; and in 1948, 20 from the Reliance Grain Company. In addition in 1948 it built 11 new elevators. At the present time 201 elevator associations own and operate 246 elevators. Handlings in 1948-49 amounted to 44,277,811 bushels of grain or 45.51 per cent of all grain delivered to licensed country elevators and mills in the province of Manitoba.

Under prudent management the Manitoba Pool has worked its way out of the difficulties that it encountered in the early thirties and has attained a generally strong financial position. With extensive handlings and heavy storage earnings when carryovers were large profits from operations have been substantial. For the year ending July 31, 1949 the net surplus on local elevator operations before provision for Dominion and provincial income taxes amounted to $1,431,792; on terminal operations to $835,423. Total assets were valued at $11,789,065. Current assets were placed at $6,624,566 and included cash in the bank and with paying agents to the amount of $1,583,306, and Government of Canada bonds valued at $1,001,000. The Pool's liabilities are chiefly to its own members. They include a fifteen-year debenture bond issue due in 1963 for $2,039,000 and loans to working capital amounting to $4,361,300. The final payment retiring the indebtedness of the Pool to the Province of Manitoba was made in October, 1949, well in advance of the date set by the agreement.

The Manitoba Pool is fully abreast of the Alberta and Saskatchewan Pools in maintaining an active field service and in promoting various other activities designed to strengthen the co-operative movement and to enrich the rural life of the province. In 1943 the *Manitoba Co-operator*, a weekly publication, was established; it is published by the Pool in association with five other provincial co-operative organizations. It now has a circulation exceeding 50,000.

Although the three provincial Pools are separate and distinct organizations they work very closely together. They own jointly and operate two subsidiary companies for the purpose of reducing agency and insurance costs. These are the Canadian Pool Agencies Limited, organized in 1928, and the Pool Insurance Company, dating from 1939. In 1924 the three Pools established the Canadian Co-operative Wheat Producers Limited to provide liaison between them and a centre for united action, to act as their marketing agency for selling grain, and to assemble and distribute information for them.   The president of each of the provincial Pools is on the executive of this body. The selling function of this central agency ended on July 31, 1930 as a result of the appointment on behalf of the Dominion Government of John I. McFarland to take over the task of disposing of the Pools' surplus stock of wheat. The central agency, however, was retained for its other purposes. It serves as a medium to unify Pool policy with respect to legislation, freight rates, and other matters where the common interest of the three organizations are affected. It also represents the Pools in its contacts with such organizations as the Canadian Federation of Agriculture, the International Federation of Agricultural Producers, and the Food and Agriculture Organization.

Pool officials occupy an important position as the spokesmen and representatives of a large sector of western farm opinion, particularly with respect to the agricultural policies pursued by the Dominion Government. The increased intervention of the Dominion Government in western agricultural affairs, begun in the 1930's and greatly expanded during the war, produced many situations where the need for representations to Ottawa were felt. On these occasions delegations of Pool officials appeared at Ottawa as the avowed champions of western grain grower interests. The forcefulness of their leadership, combined with the support of their large membership throughout the three Prairie Provinces, give their representations considerable weight at times with the Dominion Government. The Pools were active in advocating higher initial payments for grain when these were being decided upon and they are the spearhead of many attacks launched against the Winnipeg Grain Exchange and the principle of freedom in grain marketing. Hence, they have been particularly identified with the agitation to have the Canadian Wheat Board placed upon a permanent basis with monopoly powers to cover all western grains. Their strength was strikingly demonstrated with respect to the ultimate success of the policies they put forward before the Royal Grain Inquiry

Commission of 1938. They are generally credited with having been the driving force behind the negotiation of the British Wheat Agreement. They have been assiduous in keeping alive the project of an international wheat agreement, and when such an agreement was concluded in Washington in 1948, public tribute was paid to the efforts made by the Pools in consistently seeking a way to "get a steady contract for the farmer."[15]

In the distribution of honours after World War II the President of the Saskatchewan Pool, Mr. John Wesson, and the President of the Manitoba Pool, Mr. W. J. Parker, received respectively the O.B.E. and the M.B.E. in recognition of their services to Canada during the course of the struggle. Mr. Parker has served on the board of the Canadian Broadcasting Corporation and has recently become a Director of the Canadian National Railways. He has also acted as Chairman of the Board of Governors of the University of Manitoba. Mr. R. D. Purdy, General Manager of the Alberta Pool, is a Director of the Bank of Montreal.

In 1931 the three Pools assumed a debt of over $22,000,000 to their respective governments as a result of the disasters of 1929 and 1930. In 1949 this debt had been completely repaid plus $12,300,000 in interest, a total of more than $34,000,000. After twenty-five years of operations the three Pools own 1,883 country elevators and 8 terminals, nearly one-third of Canada's licensed grain storage. They operate in addition to elevators 5 plants and mills, 3 livestock yards, and 1,500 houses, coal sheds, etc., in the service of their organizations. These properties represent an investment of over $55,000,000 in which 208,000 members have an equity exceeding $32,000,000. In the last eighteen years the three Pools have not only recovered from the calamitous years of 1929 and 1930 but they have greatly strengthened and consolidated their position.

[15]Statement of J. Vesugar, head of delegation from India, Plenary Session, International Wheat Council, Washington, March 6, 1948.

11

The United Grain Growers Limited

THE United Grain Growers Limited occupies a unique position in the marketing structure of the Canadian grain trade. Originating in 1906 as the Grain Growers' Grain Company, and assuming its present name in 1917 on amalgamation with the Alberta Farmers' Co-operative Elevator Company (1913), it is rooted in the very beginnings of the grain growers' co-operative movement in Western Canada. Prior to the rise of the Pools it shared with the Saskatchewan Co-operative Elevator Company (1911) the co-operative field in the marketing of western grain. The latter company was absorbed in 1926 into the Saskatchewan Pool, but the United Grain Growers Limited retained its identity and continues to exemplify the general philosophy of co-operation in Western Canada in its earlier stages of development. The movement of the early days was of a broad agrarian nature and the old Grain Growers' Grain Company was an essential part of the initial challenge of the western grain growers to the monopoly position enjoyed by the private grain trade, by reason of the latter's arrangements with the railways, in handling grain at country shipping points. During those early years the company was under constant attack and bore the full brunt of the struggle which arose between those interested in marketing grain co-operatively and the established grain trade.[1]

As an organization the United Grain Growers Limited has been facetiously described as "having one foot in the pit [i.e., the Grain Exchange] and one foot in the Pool." In a sense this is not an unfair characterization of its position between the Pools, in the establishment

[1]See D. A. MacGibbon, *The Canadian Grain Trade* (Toronto, 1932), pp. 50, 324-5.

of which it played an important part, and the private grain trade.
Actually, the shareholders of the United Grain Growers Limited
have always prided themselves on their close adherence to the
plan of organization developed by the Rochdale Equitable Pioneers
Society, the real founders of the co-operative movement. The status
of the United Grain Growers Limited, not only as a co-operative
society but as a pioneer in agricultural co-operation in Canada, was
fully recognized by the Royal Commission on Co-operatives and by
the Canadian Minister of Finance in dealing with the taxation of
co-operatives.[2]

From the standpoint of control the organization is very like the
Pools. Its 35,000 members are grouped into 281 locals whose membership varies from 50 to 250 each. Each member has one vote in the
local to elect a delegate to the annual meeting, and each local is
represented by one delegate. General policies are determined at the
annual meeting. The delegates also elect four directors annually for
a three-year term. This gives the company a board of twelve directors,
four of whom retire each year.

Like the Rochdale Pioneers and British co-operative organizations
generally, the United Grain Growers is a co-operative with share
capital and in this respect resembles an ordinary joint-stock company.
There are, however, limitations upon the amount of stock which can
be individually held, and holdings of the voting stock are restricted
practically to active farmers. The original Grain Growers' Grain
Company had an authorized capital of $2,000,000 in shares of $25 par
value. Only farmers or their wives were eligible for membership,
and ownership was limited to 40 shares. While authority was obtained
under the charter to distribute patronage dividends, these originally
were limited to shareholders and distributed only after paying 8 per
cent on capital. The latter requirement is in accord with the Rochdale
conception of "hiring" capital for co-operative purposes. These provisions were modified in 1915 to permit payments of patronage dividends to non-member patrons while the rate of interest payable to
shareholders as a prerequisite was left to the discretion of the directors.
When the United Grain Growers Limited was formed in 1917 the
capital of the new organization was placed at $5,000,000.

The United Grain Growers operates under a charter secured by
a special act of Parliament and is the only co-operative producers'
association incorporated in this way. The Grain Growers' Grain

[2]United Grain Growers Limited, *Annual Report*, 1946, p. 18.

Company was originally formed under the Manitoba Companies Act and for some years functioned as a commission firm. When it decided to enter the field of elevator operation it obtained in 1911 a special act of Parliament which gave it the necessary powers to do so. An amendment to this Act was secured in 1917 to cover the amalgamation of the Grain Growers' Grain Company with the Alberta Farmers' Co-operative Elevator Company, and the company assumed its present name. In 1941 a further amendment to the charter was procured when the capital structure of the company was reorganized.[3]

Reorganization became necessary because the company wished to retain its nature as essentially a co-operative company controlled by its farmer members. With the passage of time an increasing proportion of the share capital was being held by persons who were no longer active farmers. To remedy this situation the shares of the company were split into Class A Preferred shares and Class B shares. Class A shares are of par value of $20, do not give voting powers, are redeemable on call for $24, and carry a dividend rate of 5 per cent. These dividends to the extent earned must be paid ahead of any other dividends. Individual holdings may not exceed 250 shares. Class B shares are of par value of $5, carry voting powers, and the issue is restricted to active farmer customers. Holdings are limited to 25 shares per person. The company has the right to repurchase these shares, but must in practice resell them, since it may not hold more than 10 per cent of the total number outstanding at any time. Under these arrangements the control and direction of the company rest with its active farmer membership.

While the payment of patronage dividends has always been part of the policy of the company its performance in this direction was limited for many years by the members' desire to build up a strong financial position and expand elevator facilities. Characteristically, a large part of its earnings were ploughed back into the company. The first attempt in 1906 to pay patronage dividends encountered the violent opposition of the private grain trade and the company was suspended from the trading privileges of the Winnipeg Grain Exchange on the technical ground that such payments violated the commission rule of the Exchange. This suspension continued for some months, causing great difficulties for the company; reinstatement only occurred when the company agreed to abide by the rules of the Exchange as then interpreted. The attitude of the Exchange later became less

[3]Statutes of Canada, 1911, c. 80; 1917, c. 79; 1940-41, c. 40.

intransigent on this question, and patronage dividends were paid by the United Grain Growers Limited for the fiscal years ending in 1926, 1927, and 1928. Since these payments, however, were only applicable to purchases of street grain the issue raised by the earlier attempt to pay patronage dividends on grain handled on a carload basis did not technically arise. There followed a lengthy period when, owing to short crops, the earnings of the company were not sufficient to provide for a return on capital stock and the payment of patronage dividends. With returning prosperity in 1940-41 the United Grain Growers Limited resumed the practice of paying patronage dividends, but upon the wider basis of payments on all grain delivered to United Grain Growers Limited elevators. These payments for the five years ending July 31, 1946 exceeded in total $2,500,000.[4]

The United Grain Growers Limited took a very active part in the discussions which followed the disappearance of the first Canadian Wheat Board of 1919, and which led to the inauguration of the Pools in 1923, but it was not itself absorbed by the new organizations. At the time the Pools were being formed the company's membership was sharply divided between Pool and non-Pool farmers. In order to assure adequate elevator services while avoiding unnecessary duplication of farmer-owned elevators, and also to assure continuing services to non-Pool farmers, the company made proposals to the Alberta and Manitoba Pools for the operation of elevators through new provincial companies to be established under the joint control of United Grain Growers Limited and the Pools. At the same time the United Grain Growers Limited firmly maintained the right of its non-Pool farmer members to make use of the company's facilities in selling their grain individually through the open market. The plan of joint operation was accepted by the Alberta Pool, to which the United Grain Growers Limited had given substantial assistance in getting started, but negotiations finally bogged down over the appointment of a manager to the new joint company. Each party wanted its own man in the position and neither would give way. In Manitoba the break came with the refusal of the Pool representatives to negotiate on the ground that the two systems of marketing were fundamentally opposed, and that the handling of pool and non-pool grain through the same elevator system was "incompatible."[5]

Although the United Grain Growers Limited and the Pools decided

---

[4]United Grain Growers Limited, *Annual Report*, 1946, p. 28.
[5]*The United Grain Growers Record*, published by the company, 1944, p. 69.

to go their separate ways an effort was made by the former to avoid the indiscriminate duplication of farmer-owned elevators. At quite a number of points the United Grain Growers Limited sold its elevators to the provincial Pools with a view to avoiding losses from duplication of facilities where there was insufficient grain to warrant two elevators. The decision to sell or not to sell to the Pool was made after consultation with the company's local shareholders. By the end of the crop year 1927-28 the company had sold a total of 53 elevators to the Pools and had also leased 20 other elevators to them. Competition, however, between the two types of farmer-owned co-operative organizations continues to exist at many local shipping points, has, in fact, increased with the expansion of their respective elevator systems. At 400 shipping points or more the United Grain Growers Limited is in competition with the Pools. At about fifty of these points the only competition is that between the two co-operatives.

While in a business way the competition between these two organizations is quite as keen as that between the co-operatives and the private elevator companies, a certain amount of ill feeling that developed at the outset between the Pools and the United Grain Growers Limited over the latter's refusal to disregard the rights of its members who were unfavourable to pooling, and to allow its absorption into the Pools, has largely disappeared. All four organizations (the three provincial Pools and the United Grain Growers) are associated through provincial agricultural federations and the Canadian Federation of Agriculture. In 1937 discussions occurred between the United Grain Growers Limited and the Alberta Pool, and later the three Pools, on the possibility of fusion but nothing developed from them.

The United Grain Growers Limited exemplifies a point of view that distinguishes it both from the Pool organizations and from the private elevator companies. When the establishment of a western wheat pool was first mooted, officials of the United Grain Growers Limited were prominent in promoting the movement, but this advocacy was always subject on its part to the overriding consideration that the individual farmer had a right to decide by what method he would market his grain. As noted above, after its insistence on this principle led to a break with the Pool organizations, the Company sold its elevators to the Pools at those points where a majority of its shareholders were in favour of pool marketing, and withdrew.

For the same reason the United Grain Growers Limited has never advocated establishing the Canadian Wheat Board permanently in a monopoly position to market Canadian wheat, though it urged the establishment of the Canadian Wheat Board in 1935 and recognized the need of its monopolistic powers to meet emergency conditions created by war and its aftermath. In advocating the retention of the Wheat Board as organized in 1935 it has always emphasized its value as an instrument by which the Dominion Government could ensure to grain growers minimum prices in years of depression, but it has also always been opposed to any compulsory system of marketing,[6] except under emergency conditions.

The United Grain Growers Limited never accepted the doctrine, made popular by Aaron Sapiro, that by means of a 100 per cent pool Canadian grain growers could exact a higher price from foreign consumers of Canadian wheat than competitive conditions would warrant.[7] The idea that international combinations of wheat producers could advance the price of wheat was not supported by the company either; it could not see that the International Wheat Agreement of 1933 would produce any useful results. Its essential view has been that the wheat growers of Western Canada are primarily engaged in the production of wheat for export, and the future prospects of this industry are bound up with greater freedom in international trade and a reversal of the trend towards rigid controls.[8] It supported, however, the London and Washington negotiations which led to the present wheat agreement and one of its directors was a member of the Canadian delegation.

In conducting its business the United Grain Growers Limited has relied upon its own elevators to handle the grain of its farmer members and employs the open market when available to afford to them the facilities of selling it on the basis of values established competitively. Hence the United Grain Growers Limited has never advocated the closing of the futures market of the Winnipeg Grain Exchange. In 1931 the President of the United Grain Growers Limited, in giving evidence before the Stamp Commission, said the opinions expressed by some witnesses, who were unfavourable to the futures market, seemed hardly fair or completely representative. He added that his own experience as a farmer and official of a farmers' grain

[6]*Ibid.*, p. 39.
[7]See MacGibbon, *The Canadian Grain Trade*, pp. 69, 354-5.
[8]*Presentation of the United Grain Growers Limited to the Royal Grain Inquiry Commission Conducted by Mr. Justice Turgeon. No. 1, General Statement* (Winnipeg, 1937), pp. 24-31.

company was that the futures market was a distinct benefit to them as a class.[9] In its principal brief to the Turgeon Commission of 1938 the company recommended the appointment of a supervisor of the Winnipeg market along the lines suggested by the Stamp Commission.[10] The solution to the problem of the western grain growers, in the view of the company as stated on various occasions, is not found in the machinery of marketing but in efficiency in production and in enlarged markets.

Moreover, as a further mark of its independence of viewpoint, in the controversies which developed in the nineteen-twenties over whether terminal elevators should be permitted to continue mixing wheat of various grades before final inspection[11] the United Grain Growers Limited took a decided stand in favour of this practice. It argued that mixing lessened the spreads between the lower grades and the highest. Provided that proper safeguards of inspection were maintained to protect the quality of the export grades, it believed that no injury would result to the quality or reputation abroad of Canadian exports of wheat, and that mixing would be a decided advantage to the western grain grower in disposing of off grades. It opposed, therefore, the prohibition of mixing in the higher grades when this step was taken by Parliament in 1929. Nor has it changed its position in this respect. In 1937 it reported at its annual meeting that investigations made by its research department confirmed its contention in that the spreads between different grades of wheat had widened following the changes in the Canada Grain Act introduced earlier.[12]

The United Grain Growers has always been subject to the levies of the Canadian Income War Tax Act. When the Income Tax Act was passed in 1917 it did not seek exemption or make any effort to avoid the tax. As a member of the Canadian Council of Agriculture it had advocated personal and corporation income taxes and felt that any other attitude would be inconsistent with its previous position. When the Income War Tax Act was amended in 1930 to exempt certain co-operative organizations, the terms of the amendment were not wide enough to apply to the United Grain Growers Limited.

[9]*Report of the Royal Commission to Inquire into Trading in Grain Futures* (Ottawa, 1931), p. 55.

[10]*Presentation of the United Grain Growers Limited to Mr. Justice Turgeon*, p. 37.

[11]See MacGibbon, *The Canadian Grain Trade*, pp. 158, 162, 168-77.

[12]United Grain Growers Limited, *Annual Report*, 1930, 1932, 1937.

Actually, until 1940 the payment of income tax did not constitute a severe burden upon the company, but this was no longer the case following the sharp increase in income tax rates as a result of the war. In the five years beginning with 1940 the company paid out as income and excess profits taxes over $900,000.

With the appointment of the Royal Commission on Co-operatives the United Grain Growers Limited set out to vindicate its status as a co-operative. As a co-operative it alleged discrimination against it in the levying of income tax in comparison with the position enjoyed by the Pools. It argued generally that patronage dividends should be deductible from earnings before the calculation of income tax. In this connection it pointed out that, if this deduction were not allowed, in addition to the income tax it had already paid from 1940 to 1944 inclusive it would be liable for a further sum in taxes exceeding $1,500,000. It also held that dividends paid by the United Grain Growers Limited to its shareholders should be exempt up to 5 per cent on the ground that "there should be no difference for taxation purposes between co-operatives organized on share capital or on a loan basis."[13] In the outcome the United Grain Growers Limited's position as a co-operative enterprise was fully vindicated. Patronage dividends secured exemption, but the company failed in its plea that dividends on its capital stock should be treated as the "hire" of capital and, therefore, be deductible as an expense of operation.

The position taken by the United Grain Growers Limited on problems of public policy emphasizes its strongly independent position. In its dislike of controls, in its opposition to the establishment of a permanent system of compulsory marketing through the agency of a centralized grain board, in its support of the mixing privilege, and in its recognition of the benefits of a futures market, the company has taken a stand similar to that of the private elevator interests. On the other hand, its advocacy of tax exemption for patronage dividends, its support of measures designed to increase the welfare of western farm producers, and particularly the generous financial assistance given to farmer organizations, mark its affiliations with the co-operative movement.[14]

As a grain marketing organization the United Grain Growers

[13]*Presentation of the United Grain Growers Limited to the Royal Commission on Co-operatives* (Ottawa, 1945).

[14]Financial assistance given to various farm organizations exceeds $350,000. *United Grain Growers Record*, p. 65.

Limited has remained distinct from the private elevator companies. It is not a member of the North-West Line Elevators Association. In buying grain, under open market conditions, at country points it buys on the basis of its own market appraisals but co-operates with the Pools and the private trade in informing local elevator agents of daily fluctuations in price. It is a member of the Winnipeg Grain Exchange and makes full use of such facilities as are now available. Membership in the Grain Exchange does not, however, distinguish it from the Pools or the Canadian Wheat Board.

While hedging the purchases of its members protected the United Grain Growers Limited from the difficulties that attended the operations of the Pools when the price of wheat fell in 1929, the period of widespread crop failures, low prices, and short crops between 1929 and 1938 brought serious problems and reduced earnings to all the elevator companies. During these years the United Grain Growers Limited's earlier policy of building up strong reserves enabled it to meet unfavourable conditions over an extended period without undue difficulty. No dividends were paid, however, for the fiscal years ending in July of 1937, 1938, and 1939.[15] With the turn of the tide, bountiful crops coinciding with the war and large carryovers, earnings have risen to high levels.

During the period as a whole the United Grain Growers Limited expanded its elevator system and at the same time strengthened its financial position. Its balance sheet as at July 31, 1948 showed an investment in elevators and other capital facilities amounting to $14,658,692 against which depreciation reserves had been set up which totalled $7,813,915. Current and working assets were $7,058,596, which, after deducting current liabilities, left it with a working capital of $2,900,337. Outstanding 3 per cent serial bonds and 4 per cent sinking-fund bonds amounted to $3,750,000. The shareholders' equity including capital stock, reserves, and surplus totalled $6,153,746. Legislation was obtained in 1950 to enable the company to increase its capital from $5,000,000 to $7,500,000.[16]

The expansion of its elevator system has been particularly noteworthy. In 1932 the total number of country elevators owned was 468. In connection with these elevators it had 53 annexes, 292 coal sheds, 224 supply warehouses, and 148 agents' cottages. By 1948 the number of its country elevators had increased to 628 with 104 perma-

[15]United Grain Growers Limited, *Annual Report*, 1937, 1938, 1939.
[16]*Ibid.*, 1949; Statutes of Canada, 1950, c. 67.

nent annexes and 329 temporary annexes, 364 coal sheds, 296 flour houses, and 348 agents' cottages. A large part of this increase occurred in 1948 when the company purchased 110 country elevators from the Reliance Grain Company. Of these 96 were in Saskatchewan. The company has its own terminal at Port Arthur with a capacity of 5,500,000 bushels and operates another terminal at Vancouver with a capacity of 2,600,000 bushels. This terminal is leased from the National Harbours Board.

For technical reasons these terminals are managed through a subsidiary company. In addition, the company owns four other subsidiary companies: the Country Guide Limited, the Public Press Limited, and the United Grain Growers' Securities Company Limited, as well as an export company. An important part of the business of the Securities Company consists in placing insurance on the main company's properties and on the grain carried in its elevators. It also handles hail insurance for farmers, as well as fire, automobile, and accident insurance.

The need of an organ to represent the grain growers' point of view was felt very early in the co-operative movement. To meet this need a paper was established in 1908 by the Grain Growers' Grain Company, which was originally named the *Grain Growers' Guide*. The paper was financed by the company until it became self-supporting. By 1913 it had the largest circulation of any farm journal published in Canada. In 1926 the *Guide* was changed from a weekly to a semi-monthly; in 1928 the name was changed to the *Country Guide*; and in 1930 it became a monthly. In 1936 the *Guide* bought out the *Nor'-West Farmer*. The magazine, now enlarged in size, has a subscription list of nearly 200,000 and the largest circulation of any publication of this nature in the Commonwealth.

In the earlier stages of its history the United Grain Growers Limited and its predecessor, the Grain Growers' Grain Company, largely as a result of the pressure of its shareholders, branched out into a variety of ventures designed to serve the farming constituency of Western Canada. These activities included the manufacture and sale of lumber, sale of farm machinery, and livestock marketing. Some of these enterprises were successful; others were not, and for this or other reasons were closed out. For a considerable period the company successfully operated an export business in grain through New York and Vancouver, but discontinued this business in 1935 because of the speculative risks involved and the reduced flow of grain for export from short crops. The United Grain Growers Limited has continued to carry on a farm supplies department through which it sells mainly binder twine, flour, and coal. An important development in recent years has been the manufacture of a line of livestock feeds, with a plant located in Edmonton, Alberta.

It is, however, as an independent, farmer-owned, co-operative grain company, with its own country and terminal elevators, that the United Grain Growers Limited must be known. As such it has registered substantial success. Moreover, in the realistic presentations it has made to various royal commissions and in public questions affecting farmer interest it has exerted a decided influence upon the nature of agrarian legislation. It is somewhat remarkable, and a tribute to the ability with which these farmer co-operators have managed their business, that the company has continued to show vigorous growth while holding its own against the competition of the Pool organizations on one side and that of the private elevator companies on the other. A recent indication of the support that the company receives from its members is shown in the announcement in its 1948 annual report that an offering of $500,000 of new capital stock had been oversubscribed and that this was being followed by another issue to the same amount.

12

The independent companies:
The Winnipeg Grain Exchange

ALTHOUGH in the last fifteen years the Pools have strengthened their position in the grain trade by reason of their greatly improved financial situation, this improvement has not noticeably occurred at the expense of the larger independent grain companies, nor, as we have seen, of the United Grain Growers Limited. A general indication of the importance of each group is afforded by the relative amounts of grain handled by the competing organizations at country points. For the crop year 1946-47 the three Pools handled approximately 41 per cent of the grain marketed. The balance was handled by the independent companies and the United Grain Growers Limited. The percentage handled varies from province to province and also somewhat from year to year, chiefly because of varying regional climatic conditions. On the whole, the situation seems to have settled down to keen but stabilized conditions of competition between the producer-owned companies and the independent interests, a condition calculated to give the producer the greatest degree of efficiency and service in the handling of his product.

One general development of interest has been an appreciable reduction in the number of country elevators serving the producers. The number of country elevators licensed for the crop year of 1947-48 was 5,326 compared with 5,652 for the crop year of 1932-33, a decrease of over 300. This reduction, however, has been more than counterbalanced by the erection of larger elevators when replacements have occurred or when new elevators have been built. In addition, many annexes have been constructed to supplement the storage capacity of other elevators in use. Licensed storage capacity at country points for the crop year of 1932-33 was reported to be 190,173,800 bushels, and at the end of 1947 to be 190,644,500. Of this capacity the Pools controlled space for 97,902,300 bushels, slightly over one-half of the total.

For the independent companies the period has been one marked by the consolidation of various companies to form larger systems. On the whole, the stronger companies have become larger but several well-known moderately sized companies have disappeared, in certain instances because of the death or retirement of the principal shareholders in the concern. Consolidation is not a new development; the trend towards concentration of control was already clearly apparent in 1932.[1] For the crop year of 1932-33 nineteen country elevator or flour milling companies operated systems of country elevators with a total of 3,167 country elevators. The average number of country elevators operated by an individual company was 167. One company had 418 country elevators and another company 326; other systems were less extensive. For the crop year 1947-48 eight country elevator companies and one flour milling company operated 2,538 country elevators with an average of 254 units per system. Of these enterprises one company owned 436 country elevators and three other companies exceeded 300 elevators each. The reduction in the number of companies has meant a decrease in head office expenses and expansion has enhanced the ability of these companies to meet and offer competition. The trend towards larger enterprises has not ceased, and the probable end result will be the gradual emergence in the independent sector of the grain trade of a small number of really large companies, with the balance distributed among relatively small enterprises, including local ventures operating a single elevator. Of the latter type there were 34 reported for the crop year of 1947-48.

Another significant feature has been the interchange of country elevator facilities at many points between competing companies. When companies have found that they owned elevators at certain points which for various reasons were not proving profitable, or were too far away from their other elevators to be convenient to service or to supervise, sales have been made to other companies located there, the transaction usually being balanced by the purchase of elevators from other companies at a similar disadvantage at points where they themselves were firmly established. Interchanges of this nature have tended

---

[1]See D. A. MacGibbon, *The Canadian Grain Trade* (Toronto, 1932), p. 319.

to increase the amount of grain handled per unit of operation for each company with a reduction in the costs of operation and supervision. The process of interchange has been one element in reducing the total number of country elevators in operation.

The country elevators owned by companies that have disappeared without being absorbed outright into another company have been disposed of piecemeal, partly to the producer-owned companies and partly to the independent companies. The object of purchase has been the desire to round out the system of a company or to strengthen its position at a certain point. Where an amalgamation has occurred, which usually involves a certain number of duplications, surplus elevators have been sold or dismantled. The National Grain Company, now with 356 country elevators, represents a fusion made in 1940 of the elevator companies controlled by the Peavey interests of Minneapolis. With its consummation the British American, Northern, National, and Grand Trunk Pacific elevator companies disappeared. Federal Grain Limited, with 436 country elevators, completely owns the Alberta Pacific Grain Company (1943), with 304 elevators. In 1940 the N. Bawlf Grain Company's country elevators were taken over by the Alberta Pacific Grain Company, Federal Grain Limited, and the United Grain Growers Limited. The last large country elevator company to disappear has been the Reliance Grain Company, which sold its elevators after the death of one of its principal shareholders, Mr. Sidney Smith. The Reliance operated 228 country elevators, the bulk of which were acquired by the United Grain Growers Limited and the Searle Grain Company. Thus, although there has been a reduction in the number of country elevators, there is no lack of facilities to meet producers' requirements. An outcome of these developments has been, by and large, that the independent companies have increased their ability to maintain their position in the face of sharp competition offered to them by the producer-owned companies. Competition between the Pools and the independent companies has not, of course, precluded equally severe competition between members of the latter group.

The reduction or the increase in the number of country elevators owned by an individual company is significant from another angle. The size of a country elevator system conditions the amount of terminal facilities a company will require. Transfers in the ownership or operation of terminal elevators at Port Arthur and Fort William have reflected developments in the country elevator field. The

Saskatchewan Pool, with its extensive line of country elevators, has three of the largest terminals at the Head of the Lakes and is increasing its terminal storage capacity to make good the loss sustained at Saskatchewan Pool Terminal No. 5 by dust explosion in 1945. Since 1932 the available storage capacity at the Head of the Lakes has declined, partly on account of the scrapping of two old terminals, each with a capacity of 2,500,000 bushels, which were owned by the Canadian Pacific Railway Company. The Northland Elevator, with storage capacity of 7,500,000 bushels, also owned by the C.P.R., has not been operated recently. The dust explosion which wrecked Saskatchewan Pool Elevator No. 5 entailed a loss of 2,100,000 bushels storage capacity. In 1932 there was total storage space at Fort William and Port Arthur for 92,782,210 bushels and in 1947 for 78,702,210 bushels.

A basic reason for the decline of terminal storage capacity at the Head of the Lakes has been the flow of a substantial volume of grain westward through Pacific ports, where terminal storage capacity has remained stable at approximately 20,000,000 bushels. When shipments via the Pacific almost ceased during the war, the urgent need for additional storage space at Fort William and Port Arthur was met by the construction of temporary storage bins with a total capacity of 50,000,000 bushels. This temporary storage space has since been removed.

The fact that a number of lives were lost in a dust explosion at Saskatchewan Pool Elevator No. 5 in 1945 led to an extensive investigation by the Ontario Government of the conditions under which employees of these terminals performed their duties. As a result, additional safety installations were required to be made. These included installing in each elevator dust removal apparatus at a cost to each terminal of from $100,000 upwards, depending upon the size of the terminal. While these installations have added to the capital investment of each elevator without bringing in additional revenue, they have greatly abated the dust nuisance and improved the working conditions of the employees. Dust removal systems are also being installed in the interior terminal elevators operated under the Board of Grain Commissioners for Canada.

Except for the general control by the Canadian Wheat Board of the flow of grain forward from country shipping points to the terminals and the mills, the technique of handling Canadian grain in its details has remained practically unchanged. The country elevator operators, when acting as agents for the Wheat Board, issue participation certificates in addition to the usual elevator receipts, but apart from this procedure grain is delivered and goes forward in the usual way. It is weighed and inspected by the officials of the Board of Grain Commissioners at the terminals, and all of the safeguards of the Canada Grain Act have been retained except where the increased powers of controlling movement given to the Wheat Board come into play. When grain intended for the Wheat Board reaches the terminals it is delivered to the Board. The fact must be clearly grasped that the Canadian Wheat Board is essentially a marketing organization superimposed upon the structure of grain handling developed through many years of growth and experience. Incidentally, one feature of the Wheat Board's activities has been a heavy increase in clerical work in the offices of the grain companies, growing out of the requirements of the Wheat Board in the fulfilling of its duties.

The establishment of the Canadian Wheat Board and the gradual expansion of its activities, particularly during the war, inevitably brought a decline in the importance of the Winnipeg Grain Exchange as the heart and focus of the grain-marketing structure of Western Canada. Public attention tended to shift away from the reduced activities of the Exchange to the policies of the Dominion Government and the administrative work of the Canadian Wheat Board. Viewed broadly, the circumstances which account for the decline in free marketing in the West were partly of a regional nature and partly of a world-wide character.

An outstanding phenomenon in the interval between the Great Depression and the close of the Second World War was the change that took place in the methods employed in the sale and purchase of wheat and other grains that enter into international trade. The older system of private trading through the medium of open markets, employed in countries of export and of import, largely gave way to bulk purchases negotiated between governments or government agencies and frequently handled in detail under the supervision of administrative officials. Trading ceased to be individual and in a strict sense became international. Under these conditions the prices that were agreed upon were determined under the influence of a variety of pressures to which governments are subject. If the prices established in this way proved to be not in accord with the marketing trend of world values, either the producer or the consumer suffered or he was protected by governmental action and the burden fell upon the taxpayer. Except through gain or loss in prestige the actual negotiators were not affected; their private capital was not at venture. All the propaganda resources of their governments were behind them to prove that the agreements negotiated were the best possible.

Under a system of private trading on an open market prices were established by the bids and offers of a large group of buyers and sellers who watched world conditions of supply and demand with a critical eye and made their appraisals in the light of their personal judgments. In so far as they were able to do so they protected themselves from losses by hedging their transactions in the futures markets, but where their judgment proved faulty and losses did occur the penalty was upon themselves. The result was the establishment of world prices for wheat and other cereals in a market of extreme sensitivity that year in and year out reflected with great accuracy the relationships between supply and demand both immediate and prospective. The growth of state trading seriously impaired this system. While state marketing in food grains did not extend to all countries, it greatly reduced the scope of free marketing, and in Canada, for the time being at least, has led to its disappearance as far as wheat is concerned.

The first shock to the free marketing system came with the First World War when the marketing of wheat under the emergency conditions which developed was brought under the control of governments or government agencies.[2] After the war free markets recovered to a large degree their former position and functioned effectively in establishing international values for wheat and other grains while facilitating the distribution of stocks through private channels of trade. Nevertheless, during this period a definite trend towards overproduction became apparent. This trend owed its origin chiefly to nationalistic government policies, particularly in Europe. It was a reaction in part, but only in part, to the attempts of producer organizations in the exporting countries to get together with a view to obtaining greater returns for their members, which meant higher prices for the European consumer. This aspect of the situation has been given wide publicity, but for military as well as political reasons the governments of European countries were predisposed on their own part to give increased protection to their domestic producers even though the effect was to encourage increased uneconomical production. Another contributing element was the prevalence of high tariffs on

[2] *Ibid.*, pp. 55-65.

manufactured goods in the wheat-exporting countries. High protective duties made it increasingly difficult for European manufacturers to secure access to markets abroad and thereby, in the balance of international trading, to provide their countries with the exchange necessary for a large import of food grains. The explanation for continued over-production thus runs in terms of national policies which were destroying the equilibrating functions of free markets. By 1929 the situation in wheat had definitely become one of serious disequilibrium between world supply and demand.

This disequilibrium was the factor in the Great Depression of 1929-32 which led to such an unprecedented fall in the price of wheat at that time. The reduction in the standard of living of very large agricultural groups compelled fresh interventions of governments, for social as well as for political reasons. Various measures were taken, but all were restrictive in nature. In the importing countries, to protect the foreign exchange position and to sustain national producers, proceedings were initiated designed to increase the use of domestic grains while the flow of imports was controlled and reduced. Regulations became rigid and complex. The methods employed included higher import tariffs, the establishment of control boards, the imposition of embargoes, quota allotments, and the negotiation of purchases through centralized government agencies of such foreign supplies as were absolutely required. In countries of export the urgent problem was to aid producers in the distress caused to them by the prevailing low prices and limited marketing outlets. Price guarantees, ultimately entailing limitations on the amount of wheat allowed to be marketed in a given year, accompanied more immediate and direct forms of government aid.[3] In certain instances surpluses were taken off the market by government agencies and disposed of in various ways, usually under conditions involving a government subsidy. In other instances grain was acquired and held in store to wait for more favourable conditions of sale. All these expedients meant that forces not purely of a commercial nature were having their effect upon the free marketing system for grains. Although the markets continued to operate, their position was being seriously undermined.[4] The decline in the importance of the open market of the Winnipeg Grain Exchange

[3] See above, pp. 17 ff.
[4] For developments in the United States see J. S. Davis, *Wheat and the A.A.A.* (Washington, 1935). Also Food Research Institute, *On Agricultural Policy, 1926-38* (Stanford, Calif., 1939).

must be viewed, therefore, as deriving chiefly from this world change in the methods of international trading in grains induced fundamentally by the protective policies pursued after the First World War and greatly extended by the measures taken during the course of the Great Depression.

In Western Canada the Exchange had not only to face the difficulties caused by the over-all change in world conditions, but had also to meet a peculiarly difficult local situation. On the prairies there has always been a strong tendency on the part of the producers to blame the Exchange and the free marketing system for low prices when these have prevailed. To this must be added a general distrust of the elevator companies stemming from various abuses, now largely eliminated by statutory control and supervision, which were prevalent in the early days of wheat growing in Western Canada. To blame the open market for low prices is to make the error of holding that the method by which exchange values for grain are reached is a cause of low prices instead of being merely a register of the strength of the really determining forces, the current world conditions of supply and demand.

Although several Royal Commissions in Canada, especially the Stamp Commission, after careful investigations found that futures trading, even with its speculative aspects, was of distinct benefit to the producer in the prices he received for his product, these findings did not convince grain growers nor allay discontent with the operations of the open market. The Pools, which had suffered so severely from their failure to estimate correctly the trend of world wheat values in 1929 and to hedge their country purchases, exploited this discontent as part of their general attack on the principles of free marketing while campaigning in favour of a permanent central marketing grain board. The upshot was that in the main the Winnipeg Grain Exchange, under continuous attack from this quarter, bore the brunt of the producers' wrath at low prices and at their unhappy situation. The reaction in Western Canada to low prices in this respect presents a contrast to the situation in the United States where the grain exchanges come under regulation to prevent abuses but where the elimination of free markets in grains has not really been an issue. United States grain growers sought a solution for their difficulties in other expedients.

The appointment of John I. McFarland in November of 1930 to take charge of the surplus holdings of the Canadian Co-operative

Wheat Producers Limited brought a powerful influence to bear upon the operations of the Exchange.[5] Mr. McFarland had been and was an expert operator in the futures market, and in taking up his task chose to work through the market in his endeavour to dispose of the supplies of wheat he had in hand at prices that would avoid loss to the Government. This decision called for operations on the Exchange of large magnitude. While his aim was to raise and stabilize the price of Canadian wheat, nevertheless it must be noted that the presence in the futures market of a bold operator who controlled large stocks of wheat and who was backed by government credit constituted an arbitrary factor in the market that impaired its efficiency both as a marketing channel and as an accurate medium of registering wheat values. This remains true even though Mr. McFarland's efforts to manipulate a rise in price without a change in world conditions proved largely ineffective, the price of wheat continuing to decline until the middle of December of 1932.

On August 15, 1933, following a sensational advance and decline of wheat prices, the Exchange, at the request of the Dominion Government, through Mr. McFarland established minimum prices on the futures market for wheat. The minimum set were the closing prices of August 14.[6] This peg continued in effect for one month, when restrictions on trading were lifted as a result of an improvement in the price situation. Thereafter for a lengthy period the Exchange, without further formal action, co-operated in an uneasy fashion with Mr. McFarland in his attempt to stabilize prices. It was becoming apparent that the Government was endeavouring to use the Exchange as an instrument of government policy, but with little success in an era of deep depression and of abundant supplies of grain.

The effort at stabilization was still in process when the federal Government in 1935 introduced legislation to establish a Canadian grain board. From the nature of the bill it appeared obvious that the effect of the Government's measure would be to eliminate the open market of the Exchange.[7] As a result of the bitter parliamentary struggle which ensued this feature was relinquished and the scope of the Wheat Board Act was limited to wheat, with a proviso that, with government approval, the Board could apply the terms of the statute to oats, barley, flax, and rye. Moreover, in dealing with wheat

[5]See above, pp. 17 ff., 33-4.
[6]Minutes of the Council of the Exchange.
[7]See above, pp. 35-6.

the Board was instructed to utilize "such marketing agencies, including commission merchants, brokers, elevator men, exporters and other persons engaged in or operating facilities for the selling and handling of wheat, as the Board in its discretion may determine." To this was added the power to conduct investigations into the operations of the futures market.[8] While the open market had taken a severe setback it was not at this time put out of business. In practice the Board utilized the facilities of the Exchange to market its holdings. "It was convenient and necessary for the Board to do so because the Exchange was almost invariably used by the trade in initiating and hedging sales or purchases of the actual cash wheat."[9]

On September 6, 1935, on the recommendation of the Wheat Board, the federal Government established delivery prices for wheat on a basis slightly above the current market quotations. Subsequently, the market price rose and remained above this minimum for nearly two months. There followed a decline which continued for about eight months, the price rising again in July of 1936. The result of these fluctuations was that when prices fell below the minimum farmers delivered their wheat to the Wheat Board, but when the open market price rose above the minimum they sold it largely to the private trade. The net effect upon the Exchange was that, when deliveries were being made to the Board, activities in the futures market fell off since the Wheat Board did not hedge deliveries made to it in the country.

This in-and-out or alternative system of marketing, one year the bulk of producer deliveries going to the Board and the next year to the elevator companies, persisted until the closing of the futures market in wheat under war conditions in 1943. For the crop years of 1936-37 and 1937-38 the delivery price was lower than the open market price and these two crops were marketed by the trade. During the crop year of 1938-39 a sharp fall in prices occurred; the delivery price of 80 cents a bushel for No. 1 Northern at Fort William was considerably higher than the open market price and practically all of the 1938 wheat crop was delivered to the Wheat Board. As a result of a further decline in wheat prices, although the initial delivery price was reduced to 70 cents a bushel for the crop year 1939-40, the Board again received a large proportion of the crop. With rising prices in 1940-41 deliveries to the Board fell to approximately 44 per

[8]Statutes of Canada, 1935, c. 53, s. 8 (k).
[9]T. W. Grindley, in Canada Year Book, 1939, p. 573.

cent of the wheat marketed. In 1942-43 there was an increase in the
initial delivery price and the Board received approximately 62 per
cent of the wheat handled. At the beginning of the 1943-44 crop year
wheat prices were rising and deliveries to the trade increasing. On
September 27, 1943 the Dominion Government, with heavy war commitments, intervened and closed the futures market for wheat, making
the Board the sole marketing agency.[10]

The inauguration of a general policy of price control during the
war also led to the shutting-down of the futures markets for coarse
grains. Before the war these markets had functioned without government interference, and continued to do so until the Wartime Prices
and Trade Board, acting through the Wheat Board as its agent, imposed ceilings upon the prices of oats and barley. These prices were
based on the maximum prices registered during the period between
September 15 and October 11, 1941. On December 2, 1941 a ceiling
price on barley was fixed at 64¾ cents per bushel and on January 6,
1942 the maximum price of oats was fixed at 51½ cents. These ceilings
remained effective until March 18, 1947 when the ceiling price of
barley was raised to 93 cents a bushel and of oats to 65 cents a
bushel. (Ceilings were eliminated on October 21, 1947.)

With prices for oats and barley rising rapidly, both grains soon
reached the ceiling level. As the demand continued strong, even
the lower grades commanded the ceiling price. The result was that
the futures market for oats and barley ceased to function since there
was no longer an element of risk or uncertainty about the price
at which grain at country points could be sold. Hence there was
no reason to hedge purchases made there. As a consequence the
futures market for these grains remained dormant during six years
of price control. When ceilings were removed the market reopened
on October 23, 1947. Prices immediately rose in the case of oats from
the ceiling price of 65 cents to a range of from 87 cents for No. 2
C.W. oats to 80 cents for No. 3 Feed oats, and in the case of barley
from 93 cents to a range of from $1.27 for No. 2 C.W. six-row barley
to $1.12 for No. 3 Feed.

In the case of flaxseed, on March 9, 1942 the Minister of Trade
and Commerce announced that the Wheat Board would be empowered to act as the sole agency to receive flaxseed from the producer for the crop year 1942-43. On March 3, 1942, on the request of
the Wheat Board, the Government suspended trading in flaxseed

[10]See above, pp. 61 ff.

futures. Trading was not resumed until August 14, 1948 following the removal of ceiling prices effective August 1, 1948.

Thus, for a considerable period, only the marketing of rye remained to the futures markets of the Exchange, but as the normal production of this cereal in Canada was under 10,000,000 bushels a year, the market was relatively unimportant, as well as being subject to the wide fluctuations in price that limited supplies aggravate.

The general consequence arising from all these restrictions was that the Winnipeg Grain Exchange no longer occupied the premier position in the grain marketing structure of Western Canada. Neither the producers nor the public were able to look to the open market for information about the trend of values. Producers focused their attention upon the acts of the federal Government. They were interested in the prices fixed at Ottawa and brought what pressure they could upon the Government to ensure that the minimum prices established should be remunerative to them. The Canadian Wheat Board, except where it was bound by Government mandate, based its price policy in making sales abroad on the values registered in the American free markets across the border.

The real problem that worries the Exchange is whether it will recover the position it occupied prior to the suspension of futures trading in wheat. With the general relaxation of controls following the close of the war futures trading in oats, barley, and flax was resumed. The negotiation of the British Wheat Agreement deferred a final decision on wheat and when it expired adherence to the International Wheat Agreement left the situation unchanged. The one point upon which all wheat producers are agreed is the importance of maintaining a minimum price to protect them against another catastrophic fall such as occurred between 1930 and 1932. The Exchange has come to accept the principle of an established minimum price even though this may involve years when the bulk of the farmers' wheat is delivered to the Wheat Board. What it is opposed to is the continuance of a state monopoly in wheat marketing. Past experience has shown that unde a voluntary system, when the price of wheat on the open market has risen noticeably above the Wheat Board's initial delivery price, producers have sold largely at current market prices to the independent trade in preference to relying upon the Wheat Board for uncertain additional returns from the participation certificates issued to them by the Board when it takes delivery.

On the other hand, although the reopening of the futures market for oats and barley coincided with a high level of prices for these grains, the Pools and other farm organizations conducted, with considerable success, a strong agitation for making the Canadian Wheat Board the sole marketing agency for all grains. It is doubtful whether they are wholly satisfied with the methods of sale that have been worked out under the Board for the disposal of oats and barley. The Pools continue adamant in their opposition to any return to the open market for wheat, even if this were supplemented by the retention of the Wheat Board to provide protection against unduly low prices by accepting grain for marketing at a guaranteed delivery price; that is, they are opposed to the Wheat Board reverting to the status it occupied before compulsory marketing was instituted as a war measure.

There are several reasons for the Pools' deep hostility to the Exchange. In the first place, the Pools were organized because of the hardships the grain growers experienced from the drop in wheat prices which followed the high levels prevailing during the First World War. The movement represented a protest, after a failure to re-establish a government board in 1922-23, against the returns the producers were receiving on their wheat in marketing it through the ordinary channels of trade. Under the influence of the fiery eloquence of Aaron Sapiro many grain growers were persuaded that, if they had control over the disposal of a large portion of the Canadian export surplus, they could not only eliminate the price hazards involved in the daily fluctuations of the open market but also exact higher prices for Canadian wheat from consumers in the markets of the world. The conjuncture of good harvests and higher prices during the boom years between 1924 and 1929 led them to believe that by organizing the Pools they had succeeded.[11] The crash of 1929 forced them to the conclusion that the Pools were not strong enough to insure their members against the effect of world-wide over-production, an inevitable decline in wheat prices. The agitation for a "100 per cent pool" developed first, but this movement quickly crystallized into a demand for a government board which would be the sole marketing agency for Canadian wheat. From this position the Pools have never wavered.

Another reason is that the Saskatchewan Pool especially contains a strong left wing, which in its political thinking leans towards state socialism. The most powerful member of this group was the late L. C. Brouillette, who was the first vice-president of the organization.

[11]MacGibbon, *The Canadian Grain Trade*, p. 69.

After the death of A. J. McPhail in 1931 he became President, holding that position until his own death in 1937. Mr. Brouillette was a farm leader before he became a Pool official and was responsible for bringing Aaron Sapiro from the United States to direct the organization of the Saskatchewan Pool. Mr. Brouillette was a crusader and in his position of President was able to exert a strong influence on the policies of the Saskatchewan Pool and on the rank and file of its membership. Adherents to Mr. Brouillette's way of thinking continue to be influential in the organization. As the largest of the three provincial Pools the Saskatchewan Pool has naturally been very important in influencing the general policies and outlook of the wider group. It is not without significance that it is in Saskatchewan that the C.C.F. has found most of the party's agrarian support.

There is also some element of competitive advantage to the Pool organizations under compulsory marketing where competition at local shipping points is limited to the receiving and handling of grain for the Canadian Wheat Board, the body responsible for marketing it. The Board's contract with the country elevator companies merely requires that the elevator agents pay not less than certain prices, but by and large local price competition tends to disappear. The Pools as part of their system have very effective local organizations at each country shipping point. These aggressive local organizations are often able to swing considerable grain deliveries to the Pool elevator when the prices available to the producer are the same at each elevator. This is the situation that normally exists although instances do occur where competing agents have broken away from fixed margins to retain valued customers. Price competition plays a much larger role when there is an open market. Skilful hedging is an element in the prices that local agents can offer to their customers at country points. Thus the area of competition between organizations is widened beyond the mere handling of the grain as agents of the Board and is extended to the whole field of marketing operations. The test then becomes which competitor can offer the highest price to the producer for his grain and ultimately dispose of it without loss. There is an additional element of risk in buying and selling which calls for a higher degree of skill to avoid loss than is required merely for warehousing grain. It was in their marketing functions that the Pools came to grief in 1929 and 1930 not in their warehousing operations.

Finally, attacks upon the open market and the Winnipeg Grain

Exchange furnish convenient rallying cries with which to maintain the morale of the Pools' membership. The history of co-operative enterprises reveals many instances where these enterprises, as time went on, have gone into decline because the rank and file have lost their original enthusiasm. The Pools, with their excellent field services, their newspapers, libraries, and radio programmes, have devoted a great deal of attention to keeping their members alert and responsive. But without the Grain Exchange as a symbol of the forces against which it is necessary to contend, much of the "bite" in their propaganda would be lacking.

There can be no doubt that the Pools will continue to support the compulsory marketing of grain through the agency of a government board, though they do not carry the logic of this position farther and advocate the nationalization of grain handling facilities. It is difficult to estimate to what degree their present stand represents the wishes of a majority of the grain growers of the West. A large group of western grain growers have never joined the Pools. Moreover, there is some evidence that many producers would not be averse to a situation where they could rely upon the Wheat Board for a minimum price in years of depressed wheat values, but would have available to them the facilities of a competitive market when prices ranged above the minimum level.

The functions of the futures market have been investigated in recent times by three Royal Commissions, and in each instance the investigators have arrived at the conclusion that free marketing, which involves the futures market, is a distinct benefit to the Canadian producer. Conditions change with time, however, and conclusions which may be perfectly sound under one set of conditions may not retain their validity if these conditions change. The importance must not be overlooked in this connection of the effect of the widespread change which has taken place in the methods of conducting international trade in grains. This is important in the Canadian situation. At the present time, with the exception of the Middle East and one or two countries in Europe, purchases of Canadian wheat for import are all negotiated through the agency of centralized government boards or departments of government. The question is whether western wheat producers would benefit if these buyers from abroad were able to purchase their Canadian supplies by operating on the open market instead of by negotiating their purchases through the Canadian Wheat Board. It is a difficult question to answer.

In recent years professional economists have made penetrating studies of the behaviour of markets where the number of buyers and sellers is not relatively equal.[12]   They have shown that theoretically there is a strong presumption that where the number of buyers is limited they possess an advantage in dealing with a multiplicity of sellers. When the chief buyers of wheat are a relatively small group of powerful government agencies, buying in substantial quantities at one time, their ability to transfer their purchasing from one exporting country to another, as well as their ability to stay out of a market altogether for a period, gives them a power of manœuvre in an open market against which a large group of independent individual sellers are at a disadvantage. The gains that may accrue to the buyers from such a situation, however, are not likely to be very large, since even a limited number of rival buyers will afford a considerable measure of competition. On the other hand, there is the weighty consideration that where control of a country's disposable surplus rests with one body, if its decisions are influenced by political considerations or if it misjudges the future trend of wheat values, the effects are widespread and may entail heavy losses which have to be borne either by the taxpayer or by the producers themselves. Recent Canadian experience would appear to confirm this conclusion.

In the United States open markets function under different conditions than those which prevail in Canada. The bulk of American grain is sold for domestic consumption, which ensures a multiplicity of buyers in the market as well as a multiplicity of sellers. But even in the United States the operation of the Commodity Credit Corporation has at times disturbed the normal functioning of the markets.

The present pattern of government buying and selling is not the most desirable form of international trading. In fact, it represents a retrograde step in the free intercourse of nations.   Politically, it represents a reversion to nationalism in trade which is susceptible to being used and is being used for the purposes of promoting extreme protectionism. Technically it is slow, bureaucratic, and inconvenient. It must be recognized that the modern development of government controls over imports was undertaken originally as a defensive measure by European countries either to protect their exchange position or to make themselves as self-sufficient as possible in food supplies in the event of war. Conditions existing since the

[12]Edward Chamberlin, *The Theory of Monopolistic Competition* (Cambridge, 1933); Joan Robinson, *The Economics of Imperfect Competition* (London, 1933).

close of the Second World War seem bound to reinforce powerfully this drive to increase home production. Success in this direction almost invariably ends up in chronic conditions of over-supply.   Present tendencies do not open up a reassuring long-run prospect to the wheat producers of Western Canada.

The advantages of an open market in wheat, where a country has a large export surplus, are part of the general advantages which derive from a freely trading international economy. Under these conditions an open market provides the most convenient method of conducting international exchange. The operations of the futures market normally give the earliest and most reliable indication of changes in world conditions of supply and demand. Information comes to these markets from all parts of the world, and its significance is translated into terms of market price. The data that such markets supply become a factor in the calculations of commerce throughout the whole trading area. Higher wheat prices in the futures market imply the prospect of dearer bread, reduced consumption, and lessened demand. Lower prices not only forecast greater abundance with increased consumption, but warn the producer against excessive production. Thus, wheat prices freely established in open markets exercise a regulative effect upon demand and supply.

It follows that the open market exerts a powerful influence in determining the best utilization of agricultural land. This is one of its main virtues. Its activities entail the diffusion of reliable information on the trend of world wheat values. When wheat prices are fixed by government fiat, the way is paved for all sorts of interested pressures and extraneous considerations to enter into the determination of the level at which prices are established. The almost inevitable result of this in the long run is to induce over-production with a recurrence of the difficulties that such a situation produces. More broadly, the results are that land that from an economic standpoint should be devoted to other forms of agriculture remains in cereals. In an agricultural area where the use of land, having regard to its qualities, is not economically adjusted to the structure of the market, the long-run result is that the area as a whole does not yield its maximum economic return. In promoting the best utilization of agricultural lands open market prices are far more likely to be permanently effective than government controls, for when prices are fixed by the Government, the prices determined upon are not likely to be as low as actual conditions warrant. Marginal and sub-marginal producers are usually sufficiently active and important politically to secure some protection. The price set does not exert the pressure necessary to divert production into possibly less attractive but sounder lines.

The problem is the more acute since there is a natural reluctance on the part of the producer to shift from familiar methods of work, to say nothing of the cost involved. A not unimportant part of this reluctance in Western Canada arises from the fact that grain growing, while one of the most hazardous types of agriculture, at the same time demands the least sustained effort on the part of the producer. The farmer engaged in stock raising or dairying is tied closely to his farm day by day throughout the year. This is not the case with mechanized grain growing. While very busy in certain seasons, the grain producer is practically idle for considerable periods and can leave his farm without difficulty. This comparative freedom of movement adds to the attraction of grain growing and is an additional reason why the grain farmer dislikes to shift to a more arduous and exacting type of agriculture such as stock production or dairying.

If compulsory wheat marketing were abolished and the Canadian Wheat Board reverted to its former status of a body to which wheat could be voluntarily delivered at an initial price, with an issue of a participation certificate entitling the holder to a proportionate share in any surplus that might be realized on the ultimate sale of the wheat, the Winnipeg Grain Exchange would be able to function on the same basis it did between 1935 and 1943. The Exchange has gone on record as considering this to be an acceptable solution of the problem of how to retain the advantages of the open market while protecting the producer against disastrous declines in price. It represents a compromise between two schools of thought, and on the whole proved a fairly satisfactory *modus vivendi* between 1935 and 1943. Western wheat producers do not deny that the system of hedging made possible by the operations of the futures market reduces the costs and hazards of grain traders in moving grain bought at country points forward to ultimate markets, but they do insist that open market selling does not protect them against a period of low world wheat prices. The continuance of the Wheat Board, authorized to accept wheat at a minimum price, would give them a measure of protection in this respect.

The basic problem would continue to exist, however; that is, the danger of setting the minimum price at a level that would tend to keep certain areas of land adaptable to other types of agriculture in wheat production. Important as this consideration is, the practical difficulties of fixing minimum prices at a suitable level are very great. A relatively low price affects in the short run all wheat producers and, therefore, is certain to be resisted even though it may be a necessary prerequisite to ensuring a more remunerative level of prices in the long run.

A possible alternative to minimum prices that would give the producer protection against violent declines in open market prices would be an application of the principle of insurance. The idea of price insurance has sometimes been discussed. It was rather superficially examined in 1931 by the Stamp Commission when investigating trading in grain futures, but created little interest. Cases were cited where such schemes had been considered but had been rejected because the premium payments would have been too high, a reason that might not weigh so heavily in Western Canada now in view of the estimated cost to western wheat producers of the temporary stability in prices secured to them through the British Wheat Agreement. Dr. Alonzo Taylor, Director of the Food Research Institute of Stanford University, stated in evidence before the Stamp Commission that "they had considered such a scheme and found it actuarily feasible, but had rejected it because it disturbed the competitive elements of the different organizations engaged in the trade."[18] This reason in itself does not appear to be an insuperable obstacle to the adoption of an insurance scheme otherwise feasible, but a system of price insurance for the producer would undoubtedly encounter difficult technical and administrative problems. Low prices are usually the result of over-production. Over-production is usually attributable to excessive acreage devoted to wheat, but in Western Canada and other exporting countries wide variations in annual yield may also be a factor in such a situation. An additional difficulty in calculating the insurable risk over a period would arise from the tendency in various importing countries to encourage for reasons of state an increased domestic production of wheat by imposing import restrictions or by subsidizing their own producers. In the past this has led to serious over-production and consequent low prices.

Within the area under an insurance scheme the insurable interest of the individual farmer would be affected by the nature of his land

[18]*Report of the Commission to Inquire into Trading in Grain Futures* (Ottawa, 1931), p. 41.

and his care in tillage. At one extreme would be the farmer who, except for an occasional catastrophe, gets either a good crop or a fair crop. At the other extreme would be the case of the farmer whose land is so poor or is in such a dry belt that he never gets much of a crop and frequently none at all. From a practical standpoint his insurable interest would be so small that on an actuarial basis the risk would be unacceptable. Dr. Taylor ventured the opinion that by using actuarial methods with data covering twenty years a premium for price insurance could be determined that would be safe.[14] This would not deal with the case of the producer located on very poor land, but at the present time there are certain areas in Western Canada that should be withdrawn from the production of wheat.

In Western Canada an approach to the principle of insurance is now partially but crudely employed with reference to crop failures. Under the Prairie Farm Assistance Act the Board of Grain Commissioners is required to collect a levy of 1 per cent of the purchase price of all western grains purchased through licensees of the Board. The funds collected by it are paid over to the Receiver-General of Canada and are placed in a special account called the Prairie Farm Emergency Fund. Out of this fund the Minister of Finance is authorized to pay awards made under the Prairie Farm Assistance Act, which is administered by the Department of Agriculture. If at any time the fund proves insufficient to meet the demands made upon it, the Minister of Finance is empowered to make an advance to the fund sufficient to meet the deficit out of unappropriated money in the Consolidated Revenue Fund of Canada. The Act became effective on August 1, 1939. It was originally operative only when the average price of No. 1 Northern wheat was less than 80 cents per bushel, thus creating an "emergency" year; by an amendment in 1942 any year might be declared an emergency year.

Since 1939 each year with the exception of 1942 has been declared an emergency year until 1947 when the regulations were changed making the declaration no longer necessary before making payments. The Act has been amended several times, in general to make it easier to grant awards. The basis of award has been the average yield per acre in areas designated to receive assistance. The insurance principle has not been carried to the point where the insurable interest of the individual producer has been actuarially calculated and the premium

[14]*Evidence and Proceedings before the Commission to Inquire into Trading in Grain Futures* (Winnipeg, 1931), p. 318.

necessary to cover his risk computed. On the whole, the measure has provided a form of relief, the expense of which has been partially borne by the grain growers as a group.

Although one might infer from the language of the Act that the levy of 1 per cent was expected normally to carry most of the cost of this relief, no one seems to have expected that the scheme would be self-liquidating. Yet the magnitude of the deficits that would ensue was probably not foreseen. The Act has now been in operation for twelve years, and it is possible to determine what burden has been placed upon the grain growers located in the more prosperous regions of the West for the benefit of those located in areas particularly subject to drought, and what burden, represented by the deficit in the fund, has fallen upon the general taxpayers of Canada.

Payments under the Prairie Farm Assistance Act from August 1, 1939 to August 1, 1948 totalled $90,623,091. Of this sum producers in the province of Alberta have received $20,043,858; in Manitoba, $2,227,117; and in Saskatchewan, $68,352,116.[15] Collections by the Board of Grain Commissioners for the same period were $33,029,802, approximately 36 per cent of the total amount disbursed. Collections from the individual provinces were: Alberta, $9,473,973; Manitoba, $5,229,853; Saskatchewan, $18,323,160. A small amount, $2,815, was not allocated to the collections from these provinces.[16]

It will be observed that while the grain producers of Saskatchewan paid into the fund roughly $18,000,000, they received from it $68,000,000, over three and one-half times the amount contributed by them under the levy and more than double the total collections made in Western Canada for the fund. Alberta grain producers as a group received $20,000,000, paying in about $9,500,000, or less than one-half of what they received. In the case of Manitoba the amount collected through the levy exceeded payments from the fund by well over one-half. From the experience of nine years it would appear that if the amount to be collected had been placed on the basis of approximately 3 per cent of the purchase price of the grain marketed the total cost of assuring the grain growers protection would have been borne by the western grain producers themselves rather than the larger part thereof becoming a charge against the taxpayers of Canada. At the same time, assessment of the levy at a flat rate is grossly inequitable as between the three provinces. Under the

[15]Dominion Bureau of Statistics, Ottawa, Oct. 27, 1948.
[16]Board of Grain Commissioners for Canada, Winnipeg, Nov. 8, 1948.

scheme as presently constituted the producers of Saskatchewan have been the greatest beneficiaries while the producers of Manitoba, if such a scheme were operated on a provincial basis, could have provided themselves with the protection they now receive at one-half the present rate of the levy.

The magnitude of the disbursements in Alberta and Saskatchewan for seven of the nine years under review confirms the conclusion that there are certain areas in these provinces where crop failures recur so frequently that the land should be devoted to other forms of agriculture or withdrawn from cultivation altogether. To the objection that this would mean drastic reorganization of the life of the communities affected there is the reply that there is no reason to suppose that climatic conditions will radically change. The situation is likely to be a permanent one. Many of the agricultural areas of Eastern Canada in their earlier history were forced to undergo drastic reorganizations of their community life for similar causes.[17] There is a real reluctance to face the harsh fact that through subsidies, direct or concealed, grain growing is being continued in certain districts of the West without providing of itself a decent living for the producer or strengthening the economic life of the state. If payments under the Prairie Farm Assistance Act were taken out of the category of relief and based upon a fund accumulated by assessments levied on an actuarial calculation of risk this situation would tend to disappear.

The most substantial grievance that western grain producers have against a system of free marketing is that it does not protect them against disastrous declines in prices. One might regard the last twenty-five years as an era of experimentation in which various expedients have been resorted to with a view to ensuring to producers reasonable stability in returns. But at the end of this period there continues to be great uncertainty over what direction the marketing system will ultimately take. It is conceivable that a return to the open market, complemented by a comprehensive system of price insurance, would eliminate the weaknesses disclosed in fixed minimum and maximum prices and long-term contracts while affording the grain producer an adequate degree of protection. But it is important to emphasize that no conclusion with respect to the merits of price insurance should be reached without the most thorough investigation of its possibilities.

[17]Dominion Bureau of Statistics, Education Statistics Branch, *Analysis of the Stages in the Growth of Population in Canada*, by M. C. Maclean (Ottawa, 1935).

13

Summary and conclusion

In 1932 the wheat economy of Western Canada was reeling under the full impact of the Great Depression. The outlook was most depressing, and farm welfare was at a very low level. The interval between that period and the present has been crowded with events bringing to the fore a variety of problems that have engaged the attention almost continuously of the producers, the Pools, the independent trade, and the Government. In 1932 the immediate problem was the disposal of excessive surpluses without undue loss, a problem that led to acrimonious public controversy. In 1937 a severe drought reduced the average yield of wheat to 6.38 bushels per acre and brought distress to large areas. In 1939 the outbreak of war, coinciding with a return to abundant harvests, cut off a large part of Canada's export markets, piled up surplus stocks, and channelled the bulk of Canadian exports to Allied countries. With the conclusion of the war the breakdown in international trade and the virtual bankruptcy of western Europe made the financing of export shipments the dominant concern.

National wheat policy has been shaped largely by attempts to solve the problems created by these circumstances one after another as they arose. The Canadian Wheat Board was established as an agency to liquidate the surplus accumulated by the Pools in 1929 and 1930 plus supplies acquired in an effort to stabilize the market. Controversy over the best methods of selling Canada's export surpluses led to the Royal Grain Inquiry Commission of 1936-38. The Commissioner's suggestion that the Government should remain out of the grain trade, with the retention of the Canadian Wheat Board as a stand-by organization to ensure a minimum price to the producers, was rejected because of the latter's fear that prices might again fall to unprofitable levels on the open market. The Board became the sole instrument for marketing Canadian wheat as part of the policy of controls instituted in connection with the Canadian war effort. Its status has been maintained to guarantee minimum prices to the producer. A by-product of the war arising out of the fiscal necessities of the Dominion Government was the taxation of the Pools under the Income War Tax Act. The threat of unmanageable surpluses led to acreage controls; the various measures enacted to provide for relief in the event of short crops and to encourage farmers to increase livestock production were due partly to the requirements of the war effort and partly to an attempt to persuade western wheat growers, in the interests of greater stability of income, to diversify their output. The British Wheat Agreement was an effort to safeguard Canada's principal export market under post-war conditions. The International Wheat Agreement of 1949 which overlapped and followed it represents the fulfilment of an ideal which has been cherished by the wheat growers of exporting countries for over twenty years.

The mechanics of receiving grain at country elevators, shipping it, grading, weighing, storing, and moving it forward to its final markets have remained practically unchanged, but the marketing of wheat, the principal export crop, is now completely under the control of the Dominion Government. The open market for wheat has disappeared. Legislation has also been put into force providing for the marketing of oats and barley under the Wheat Board and it now appears to be established firmly as the controlling marketing instrument for these grains. The result of the recent plebiscite in Manitoba supports this conclusion. The Dominion Government's constitutional authority to legislate for compulsory grain marketing remains insecure. At present in the case of oats and barley it rests upon complementary legislation by the provinces; in the case of wheat upon the Government's ability to enter into agreements with other countries.

Although all the actions of the present Liberal administration at Ottawa imply a continuance of monopoly control, if legally feasible, the Liberal party has not specifically committed itself to state marketing as a permanent policy. On the other hand, the Progressive Conservative party has endorsed the principle of allowing the producer to market his wheat or other grains by any means he may choose. The Co-operative Commonwealth Federation supports in principle state socialism.

While western farm organizations adhere, under the militant leadership of the Pools, to the policy of a state marketing board, the oldest of the producer-owned organizations, the United Grain Growers Limited, a strong and expanding company, has consistently championed free marketing as being in the producers' interests. The Winnipeg Grain Exchange naturally has bitterly opposed the Dominion Government's adoption of state socialism with respect to grain marketing, but up to the present has been fighting a losing battle. Nevertheless, the private elevator companies remain in a strong position.

Canada is so deeply committed to an export trade in wheat that any developments in this field of international trade are of the highest importance to her. The general trend towards negotiating purchases and sales through the agency of government bodies was strengthened by the chaotic conditions in Europe following the Second World War. This trend itself is one phase of the swing towards more socialistic forms of government. The repeated and finally successful effort to achieve an over-all international wheat agreement is in accord with theories of this nature. As long as this trend continues it will influence the methods by which Canada sells her wheat for export. But it must be recognized that neither the outcome of the British Wheat Agreement nor the prices currently being obtained from sales made under the terms of the International Wheat Agreement provide evidence that long-term contracts of this nature are advantageous to the producer.

Marketing arrangements are only one aspect of the larger problem of agriculture in Western Canada. Much of the land in the West is better adapted to the cultivation of cereals than to other forms of agriculture. As far as the predictable future is concerned Western Canada will continue to be an important exporter of wheat.   But variations in rainfall from year to year in this region, in conjunction with fluctuating world supplies, make wheat farming a hazardous type of agriculture.   Within the last two decades annual western wheat production has twice exceeded 500,000,000 bushels, and in one year has fallen below 200,000,000 bushels. Prices for No. 1 Manitoba Northern wheat within this period have ranged from below 50 cents per bushel to over $3.00 per bushel. These violent fluctuations have meant that the western wheat producers have enjoyed years of high prosperity and periods of painful depression.

The problem of the western farmers who must rely upon the production of cereals for their income is to endeavour to secure a reasonable stability of returns from one year to another. Hence the strong tendency to look to the state for assistance and protection. Legislation in keeping with these ends, however, entails the danger of placing wheat growers in a preferred position, thereby delaying the development of a desirable balance between the production of cereals and that of livestock and of dairy products. There is a constant drive in Western Canada towards expanding the production of wheat, a propensity which is not in the interest of developing a stable agricultural economy. This tendency requires to be kept in check by firm administrative control if the consequences that normally flow from price declines on a free market are to be cushioned by basic minimum prices or other measures. Unless the necessity for control receives the weight it deserves in the formulation of agricultural policy, areas eminently suitable for stock raising or dairying will continue to be devoted to the production of wheat. It is of the highest importance that the long-run effect of immediate policies should be constantly kept in mind.

The maintenance of the Canadian wheat export trade on a sound basis requires wheat production in areas capable of growing wheat of high quality at relatively low cost, the handling of stocks in the least costly method possible without deterioration of quality, and a sales policy of offering wheat at prices "as low as is consistent with actual cost of production." Regard for these factors in the past largely accounts for the important position Canada now occupies in international wheat trading, and it lies within Canada's own power to continue to be guided by this fact. Canada, however, is only part of an international trading community in which the wheat trade is an important item. International trade will languish if nationalistic restrictive policies impair it. For the Canadian West the most propitious circumstances for the continuance of its export trade in cereals are those that make for the freest possible international exchange of goods and services.

Index

AGRICULTURE, Minister of (J. G. Gardiner), 50, 52, 54, 76, 111, 120, 126, 127, 128, 131, 134, 139, 141, 144

Alberta, 12, 51, 219-20; Government of, 168, 169; Minister of Agriculture for, 52

Alberta Pacific Grain Company, 201

Alberta Wheat Pool, 74, 84, 166, 173, 176-9, 187

Alberta Wheat Pool Budget, 179

Annexes, temporary, 107

Argentina, 22, 25, 27, 90, 145, 148, 150, 157, 159

Assiniboia, by-election, 76

Australia, 27, 44, 46, 75, 145

BARLEY, 60, 78, 109, 111, 164-7, 169-70, 209, 222

Bennett, R. B., 20 ff, 26, 38, 72

Board of Grain Commissioners, 21, 54, 202, 203, 218

Bonus, acreage, 46

Bracken, John, 31, 84, 123

British Wheat Agreement, 119-44, 164, 170, 187, 210, 222, 223

Brouillette, L. C., 73, 74, 211, 212

CANADA, Government of, 9, 17-32, 34, 36, 38, 45, 49, 52, 58-9, 90, 93, 119, 140, 186, 209, 210, 215, 222, 223

Canada Grain Act, 194, 203

Canadian Co-operative Wheat Producers Limited (central selling agency), 17, 68, 71, 73, 173, 186, 206

Canadian Federation of Agriculture, 137, 166, 186

Canadian Pool Agencies Limited, 186

Canadian Wheat Board (1919), 191; (1935), 33-8, 40, 44, 45, 47, 49, 55, 64-5, 72, 73, 77, 89-118, 143, 144, 162-4, 164-9, 171, 186, 196, 202, 203, 208-10, 213, 216, 221, 222

Canadian Wheat Board Act, 34-7, 38, 90-2, 95, 96, 141, 162-4, 167-70, 207

C.C.F.; *see* Co-operative Commonwealth Federation

Central selling agency; *see* Canadian Co-operative Wheat Producers Limited

Cereal Imports Committee, 63, 102

Commodity Credit Corporation, 214

Companies, independent grain, 199-203

Conference, Imperial, 1930, 18; Imperial Economic, 21; Monetary and Economic, 26

Contract, five-year, 69, 173, 174, 176, 179

Co-operative Commonwealth Federation, 83, 123, 139, 165, 167, 212, 222

Corn Trade News, 125, 126

Country Guide, 197

Crerar, Thomas, 100

Crown, prerogatives of, 117, 163

DEPRESSION, the Great, 3-16, 205

Dividends, patronage, 81, 83, 88, 175, 179, 184, 190

Economist, 29, 124, 148

Elections, Dominion, 35

FARM LANDS, value of, 11

Federal Grain Limited, 201

Finance, Minister of (J. L. Ilsley), 81, 84
Fitzgerald, Dennis A., 129
Flaxseed, 78, 113-15, 209
Food and Agriculture Organization (F.A.O.), 147, 186
France, 151, 157
Fraser Valley Milk Producers' Association, 82
Futures, grain, 36, 45-6, 101, 165, 204

GARDINER, J. G., 74; *See also* Agriculture, Minister of
Gardiner, Robert, 60
Gillespie Grain Company, 183, 184

HALLET & CAREY LIMITED, 112

INCOME, of western farmers, 8
Income War Tax Act, 81-8, 194, 222
Insurance, price, 217-20
International Federation of Agricultural Producers, 186
International Wheat Advisory Committee, 28-9, 145, 146
International Wheat Agreement (1933), 26-32, 145; (1949), 131, 145-61, 170, 187, 210, 222, 223
International Wheat Council, 146, 148, 156

JONES, Stanley, 137
Justice, Minister of (J. L. Ilsley), 165

KING, W. L. Mackenzie, 58, 74, 75, 127

LIBERAL PARTY, 36, 46, 74-5, 112, 119, 134, 139, 165, 222
Lumber, controller, 116

McFARLAND, John I., 17, 25, 33, 35, 37, 38, 41, 43, 53, 67-8, 70-2, 73, 75, 78, 79, 99, 141, 186, 206, 207
McIvor, George, 100, 162, 171
McNamara, W. C., 129
McPhail, A. J., 212

Manitoba, 12, 51, 219-20; Government of, 31, 168, 169, 170, 180, 182, 183
Manitoba Co-operator, 185
Manitoba Wheat Pool, 166, 173, 179-85, 187
Marshall Aid, 135
Murray, James R., 37, 39, 43, 180-1

NATIONAL EMERGENCY TRANSITIONAL POWERS ACT, 112, 143
National Grain Company, 201
National Revenue, Minister of (C. W. Gibson), 82-3
North West Line Elevators' Association, 196
Northern Grain Company Limited, 177

OATS, 60, 78, 109, 108-12, 164-7, 169, 170, 209, 222
Oatway, 117-18

PARKER, W. J., 187
Plumer, Ben S., 132, 179
Pools, Wheat, 17, 19, 35, 41, 67-9, 77, 80, 87, 88, 134, 137, 186, 188, 173-87, 191, 196, 199, 211, 212, 213, 222, 223
Prairie Farm Assistance Act, 46, 50-2, 58, 218-20
Progressive Conservative party, 84, 167, 172, 222
Public Press Limited, 197
Purdy, R. D., 179, 187

RALSTON, J. L., 141
Rapeseed, 115
Reliance Grain Company, 201
Relief expenditure, 9
Rochdale Equitable Pioneers Society, 189
Ross, J. A., 137
Royal Commission on Co-operatives, 84-7, 189, 195; on Trading in Grain Futures (Sir Josiah Stamp), 36, 42, 193, 217; on Manitoba Pool Elevators Limited, 180-2

Royal Grain Inquiry Commission, 1938 (W. F. A. Turgeon), 38-45, 80, 141, 186-7, 221
Russia, 148, 150, 158, 159

St. Laurent, L., 130, 136
Sapiro, Aaron, 193, 212
Saskatchewan, 12, 14, 51, 219-20; Government of, 19, 38, 168
Saskatchewan Co-operative Elevator Company, 188
Saskatchewan Livestock Pool, 175
Saskatchewan Wheat Pool, 19, 59, 60, 139, 165, 173-6, 187, 188, 202, 211, 212
Searle Grain Company Limited, 8, 201
Senate, of Canada, 163-4; of United States, 149
Smith, Sidney, 201
Snowden, Philip, 21
Social Credit party, 123, 167
Soybeans, 115
Stamp, Sir Josiah; see Royal Commission on Trading in Grain Futures
Standard of living, 9, 12, 160
Strachey, John, 120, 124, 126, 143
Sunflower seed, 115

Taxation, of co-operative profits, 81-8
Taylor, Dr. Alonzo, 217, 218
Times, The, 148
Trade and Commerce, Minister of (W. D. Euler), 75; (James MacKinnon) 54, 61, 65, 93, 94, 119, 120, 127, 142, 143, 164; (C. D. Howe) 132, 133, 135, 144, 167, 169

Turgeon, W. F. A., 38, 43, 44, 53, 80-1; see also Royal Grain Inquiry Commission, 1938

United Grain Growers Limited, 166, 180, 188-98, 199, 201, 223
United States, 22, 25, 27, 90, 145, 149, 150, 151, 214

Waines, W. J., 9
War Measures Act, 1914, 140
Wartime Prices and Trade Board, 102, 116
Wesson, J. H., 60, 93, 120, 166, 187
Western Producer, 175
Wheat, allocations of, under international wheat agreements (1933), 27, 32 (1949), 152; British preference on, 22-5; bonus, 21; cash income from, 7; Class B, 97; in Eastern Canada, 103-5; "floor" price for, 65; limit on marketing of, 55, on deliveries of, to Wheat Board, 91, 95; liquidation of surplus, 37; minimum price of, 45, 47, 50, 60, 90, 95, 208; 100 per cent pool, 19; permits for delivery of, 105; processing tax on, 92; purchasing power of, 8; quota deliveries of, 105; statistical data for, 5, 6, 7, 14, 29, 52, 56, 61, 62, 106, 116, 152, 157, 158, 223
Wheat Acreage Reduction Act, 57
Wheat Board Advisory Committee, 166
Williams, E. K., 181
Winnipeg Free Press, 73, 123
Winnipeg Grain Exchange, 20, 36, 40, 42, 45, 63, 81, 96, 101, 133, 137, 142, 186, 188, 190, 196, 199-200, 223